Drugs and Democracy

Drugs and Democracy

In Search of New Directions

Edited by
GEOFFREY STOKES, PETER CHALK
AND KAREN GILLEN

MELBOURNE UNIVERSITY PRESS

MELBOURNE UNIVERSITY PRESS
PO Box 278, Carlton South, Victoria 3053, Australia
info@mup.unimelb.edu.au
www.mup.com.au

First published 2000

Typeset by Syarikat Seng Teik Sdn. Bhd., Malaysia, in 10 point Sabon
Printed in Australia by RossCo Print

National Library of Australia Cataloguing-in-Publication entry

Drugs and democracy: in search of new directions.
  Bibliography.
  Includes index.
  ISBN 0 522 84891 5.
  1. National Drug Strategy (Australia). 2. Narcotics,
  Control of—Australia. 3. Drug traffic—Australia.
  4. Drug abuse and crime—Australia. 5. Drug abuse—
  Government policy—Australia. I. Stokes, Geoff (Geoffrey),
  1949– . II. Chalk, Peter. III. Gillen, Karen.
362.2930994

Contents

Preface

THIS BOOK WAS INSPIRED by the contributions to an inter-
disciplinary conference on illicit drugs sponsored by the Centre
for Democracy at the University of Queensland in December
1998, and supported by the Department of Government. A major
concern was to shift the terms of policy debate on illicit drugs away
from a focus upon the dogma of 'zero tolerance'. On reviewing
the contributions to the conference, it became obvious that most
studies of the issue of illicit drugs in Australia (and elsewhere)
have approached the problem from either a purely law enforcement or a purely health perspective. In searching for new directions to tackle the problem, we were encouraged to think that a
broader outlook, drawing upon more enlightened political, legal
and social strategies, would be fruitful. A particular strength of
this book therefore is that it examines the implications of the issue
of illicit drugs for the country's liberal democratic institutions and
criminal justice tradition. In this vein, the problem of illicit drugs
becomes multi-faceted, having relevance for issues of international
security and political rights as well as law, policing and health.
The chapters are written by national experts and practitioners
within various fields, and offer innovative options for future policy
and its formulation. We are pleased to have the opportunity of
bringing together these views on a major, contemporary problem
of Australian public policy. We are especially grateful to Dr Alex
Wodak for his valuable comments on the manuscript.

Geoffrey Stokes
Peter Chalk
Karen Gillen

Contributors

David Brereton is the Director of the Research Division of the Queensland Criminal Justice Commission, a position which he has held since 1993. Dr Brereton holds a PhD in Political Science from Stanford University (1989) and a BA First Class Honours from the University of Melbourne. His previous positions have included: Senior Lecturer in Legal Studies at La Trobe University, Melbourne; Principal Consultant for the Victorian Law Reform Commission on several projects; and Director of the Victorian Bureau of Crime Statistics and Research.

John Broome was the Chairperson of the National Crime Authority from February 1996 to September 1999.

Peter Chalk now works for the Rand Corporation and is based in Washington, DC. Prior to this he was a Lecturer in International Relations in the Department of Government, University of Queensland. He is Associate Editor (Asia) for the journal *Studies in Conflict and Terrorism,* has published widely on terrorism and security issues, and has close links with the Australian police community.

David Crosbie is Chief Executive Officer of the Alcohol and other Drugs Council of Australia (ADCA), the peak national non-government organisation in the field. He currently serves on the National Alcohol Strategy Committee and the National Expert Working Group on Illicit Drugs. Prior to taking up his current role, he managed a broad range of alcohol and drug programs and services, and has written and published many papers and submissions on drug-related issues.

Keith Evans is State Manager, Alcohol, Tobacco and Other Drug Services, Queensland Health. He has worked in the alcohol and drug field for over twenty years. During this time he has worked in clinical service delivery, program management and international consultancy with the World Health Organisation.

Karen Gillen is a postgraduate student in anthropology, in the Department of Anthropology and Sociology at the University of Queensland. She has also taught and researched in the fields of Australian politics and public policy.

Stephen James is a Senior Lecturer in the Criminology Department at the University of Melbourne. He specialises in law enforcement, and his recent publications include works on young people and policing, community policing, drug law enforcement and police culture.

John McFarlane is the Australian Federal Police Visiting Fellow at the Australian Defence Studies Centre, University College, Australian Defence Force Academy in Canberra, where he is researching the impact of transnational crime on regional security and stability. He is the Australian Co-Chair of a Working Group on Transnational Crime set up under the auspices of the Council for Security Cooperation in the Asia–Pacific. He is also investigating cross-border crime affecting the Torres Strait and the impact of transnational crime on Australia's bilateral relationships with Papua New Guinea and the countries of the South Pacific.

Paddy Mahony and his co-authors are members of the Australian Bureau of Criminal Intelligence in Canberra. Some of the contributors belong to the Australian Federal Police, some are seconded from State and Territory police services and one is a statistical consultant. Holding qualifications in sociology, applied science, and Asian and justice studies, they come from various backgrounds, including defence intelligence, and police operational and intelligence duties.

Andrew Parkin is Professor of Political and International Studies at the Flinders University of South Australia. His research interests encompass many aspects of government, politics and public policy, with particular emphasis on debates about criminal justice, immigration, ethnic affairs, housing, urban planning, education and intergovernmental relations.

Ann Roche is a Senior Lecturer within the Department of Social and Preventive Medicine at the University of Queensland, and is Director of the Queensland Alcohol and Drug Research and Education Centre (QADREC). She has over twenty years' experience in the field of public health, has worked as a researcher, educator, and policy analyst in various public health areas, and has held academic posts at the University of Sydney and the University of Newcastle.

Timothy Rohl is Director of the Australian Institute of Police Management. He was Co-Evaluator (with Professor Eric Single) of the National Drug Strategy 1993–97, and co-produced a report entitled *The National Drug Strategy: Mapping the Future* (1997).

Geoffrey Stokes is Associate Professor in Social and Political Theory and Director of the Centre for Democracy in the Department of Government at the University of Queensland. He was co-editor of the *Australian Journal of Politics and History* (1994–99), has edited three books of collected essays, and is the author of a book on the philosophy of Karl Popper.

Adam Sutton is a Senior Lecturer in the Criminology Department at the University of Melbourne, specialising in crime prevention, white-collar crime, crime policy and drug-law enforcement. His recent publications include work on crime prevention, drug law enforcement and 'criminology as a religion'.

Alex Wodak is Director of the Alcohol and Drug Service at St Vincent's Hospital, Sydney. He was trained as a physician and became interested in drug policy while involved in efforts to maintain control of HIV infection among injecting drug users in Australia and developing countries in Asia. Dr Wodak is closely linked with a growing international drug law reform movement and is currently President of the Australian Drug Law Reform Foundation.

Abbreviations

AFP	Australian Federal Police.
AIDS	Acquired Immune Deficiency Syndrome. See also HIV.
AMA	Australian Medical Association.
APG	Asia–Pacific Group on Money Laundering.
APMC	Australian Police Ministers Council.
ASEANPOL	Association of South-East Asian National Police.
AUSTRAC	Australian Transaction Reports and Analysis Centre. Created in 1989 to analyse cash transactions of $10 000 or more, suspect transactions and all international telegraphic transfers of money.
BCCI	Bank of Credit and Commerce International.
BMA	British Medical Association.
CGSB	Simon Bolivar Guerrilla Coordination. This is an ultra-leftist umbrella guerrilla group which uses profits from the drug trade to finance rural insurgency in Colombia.
CMO	Comprehensive Multi-Disciplinary Outline. The CMO, adopted in 1987, elaborates the UN's international drug strategy framework. It serves as a basis on which national authorities can formulate their plans to combat the spread of illicit drugs, and comprises recommendations covering prevention and reduction of illicit demand; control of supply; action against illicit traffic; and treatment and rehabilitation.
CND	United Nations Commission on Narcotic Drugs. The CND is the central policy making body within the United Nations system for dealing with all questions related to drug control.

CSCAP	Council for Security Cooperation in the Asia–Pacific.
DATs	Drug Action Teams. As part of the National Community-Based Approaches to Drug Law Enforcement (NCBADLE) project in Australia, these teams work at the 'grassroots' level bringing together operational police and other local service providers in the drug and alcohol related areas to apply harm reduction strategies to areas of identified concern.
DEA	USA Drug Enforcement Agency.
DMA	3,4-dimethoxyamphetamine, a synthetic euphoric drug.
DPRK	Democratic People's Republic of Korea, the official name of the state of North Korea.
DRGs	Drug Reference Groups. As part of the National Community-Based Approaches to Drug Law Enforcement (NCBADLE) project in Australia, the purpose of the DRGs is to bring together senior managers from the agencies whose personnel are involved with the Drug Action Teams (DATs) in order to provide advice, advocacy and organisational support for DAT strategies.
ECOSOC	United Nations Economic and Social Council.
FANC	Foreign Anti-Narcotics Community. A group of foregin narcotics liaison officers based in Bangkok and Islamabad, who meet regularly to exchange information.
FARC	Fuerzas Armadas Revolucionarias Colombias, the Colombian Communist Party.
FATF	Financial Action Task Force of the Group of 7 (G7) nations.
GDP	Gross Domestic Product.
HIV	Human Immunodeficiency Virus, the virus responsible for AIDS.
HONLEA	Heads of National Drug Law Enforcement Agencies. A subsidiary of the United Nations Commission on Narcotic Drugs (CND), HONLEA consists of

	four regional groupings covering the Asia–Pacific, the Americas, Africa and Europe.
IIDM	Integrated Intervention Drug Model. The IIDM attempts to provide a comprehensive framework for drug policy and strategy which can take account of the various perspectives of the different professional areas involved (see chapter 10).
IMF	International Monetary Fund.
INCB	International Narcotics Control Board. The INCB is the independent and quasi-judicial control organ for the implementation of the UN drug conventions, established in 1968 by the Single Convention on Narcotic Drugs of 1961. It is responsible for the administration of treaties relating to the international control of narcotic drugs, psychotropic substances and precursors.
INTERPOL	International Criminal Police Organisation.
LTTE	Liberation Tigers of Tamil Eelam, a Tamil separatist group in Sri Lanka.
M–19	19th April Movement, a terrorist group in Colombia.
MBDB	N-methyl-1-(3,4-methylenedioxyphenyl)-2-butanamine, a synthetic euphoric drug.
MCDS	Ministerial Council on Drug Strategy. This is the principal drug policy-making body in Australia, and comprises Commonwealth and State Health and Police Ministers.
MDEA	3,4 methylenedioxy-N-ethylamphetamine, a synthetic euphoric drug, also known as 'Eve'.
MDMA	3,4 methylenedioxy-MA, a synthetic euphoric drug, also known as 'Ecstasy'.
MTA	*Mong Tai* Army. The 15 000-strong private militia of Chang Chifu (more commonly known as Khun Sa), the principal heroin warlord in Burma and a key player in the Golden Triangle heroin nexus.
NCADA	National Campaign Against Drug Abuse. The campaign was launched in 1985, by the Hawke Government, when it was recognised that continued

	evaluation and reform of drug-control policy would be required. Now replaced by the National Drug Strategy (NDS).
NCBADLE	National Community-Based Approaches to Drug Law Enforcement. Australia's Police Commissioners have established and funded a NCBADLE project, to implement localised drug law enforcement initiatives (see chapter 10). See also DRGs and DATs.
NDS	Australian National Drug Strategy. Established in 1993, the NDS defines policies designed to co-ordinate the efforts of the numerous agencies and individuals involved in drug control.
NGO	Non-government organisation.
NPDC	Nardoni Proti-Drogovy Central, the main anti-drug squad in the Czech Republic.
ONCB	Office of Narcotics Control Board in Thailand.
SAARC	South Asia Association for Regional Cooperation.
UN	United Nations.
UNDCP	United Nations Drug Control Program, established in 1991 to integrate into a single program the structures and functions of three former UN drug control units. It carries responsibility for co-ordinating and providing leadership for all United Nations drug control activities, and is geared towards assisting developing countries in meeting their obligations in implementing provisions of the international drug control treaties.
UNGASS	United Nations General Assembly Special Session.
WCO	World Customs Organisations.

Introduction: Broadening the Political Agenda

THE OBJECTIVES OF this volume are to examine: the history and politics of drug policies; the scope of the contemporary drug problem in Australia; the general effectiveness of the contemporary responses to the drug problem in Australia; and how Australia's national drug strategies might be improved within the confines of liberal-democratic values and culture.

The terms of the political agenda in which we determine drugs policy in Australia need to be expanded, and this requires broadening the context in which we understand the various problems of illicit drug taking. Besides recognising drug taking as both an individual and social problem, we may also see it as a political problem. Approaches which simply criminalise and medicalise the problem of illicit drug taking are inadequate, as they ignore its wider political implications. Effective policy responses to illicit drugs have to be based upon an understanding of its inherently multidimensional character. Such responses ought to take account of impacts upon democratic institutions and political culture. Policies that weaken our commitments to democracy and which bring Australian political institutions into disrepute need reappraisal.

Defining the Problem

A short account of the origins of the word 'draconian' may prove a useful starting point for considering the problem of illicit drugs in contemporary Australian society. We learn from the Roman historian Plutarch about the decision of the people of Athens to repeal the laws of King Draco (*c.* 600 BC). The Athenians had come to the conclusion that Draco's laws were too severe. They based their judgement upon the fact that Draco assigned the one penalty for virtually all crimes—that of death. Plutarch tells us that even those convicted of idleness were put to death, and that this was the same penalty as for those who stole fruit or committed sacrilege or murder. According to Plutarch (1914: 40), when Draco was asked why he made death the penalty for all these offences he replied that 'in his opinion the lesser ones deserved it, and for the greater ones no heavier penalties could be found'. Certainly Draco's legal strategy provided a simple solution to the problem of crime, but it created many further problems and led to political efforts to remedy matters. This created quite a task of law reform for Solon (*c.* 640–559 BC) who was appointed Archon of Athens to reform the constitution and make new laws that were more just.

This account raises important questions for thinking about the problem of illicit drugs before us today. What precisely is the problem? What is the extent of it? What are sensible and politically acceptable solutions to the problem? How can we avoid responses that create more problems than those they are designed to solve? While the following chapters in this book provide informed and substantive answers to these questions, in this introduction we offer a preliminary framework for thinking about them.

Drug taking is not inherently a social or political problem. It is we—as individuals, public servants, educationalists and members of governments—who determine what counts as a public problem. All societies appear to have used intoxicating or consciousness-altering substances to different degrees. Historically, there have been many ways of regulating the use and punishing the excess use of different substances. Much of this has depended on the community's understanding of whether the substance was used for public, ritual or religious purposes, or for private personal gratification. These different regimes of regulation are founded upon the kinds of behaviour the society classifies as abuse and what levels of use and trafficking it is prepared to tolerate.

Any society will always mark out the limits of unacceptable behaviour, if only to indicate more clearly what it values. But this set of limits is rarely fixed and what is prohibited in one generation may be accepted as normal in the next. This is not to claim that we cannot choose rationally between different standards, or arbitrate between them, or that we must accept whatever may appear to be the current fashion or trend. It is simply to say that in dealing with the problem of illicit drugs, we must avoid self-righteous moralism and one-dimensional responses. It also suggests that how we define the problem will reflect our own history and political context.

Given this brief sketch, the issues before us may be summarised in the following questions:

- *What kinds of individual and social behaviour do we want to specify as valuable?* How do we want to promote these values? Negative strategies of stigmatisation are commonly used to deter drug taking, but are positive models sufficiently discussed and articulated? None of us are saints, however, and ideal models of social behaviour represent aspirations, not rigid personal blueprints.

- *What kinds of behaviours do we want to specify as unacceptable, if not outright physically dangerous, to the individual and to others?* Here we always need to keep in mind that there will have to be different levels or degrees of unacceptability. How do we want to treat those who cannot live up to those standards? What are the limits to our tolerance?

- *How ought we understand or explain these forms of unacceptable behaviour?* Are they the product of personal weakness, larger social forces, unjust laws, or any variation or combination of these?

- *How ought we treat or respond to unacceptable behaviour?* Do we 'medicalise' them or 'criminalise' them, or, as in some other countries, do we respond so that the problem becomes one of political security and stability? Do we continue to stigmatise them through publicity campaigns? How should we discriminate between different kinds of behaviour and order priorities?

- *What are the various consequences of the different kinds of policies?* Here we have to consider the individual, the society, the law enforcers, the democratic polity, and also the impact upon other countries.

- *How should we make policy on these subjects?* What are the major assumptions, indicated above, underlying our policy responses? Are the current policy arrangements appropriate to the problem, or has one policy model become dominant and excluded other approaches?

The following chapters in this book indicate that the existing policy-making process on illicit drugs is somewhat less than satisfactory. This may be because of the dominant assumptions about the nature and origins of the problem. That is, just how we understand the problem of illicit drugs is crucial for policy making. For example, we can understand the problem as an *individual* problem, a *social* problem, or as a *political* problem. For others it is also an *economic* and *security* problem.

First, we often tend to think that the taking of drugs, whether illicit or licit, is a purely *individual problem* best understood as a weakness of individual will and morality. This tends to lead us to search for legal solutions that make criminals out of those who transgress. Alternatively, we may see the problem as one of personal health and tend to medicalise it. This usually requires that we treat illicit drug taking as a medical issue and often within strict legal parameters. Acute political conflict, based upon struggles for control of agendas and resources, often occurs between those who would 'criminalise' and those who would 'medicalise' the problem.

Depending on our values and the perceived scale of the problem of illicit drugs, we may see it primarily as a *social problem*. This requires us to understand its larger social origins and also calls for a collective social response. For the legalists and moralists, this may require addressing public morality and maintaining a stronger criminal justice approach. Stronger penalties and the publicising of these penalties may be part of this type of strategy. For the 'medicalists' with a social orientation, illicit drug taking is not just an individual matter. It becomes a public health problem requiring coordinated public action and resources to match. Both approaches, of course, may overlap.

Another important perspective to be considered is that which views illicit drugs as a problem important to the *political health* of Australian democracy. By this we do not mean the economic costs of regulation and enforcement, or the loss of taxation revenue, although both are significant. Rather, we want to draw attention to a number of less tangible, but no less vital consequences of poor policies and policy making. Democracy requires both effective institutions and a strong democratic political culture to support them. Policies that weaken our commitments to democracy and which bring the political institutions into disrepute need reappraisal. It is arguable that current policies on illicit drugs tend to do both.

If we set the boundaries of unacceptable drug taking behaviour too wide, we risk criminalising or threatening to criminalise large numbers of Australian citizens. If, like King Draco, we treat all illicit substances, such as cannabis and heroin, in the same way we are encouraging a number of undemocratic political consequences. By adopting such an approach, we not only expand the potential net of criminality, we also invite a loss of respect for law and the rule of law. One of the great achievements of European liberalism and one of the cornerstones of Australian democracy is the principle of the rule of law. Without respect for the principle and practice of rule of law, we cannot have a secure and peaceful democracy. Decisions that fail to discriminate between levels of harm and degrees of appropriate response undermine respect for the rule of law. Such decisions also put law enforcement officers under increasing strain in both the allocation of resources and in resisting the inevitable pressures of corruption. This, in turn, reduces respect for particular laws, the rule of law and the justice system as a whole. The draconian response will, sooner or later, end up by appointing or electing a Solon to fix up the mess.

This leads us to the issue of policy making. For people to retain faith in democratic procedures, they need to know that governments can make good policies and implement them effectively. If a polity cannot make intelligent policy decisions on difficult and controversial issues such as gun control or illicit drugs, then it risks loss of political legitimacy. It risks increasing what is often referred to as the 'democratic deficit'. This is the term given to the loss of faith that results from governments being unable to satisfy the growing expectations of their citizens. Given the extent of illicit drug use among certain age groups, ineffective and unjust responses to the problem run the risk of alienating generations of young people from our political system. On the other hand, living in a drug-induced stupor does little to enhance one's civic capacity. Balancing such considerations is part of the dilemma.

Chapter Outline

This book considers the following questions:
- What is the extent of the contemporary drug problem in Australia and how is it impacting on the country's liberal-democratic institutions and political culture?
- How effective has the contemporary Australian response to its drug problem been?
- How might Australia's overall National Drug Strategy be improved within the confines of the country's liberal-democratic values and culture?

The book is divided into three sections. The first three chapters provide an overview of global trends in drug trafficking and the various impacts of illicit drugs on Australia and in the Asian region. The chapters in the second section examine a number of general issues and constraints upon the setting of public agendas and responses to the problem of illicit drugs. The final set of chapters explores the range of possible responses and policy options for minimising the problem of illicit drugs in Australia.

Australia in the world and region

In the first chapter of this section, Peter Chalk assesses the scope and political impact of global production and trafficking in illicit drugs, concentrating primarily on the trade in heroin and cocaine. His chapter begins with a brief overview of main production areas, trafficking routes and statistical trends. The nature of the threat posed by the illicit drug trade is then examined, particularly in relation to its impact on social, economic and political stability. Having set out the dimensions and impact of the global illicit drug trade, Chalk goes on to consider the growing nexus between drug trafficking and other emerging threats to international stability and security. Two in particular are examined: organised white-collar crime (especially money laundering) and narco-terrorism, both of which have the potential to seriously weaken liberal-democratic governments and destablise relations between countries. In chapter 2, John McFarlane examines the impact of illicit drug trafficking in South-East Asia and considers transnational crime as a regional security and stability issue. He describes how transnational crime, especially drug trafficking, can affect military, political, economic, societal, environmental and human dimensions of security. Next, he explores the scale and significance of transnational organised crime in South-East Asia, concentrating, particularly but not exclusively, on Chinese, Japanese and Vietnamese criminal groups involved in the regional drug trade. He then considers the specific problems of heroin, cannabis, amphetamine and cocaine trafficking in South-East Asia. In the second part of the chapter, McFarlane examines the role of the United Nations (UN) in proposing and implementing international drug policies, especially the three UN Conventions on narcotic drugs and psychotropic substances. He then considers the role of other international and regional organisations involved in countering the drug problem, particularly in South-East Asia. McFarlane concludes that strategies have been developed which, if adopted by countries in the region, would go a long way not only to combating the supply of illicit drugs, but also to addressing the demand problem.

Paddy Mahoney, in chapter 3, describes statistical trends and events in the illicit drugs trade and predicts likely developments. Focusing on the domestic scene, it also discusses briefly the international trends that impact on Australia, and the place of illicit drugs in the National Drug Strategy. The chapter outlines law enforcement successes and difficulties in dealing with a range of illicit drugs, including some of the more recently marketed types, as well as the outcomes of legal action to confiscate the proceeds of drug-related crime. The chapter also describes a number of national law enforcement initiatives in the illicit drugs field, discusses issues such as targeting specific groups and decriminalising cannabis production and use, and suggests approaches that could be taken in formulating policy responses.

Illicit drugs and Australian democracy

Drugs such as cannabis and opium have been in existence for many hundreds, if not thousands, of years. Anti-drug laws, however, are a relatively recent phenomenon. Since the first anti-opium laws were passed in the 1890s, there has evolved in Australia a comprehensive and complex legal framework to enforce legal prohibitions against a wide range of drugs. In chapter 4, David Brereton provides a brief overview of some of the factors which have shaped the development of these laws. Two in particular have been of primary importance: the various international drug control treaties to which Australia has been a party; and the emergence of an illicit drug market in Australia during the 1960s and 1970s. Chapter 4 also analyses some recent trends that are taking place in Australian anti-drug legislation, relating these developments to a policy debate that increasingly appears to be driven by a demand for an easing of existing legal prohibitions. Finally, Brereton examines some of the main factors that continue to constrain the pace and direction of anti-drug reform in Australia, and discusses the prospects for future possible change.

In chapter 5, Andrew Parkin describes the characteristic liberal democratic mode of policy engagement and its character in recent political debates about illicit drugs. According to Parkin, liberal democratic states like Australia engage with the issue of illicit drugs, as they engage with other contentious policy issues, in a way which reflects an in-built tension between liberal and democratic values. That is, liberal democracies are responsive both to liberal claims and to democratic claims. Policy debates and strategies can oscillate between (on the one hand) liberal sensitivity to individual rights and opposition to enhanced state capacity; and (on the other hand) democratically legitimised community norms and collective values. Parkin argues that this spectrum of policy responses corresponds to an analogous spectrum within criminology which contrasts individualistic with structuralist conceptions of the nature and causes of crime.

John Broome, in chapter 6, examines illicit drugs in Australia from two main perspectives: supply and demand. He explores some of the issues relating to not only the social and political impact of the illicit drugs trade on Australia, but also the public policy dimensions of that trade. In particular, his chapter examines what we know about the illicit drugs trade, and highlights those areas where further research is required. In addition, chapter 6 examines the cost to Australia in social, economic and political terms, not only of the illicit drugs trade itself, but of our ignorance of the causes of that trade. Broome argues that without more publicly funded research and a well-informed policy debate, our choices on how to reduce the impact of the illicit drugs trade will remain limited and ineffective. He offers an acute practitioner's perspective on some of the issues raised in chapter 5.

Policy responses

Chapters 7–11 provide a series of critical perspectives upon national drugs policy in Australia. The main subject of discussion is the National Drug Strategy (NDS). Each contributor offers valuable insights into the strengths and weaknesses of the NDS. Key issues include political leadership accountability, policy formulation and the guiding principle of harm minimisation.

Chapter 7 is Timothy Rohl's account of his joint evaluation of the Australian National Drug Strategy (NDS) as implemented between 1993 and 1997. While recognising the importance of the NDS in terms of providing a more innovative and inclusive response to the Australian drug problem, the chapter criticises the performance of the NDS largely on the grounds that it lacks political commitment and democratic leadership, and is too fragmented in structure. Rohl outlines a number of ways to refocus the NDS and give it a new sense of purpose. In particular, he recommends that: NDS partnerships should be strengthened and expanded to the local level; a dedicated NDS Unit should be established; the NDS should be made more accountable for its performance; mainstream health, law enforcement and community officials should be trained to respond proactively to drug issues. He argues that the involvement and effectiveness of law enforcement in preventing drug-related harm should be enhanced—especially with respect to long-term strategic planning. Rohl concludes that despite its achievements and accomplishments, the NDS is currently in danger of sliding off the political agenda. What is required is for the Commonwealth Government to demonstrate political leadership by committing itself to the NDS and its reform. Only then will Australia move closer to the vision of becoming a society which deals effectively with drugs.

In chapter 8, David Crosbie also takes issue with current Australian procedures for drug policy development and accountability, arguing for increased accountability and more rigorous policy analysis. According to Crosbie, Australia's national drug-policy-making bodies represent an outstanding example of 'dysfunctional policy-making bureaucracy' by government. The structures generally exclude expert knowledge, community or consumer input. The ultimate decision-making power theoretically lies with a group of eighteen politicians representing nine different jurisdictions and both law enforcement and health interests. In recent years this main decision-making committee has met for around four hours per year to consider a very broad range of issues listed on an agenda that no one outside of senior government officials is allowed to see. Crosbie suggests that such structures avoid public accountability and discourage serious policy analysis. Currently in Australia, it is almost impossible to describe accurately the extent of drug problems, the response of different governments to these problems, and the effectiveness of these responses. While Australia may be a world leader in some areas of drug policy and practice, Crosbie argues that this has been achieved despite secretive government policy processes which have, at best, diluted efforts to reduce drug-related harm in Australia.

Ann Roche and Keith Evans, in chapter 9, provide an overview of the strengths and weaknesses of *harm reduction*—or harm minimisation as it is sometimes known. Harm reduction is one of the major policy and philosophical responses to drug use over the past decade in Australia and a number of other countries. These writers acknowledge that harm reduction—either as an end goal or as a set of strategies—has been a successful approach to dealing with drug issues. Nonetheless, they argue that to focus exclusively on abstinence or on harm reduction limits opportunities to recognise and address the contribution of other significant factors. A narrow approach also curtails scope for prevention efforts. Roche and Evans suggest that a broader model is needed to provide the overarching guidelines for formulating drug policies. Such a model could encompass a wider range of positions, some of which are antithetical to each other. They therefore recommend an integrated model in which no single approach is given priority over another. In this context, harm reduction is an essential element but one which operates among a range of other approaches.

In chapter 10, Adam Sutton and Stephen James review a unique attempt to assess the work of dedicated drug law enforcement agencies (e.g. state and territory drug squads, relevant sections of the Federal Police, Customs Australia and the National Crime Authority) throughout Australia. The study, conducted in 1993 and 1994 for Australia's National Police Research Unit, found that Australian drug law enforcement fell far short of being a 'rational' system with practices based on accurate and systematic assessment of problems, and operations continuously monitored for both intended and unintended consequences. Drug squad and other relevant officers often acknowledged that their work may have had little impact on the availability of illicit drugs. Even more disturbing, most exhibited little or no interest in implementing systems and indicators which would allow more accurate assessment of the effects of enforcement activity. Sutton and Jones outline the innovative pilot reforms currently being implemented in three different Australian jurisdictions. They acknowledge, however, that police and other enforcement authorities will encounter significant problems in trying to move away from reactive, 'zero tolerance' models toward more 'rational' approaches which place the emphasis on reducing drug-related harm and risk. Nonetheless, this pilot program offers an important initiative designed to increase the levels of accountability necessary for evaluating Australian policies on illicit drugs.

In the final chapter, Alex Wodak critically examines the historical development and outcomes of Australia's illicit drug policy. He then reviews the alternative strategies being pursued in Switzerland and the Netherlands. In the light of this comparison, Dr Wodak argues that the problem of illicit drug use in Australia should be redefined as primarily a health and social issue rather than a criminal justice one. Whilst maintaining that law enforcement is a necessary complement to health and social interventions, he stresses that it should not dominate policy, funding allocation or public rhetoric. He rejects as both unrealistic and socially harmful the objectives of a 'zero tolerance' strategy.

Conclusion

It is apparent that any effective response to illicit drugs will have to accept the inherently multidimensional character of the issue. It must be understood as a problem for individuals, society and democratic institutions. For this reason we must evaluate our policy responses in terms of a broader range of consequences and not just against legal and medical criteria. We must also be aware of what professional and political interests we are serving when we argue for one policy response rather than another. We must avoid at all cost, however, policies and policy making that are draconian and one-dimensional, and which undermine the system of democratic government. Given these considerations, can we afford not to take up policy options and 'experiments' that bolster rather than undermine our faith in the policy process? The task of broadening the political agenda is therefore not only one for democratic leadership and political will, but also one of creating effective partnerships within and between countries.

Australia in the World and Region

1

The Global Heroin and Cocaine Trade

Peter Chalk

WITH THE COLLAPSE of the Soviet bloc in Eastern Europe in the late 1980s and early 1990s, it appeared that the international system could be on the threshold of an era of unprecedented peace and stability. Politicians, diplomats and academics alike began to forecast the imminent establishment of a new world order, increasingly managed by democratic political institutions. These, it was believed, would develop within the context of an integrated international economic system based on the principles of the free market (International Monetary Fund 1991: 26–37). It was assumed that as this new world emerged, serious threats to international stability would decline commensurately.

The initial euphoria evoked by the end of the Cold War has now been replaced by a growing sense of unease that threats at the lower end of the conflict spectrum may soon assume greater prominence. Such concern has been stimulated largely by the remarkable fluidity that now characterises international politics—an environment in which it is no longer clearly apparent who can do what to whom and by what means. As Richard Latter (1991: 2) observes, the establishment of a new global security may reduce inter-state conflict only at the expense of an increase in so-called 'soft' security threats that fall below the level of conventional war.

One such issue now recognised as posing a significant threat to both national and international security is the illicit trade in drugs. The end of the Cold War has brought greater freedom of movement for people and goods in many countries, particularly those of the former Soviet Union and Eastern Europe. At the same time, the economic success of capitalism and its accompanying system of materialism has led to the so-called 'dollarisation' of the globe, whereby to possess money is now also to possess power, success and influence. While these effects of economic liberalisation and financial imperatives have led to a huge increase in legitimate transnational commercial enterprises, they have also helped to fuel a parallel underground international drug economy whose annual profits are now believed to be between $US200 billion and $US400 billion.*

Few areas of the world have been untouched in recent years by the illicit trade in narcotics. Its impact has been felt throughout Australasia, Europe, North America, South America, Africa and Asia, contributing to such corrosive effects as AIDS, social instability, a lack of economic performance, official corruption and the growing force of organised crime. Certainly recognition of the global threat currently posed by the drugs trade is evident in the decision to declare 1991–2000 the UN Decade Against Drug Abuse. It is also reflected by the numerous national and international bodies created specifically to address this problem (Kumar 1996: 209).

The purpose of this chapter is to assess the scope and impact of global production and trafficking in two prominent drugs of abuse: heroin and cocaine. The chapter will begin with an overview of the main statistical trends, production areas and trafficking routes of these two narcotic substances. The nature of the threat posed by the illicit trade in heroin and cocaine is then examined, particularly in relation to its impact on social, economic and political stability. Having set out the dimensions and impact of the global trade in these two drugs, the chapter examines the growing nexus between heroin and cocaine trafficking and two other threats to international stability and security: money laundering and terrorism.

---

* Throughout this volume the unit 'billion' is employed as being equivalent to a thousand million.

Major Production Areas and Trafficking Routes

Heroin

There are two main production areas for heroin: the Golden Crescent of South-West Asia; and the Golden Triangle of South-East Asia. It should be noted that a third, increasingly prominent heroin production area is now also emerging: Colombia. According to the Counselor for Narcotics Affairs at the US Embassy in Bangkok, Allen Nugent (personal interview, Bangkok, February 1998), Colombian cocaine syndicates have been diversifying into the heroin trade since the early 1990s, largely as a result of the saturation of the global cocaine market. According to Nugent, latest US Government figures show that at least 15 per cent of the heroin that is now trafficked to the USA comes from Colombia. In global terms, however, Colombia still accounts for only about 2 per cent of overall world heroin production.

Opium bound for the European market is produced principally in the Golden Crescent of South-West Asia, an area comprising southern Afghanistan, northern Pakistan and eastern Iran. In 1997, Afghanistan and Pakistan collectively cultivated a total of 43 250 hectares of opium poppy, generating a potential yield of 1350 metric tons of dry opium gum. Although current statistics for Iran are unavailable, in 1992 the US State Department estimated that the country had cultivated approximately 3500 hectares of opium, representing a potential yield of between 35 and 70 metric tons of opium gum. The main producer country in the Golden Crescent is Afghanistan, accounting for roughly 93 per cent of all opium cultivated in the region. In 1997, Afghanistan produced 1265 tons of opium gum, a 3 per cent increase on the 1996 yield. This translates into an approximate heroin output of 120 metric tons, most of which is refined in laboratories located along the Afghan—Pakistani border (US State Department 1998). Information obtained by the Australian Federal Police (AFP) liaison officer in Islamabad suggests that the Afghan opium yield in 1998 is likely to continue to grow. This is largely due to the continuing high levels of political instability in the country, and the Taliban's own willingness to fund its civil war on the back of heroin funds (Mahony et al. 1997: 14).

Most of the heroin that is produced in the Golden Crescent is smuggled to Europe by sophisticated Pakistani trafficking organisations operating out of the city of Quetta. These groups place orders with Afghani producers and arrange for transshipments of refined heroin to Iranian or Turkish buyers, who then move it into the European market. Considerable use is made in this regard of the so-called Balkan Corridor, a trafficking network that distributes heroin to major West European cities via one of two runs: northwards from Turkey through Bulgaria, Romania, Hungary and the Czech and Slovak Republics; or westwards through Greece, Albania, Macedonia, Croatia and Slovenia. The main transit countries within Western Europe are Austria and Germany for the northern route, and Italy for the western route (US State Department 1998; Jamieson 1992: 5; Economist Intelligence Unit 1991).

With the collapse of the Soviet Union, ethnically based gangs from Central Asia are also playing an increasingly pivotal role in the distribution of South-West Asian heroin. A secondary, increasingly used trafficking route run by Russian organised crime has thus emerged. This makes use of a distribution channel that runs from Afghanistan through refining centres in Turkmenistan, Uzbekistan, Kyrgyzstan and Kazakhstan to Moscow and from there to destinations in the Baltics and Western Europe (US State Department 1998). So extensive is this secondary refining and trafficking route that certain analysts are now referring to the four Caucasus states that comprise Central Asia as the 'new Colombia' (Kumar 1996: 213).

The second main production area for heroin is the Golden Triangle of South-East Asia, a region comprising the Shan hills of eastern Burma, the mountain crests of northern Thailand, and the high plateau of northern Laos. The vast majority of refined opium produced in this area is exported to North America and Australia, though significant quantities are also trafficked to Africa. In 1997, the Golden Triangle countries collectively cultivated approximately 184 950 hectares of opium poppy, generating a potential yield of 2600 metric tons of opium gum (US State Department 1998). In global terms, the Golden Triangle presently accounts for approximately 60 per cent of all known illicit opium production, fuelling an underground industry which is now thought to be worth at least $US160 billion (Chalk 1997: 42–3).

The main producer country in the Golden Triangle is Burma, currently accounting for roughly 91 per cent of all opium that is generated in the region. According to the US State Department (1998), the area under poppy cultivation in Burma increased from 92 300 hectares in 1987, through 154 000 hectares in 1995 to 155 150 hectares in 1997. The potential heroin output from this crop soared from 54 metric tons in 1987 to 197 metric tons in 1997, enough to satisfy the US market many times over (US General Accounting Office 1996: 24). According to a 1996 report issued by the US Embassy in Rangoon, the exports of opiates alone from Burma now appear to exceed the value of all legal exports combined (Lintner 1996: 435–6).

The principal heroin warlord in Burma for many years was Chang Chifu, more commonly known as Khun Sa. During the 1960s, 1970s and 1980s he developed an increasingly powerful opium—heroin 'empire', thanks largely to the backing he received from both the Rangoon Government and the CIA. By the 1980s, over 50 per cent of the heroin that was produced in the country was refined by Khun Sa. The remainder was largely accounted for by Chifu's main rival, Lo Hsiung-Han, who also benefited from Burmese and US backing. Chang Chifu used the extensive profits from his drug trade to finance his own private militia (the 15 000-strong *Mong Tai* Army/MTA) as well as a thriving Shan 'capital' in Ho Mong (The Shan Connection, *Economist*, 6 January 1996; Former MP turned over to USA on drug charges, *South China Morning Post*, 27 January 1996).

In January 1996 Khun Sa was reported to have surrendered to the Burmese Government, raising hopes that a key player in the Golden Triangle's heroin nexus had been 'neutralised' (The Shan Connection, *Economist*, 6 January 1996). Nevertheless, the surrender is unlikely to have any discernible effect on heroin movements coming out of the region, for two main reasons. First, it now appears that, far from giving himself up, Khun Sa has actually struck a deal with the Burmese junta. According to Western observers in Rangoon, Khun Sa has agreed to end the *Mong Tai* separatist war only on condition that he be allowed to remain in charge of his current drug operation and trafficking routes (personal interview with Gavin Greenwood, Senior Asian Analyst of the Control Risks Group, London, January 1997).

Second, Khun Sa no longer dominates the heroin trade in the Golden Triangle as he previously did. Since 1989 he has progressively lost ground to a new generation of more influential and better connected traffickers located in the Kokang area of northern Shan State on the Burma–southern Chinese frontier. According to the US Drug Enforcement Agency (DEA), the main players in the Golden Triangle's opium trade now appear to be Chao Nyi Lai, who heads the United Wa Army and works in conjunction with the Wei brothers, two traffickers who operate a network of smuggling routes along the Burmese—Thai border; and Lin Mingxian and Zhang Zhiming, two former Red Guards who control several refineries in eastern Shan State (personal interview with Allen Nugent, Bangkok, February 1998). Certainly there is, as yet, no sign of Khun Sa's surrender leading to any significant reduction in the supply of heroin from the Golden Triangle.

A large amount of the heroin that is produced in the Golden Triangle is smuggled across the Burmese—Thai border, transported to Bangkok, Malaysia or Singapore, and trafficked from there to Japan, Australia or the USA in shipping containers or on board commercial and passenger flights. A secondary, increasingly used, route makes use of Laos as a transit point for shipments bound for Cambodia and Vietnam. The Cambodian heroin is exported to international markets either in shipping containers from the south-western port of Koh Kong or by human couriers from Phnom Penh's Pochentong international airport. Most of the Vietnamese heroin is trafficked north through the southern Chinese provinces of Yunnan and Guangxi to Guangdong and then taken either overland or by boat to neighbouring Hong Kong, where local triad gangs operate sophisticated transit routes to Asia and North America (Chalk 1997: 43; Lintner 1996: 13; Economist Intelligence Unit 1995: 5).

A final route makes use of Nigeria as an intermediary transshipment point for heroin bound both for Africa (most of which goes to South Africa) and the USA. Rampant corruption at virtually all levels of Nigerian Government administration has ensured that this country is now playing an increasingly pivotal role in the international distribution of South-East Asian heroin, especially to the North American market (US State Department 1998).

Cocaine

Virtually all of the world's cocaine originates from the Andean region of South America. The main producer countries are Peru, Bolivia and Colombia. In 1997, these three countries collectively produced 194 100 metric tons of coca leaf, generating a base of sufficient quantity to yield a potential output of 650 metric tons of refined cocaine. Despite a concerted crop eradication program in Peru (giving the country its lowest coca yield in over ten years), the 1997 figures only represent a modest decline of 5 per cent from the 1996 estimate of 48 100 hectares. This is largely because gains made in Peru were offset by a major increase (18 per cent) in Colombian coca production (US State Department 1998; Mahony et al. 1997: 32–3).

The majority of the coca that is grown and cultivated in South America is refined in Colombia—the world's leading producer and distributor of cocaine. According to the US State Department (1998), in 1997 three-quarters of all known illicit cocaine originated from Colombia, most of which was trafficked to markets in North America and Western Europe. Prior to 1994, virtually every aspect of cocaine refining and trafficking in Colombia was dominated by two syndicates: the Cali Cartel and (especially) the Medellin Cartel. Since the killing of the Medellin leader Pablo Escobar in December 1993, however, as well as the capture of leading members of the Cali 'inner circle' in 1996 (including the group's two alleged founding members, Gilberto and Miguel Rodriguez Orejula), control of the country's cocaine trade has become more fragmented and dispersed. In particular, newer, smaller organisations based to the north of Cali, as well as the ultra-leftist Simon Bolivar Guerrilla Coordination (CGSB, an umbrella guerrilla group which uses profits from the drug trade to finance its continuing rural insurgency against the Bogotá Government), now appear to be in the ascendant. This is a trend that is expected to accelerate over the coming years (US State Department 1998; Control Risks Group 1997: 117; Kumar 1996: 211).

A variety of trafficking methods are used to export cocaine from Latin America. Cocaine intended for the North American market is smuggled out of Colombia by light aircraft, flown up the Pacific coast of Central America to Mexico, where it is transported overland to the USA. To facilitate the transshipment of cocaine into the USA, considerable use is made of Mexican crime syndicates who have both experience and expertise in running sophisticated smuggling operations across the heavily guarded southern US border (most of which has been gained as a result of trafficking illegal aliens into Texas and California) (Mahony et al. 1997: 32; P. Williams 1995: 243; Paternostro 1995: 43–4).

Cocaine bound for Europe (the majority of which is handled by the Sicilian Mafia or *Cosa Nostra*) is exported largely by sea, mainly from ports in Venezuela and Brazil. Most is concealed in legitimate shipping cargo destined for European ports such as Rotterdam, Genoa, Barcelona, and, increasingly, northern coastal locations on the Baltic Sea, such as the Polish city of Gdyina. A secondary route runs via territories with British, French or Dutch links in the eastern Caribbean. In this instance, the cocaine is first smuggled from Latin America on board small, privately owned ships and yachts to a variety of ports in the Lesser Antilles such as Dominica, St Kitts, St Lucia, the Virgin Islands, Martinique, Guadeloupe and Aruba. It is then off-loaded onto larger commercial vessels (particularly European-based fishing trawlers) for the final trip across the Atlantic (US State Department 1998; US State Department 1997: 8–10).

West Africa has also emerged as an increasingly used trafficking transshipment point for heroin, as for cocaine. This alternative route makes use of Nigerian and Ghanaian couriers who smuggle cocaine directly from the Andean countries via West Africa to major West European capitals, as well as secondary destinations in Southern Africa (such as Johannesburg, Durban and Cape Town). These human 'mules' typically 'carry' their product internally in cocaine-filled condoms, earning on average about $US2000 per trip (US State Department 1998; Drugs courier dies after swallowing 500g of cocaine, *Independent*, 10 November 1992). According to Allen Nugent (personal interview, Bangkok, February 1998), West Africans (especially Nigerians) are playing an increasingly pivotal role in global heroin and cocaine trafficking. Nugent asserts that extremely sophisticated smuggling rings are now being run from capitals such as Lagos, where human mules are supplied with everything from false identification documents to counterfeit money. Nugent argues that in terms of the illicit trafficking of narcotics, West Africans probably now pose one of the greatest threats of any group in the world.

Heroin and Cocaine Addiction

Not surprisingly, the huge quantities of heroin and cocaine that are currently being trafficked around the world can be linked to a growing global addiction problem. This has affected not only the developed countries of Western Europe, North America and Australasia, where most of the drugs are consumed. It has also impacted on producer and/or transit countries, many of which have suffered substantial rises in addiction in recent years. The following figures (US State Department 1998; Congressional Research Service 1997: 30; Chalk 1997: 47; Mahony et al. 1997: 32; Lintner 1996: 5) are merely some of the more dramatic examples that could be used to illustrate the extent of cocaine and heroin addiction around the world:

- By 1994, Colombia had an estimated 600 000 cocaine addicts.
- Approximately 1.5 million Americans are currently believed to use cocaine regularly (of which 420 000 use crack cocaine), with a further 548 000 addicted to heroin.
- Experts believe that at least 250 000 Canadians are addicted to cocaine.
- In Italy, approximately 140 000 people are addicted to either heroin or cocaine.
- Roughly 500 000 people are addicted to heroin in Thailand.
- In 1996, the Government of Iran stated that the number of heroin addicts in the country was 500 000; non-official estimates, however, run as high as 2 000 000 (although these statistics often fail to distinguish between 'users' and 'addicts').
- Anecdotal evidence suggests that the official figure of 520 000 heroin addicts in China significantly underestimates the scale of the problem there.
- It is believed that the number of heroin addicts in Pakistan is now as high as 3.5 million.

• According to official figures, there are presently over two million drug users in Russia, a significant proportion of whom are believed to be hard-core heroin addicts.

The Threat Posed by the Trade

There are four main dimensions to the threat posed by the global trade in heroin and cocaine. First, and most visibly, it contributes to growing social instability by encouraging high rates of crime. This emanates from users struggling to finance their habit as well as traffickers and distributors striving to gain control of a greater share of the narcotics market. Drug-related arrests in the Chinese province of Guangdong have risen nearly fifty times between 1990 and 1996 on account of the South-East Asian heroin trade. It is estimated that 80 per cent of all crimes committed in the southern Chinese provinces are currently committed by heroin addicts (Chalk 1997: 47; Lintner 1995: 16). Figures in the Czech Republic are even more dramatic. In 1997, the country's main anti-drug squad, the Nardoni Proti-Drogovy Central (NPDC), reported a staggering 300 per cent increase in drug-related crime, with street-level violence linked to the heroin trade becoming almost a daily occurrence in Prague (Slatem 1998: 40).

In the USA, cocaine and crack (a smokeable derivative of cocaine) sales fuel much of the country's drug violence, as gangs compete for lucrative sales territory and addicts steal to feed their habit (US State Department 1998). Throughout Colombia in early 1993, a wave of violence exploded as a result of inter-factional fighting within the Medellin cartel between Pablo Escobar and a rival group calling itself Pepes. In one month, Pepes killed over twenty Escobar loyalists and carried out eleven dynamite attacks, causing approximately $US8 million worth of damage to prop- erties owned by the Escobar family (In a 'Dirty War,' former drug allies are terrorizing Escobar, *New York Times*, 14 March 1993). At least up until the death of Escobar in December 1993, 40 per cent of all killings in Colombia were believed to be related to the country's cocaine trade. In Russia, the period since 1990 has seen a series of highly destabilising drug turf wars, with most violence connected to the attempts by the *Mafiya* to eliminate new threats from the *bespredel'chiki*, a younger, newer generation of narcotics criminals (Galeotti 1998b: 10). In Australia, it has been estimated that more than $A312 million is raised each year by heroin users and dealers engaging in various forms of property crime (Broome 1997); while in Switzerland in 1994, over 2000 Albanians were being held on heroin-related offences (Crime and corruption foster calls for greater police power, *Criminal Justice Europe* 4(1) 1994: 10.)

Virtually all countries experiencing increased cocaine and heroin use in recent years have suffered from similar patterns of endemic crime and violence. In certain inner-city ghettos of Peru, Brazil and Mexico, the problem has become so great that any notion of civil society has largely disappeared. As John McFarlane (1997), observes, in these instances crime is not only seen as the fast track to success; it is often regarded as the only path to survival. The ensuing instability encourages yet more crime, thus perpetuating the problem. The end result is an extreme case of societal dislocation.

Second, heroin and cocaine use is helping to foster the spread of one of the most lethal diseases of our time—AIDS (Acquired Immune Deficiency Syndrome). This has been particularly evident in South-East Asia as a result of the intravenous injection of heroin. According to the Office of Narcotics Control Board (ONCB) in Bangkok (personal interview July 1997), Thailand currently has to administer at least 50 000 confirmed heroin addicts, the majority of whom are also HIV positive as a result of sharing needles. Similarly Burma, which was free of AIDS only a few years ago, now has an estimated 200 000 people carrying the HIV virus, 74 per cent of whom are tested heroin users (Lintner 1995: 19). China has been especially hard hit. The Beijing Government officially admits that the outbreak of an AIDS epidemic is directly related to drug addicts sharing needles to inject heroin. Indeed the small border town of Ruili in Yunnan has one of the highest concentrations of opium addicts in the province, and is now in the unenviable position of also being the AIDS capital of China (Lintner 1995: 16).

Third, the costs associated with trying to control the global cocaine and heroin trade are contributing to a lack of economic performance in source, transit and consumer states. As production and trafficking of these narcotics increase, so more and more resources have to be diverted to treat addicts through detoxification, health and rehabilitation programs, as well as to finance the clinics to treat those afflicted with AIDS on account of their habit. Moreover, the violence and crime that have come to surround heroin and cocaine addiction and trafficking mean that public resources also have to be channelled into law enforcement —further reducing the availability of funds to stimulate economic productivity (Chalk 1997: 48).

The true extent of the finances needed to control the drug trade is well exemplified by the United States. In February 1998, President Clinton allocated almost $US16 000 million to fund the country's anti-drug effort. Over the last ten years, the US Government has spent, at the federal level, $US110 000 million to fight drugs. If one includes monies allocated by state and local governments in addition to out-of-pocket efforts by businesses, communities, schools and private individuals, the total rises to an incredible $US500 000 million (a sum which does not include the indirect costs of drug use measured in terms of human suffering, increased violence and lost lives). Every year, the US anti-drug effort consumes the overwhelming majority of federal state funds as well as the resources allocated by state, local and private groups. On average, this amounts to more than $US30 000 million annually (Grassley 1997: 10–11; McCaffrey 1997: 5). As the table below illustrates, 1998 was likely to be every bit as costly, at least at government level:

Costs of fighting drug abuse in the USA, 1997–98 (federal allocations, $US million)

DRUG FUNCTION	FY97	FY98
Law Enforcement	7 835	8 126
Treatment	2 808	3 003
Prevention	1 648	1 916
International	450	487
Interdiction	1 638	1 609
Research/Intelligence	723	831
TOTAL	$15 102	$15 972

Source: USA Electronic Information Agency

Fourth, drug money from the illicit trade in cocaine and heroin is playing a key role in weakening and undermining already weak and vulnerable regimes by encouraging official corruption in government and military circles. The profit margins involved in the sale of illicit narcotics are truly colossal, and all the more so because they are untaxed. The wholesale price for one kilogram of heroin in Thailand, for instance, is estimated to be between $US3400 and $US5600. It is believed that the same kilogram would cost a British wholesaler up to $US51 000, with the price rising to $US250 000 in the USA. The current cost of a single 'hit' of heroin (less than one gram) in London is around £10 sterling, while the street price for a whole kilogram sold in New York is well over fourteen times the purchase price in Yunnan (personal interviews with Gavin Greenwood and Allen Nugent in London and Bangkok, January 1997 and February 1998; Jamieson 1990: 23–4).

The potential profits from the cocaine trade are just as dramatic. As the US State Department (1998) observes:

> Assuming an average retail street price of $US100 per gram, a metric ton of pure cocaine has a retail value of $US100 million on the streets of a US city—two or three times as much if the drug is cut with adulterants. By this measure, the 100 or so metric tons of cocaine that the US Government typically seizes each year are theoretically worth as much as $US10 billion to the drug trade, more than the gross domestic product of many countries.

Mexico, Colombia, Thailand and Italy are all examples of states where the problem of drug-induced corruption has been especially serious. In Russia, none of the country's main institutions have escaped allegations of links with the *Mafiya*, including the Prime Minister's office, the civil service, armed forces, big business, regional authorities and the Duma (Galeotti 1988b: 6; Attanasio 1994: 91–3). In 1996, forty-three high-ranking officials in Colombia were detained in a series of narcotics-related investigations, including members of President Samper's cabinet; an additional 2000 policemen suspected of corruption were removed from their positions (US State Department 1998). In Thailand, numerous MPs—including Vatana Asavaname, a former deputy interior minister and deputy leader of Chart Thai, and Narong Wongwan, leader of the prominent Justice and Unity Party—have been 'fingered' by the US Government for their involvement in the Golden Triangle's drug trade (Kumar 1996: 219; Lintner 1995: 11; Former MP turned over to USA on drugs charges, *South China Morning Post*, 27 January 1996; Smells in high places, *Economist*, 28 May 1994.). According to Lintner (1995: 14), drug-induced corruption in Thailand has much to do with the country's long-established practice of vote buying:

> In every election, millions of dollars are spent on securing votes for powerful candidates [as much as 20 million baht/$US1 billion in the November 1996 general election]. Only a tiny fraction of this money actually goes to paying off voters. The bulk is spent on financing gangsters who enforce the will of politicians and make sure the people vote for the 'right' candidate. Money rules politics in Thailand's provinces and in cities like Chiang Rai the fastest and easiest money comes from the local drugs trade.

And in Italy, over 3000 executives, politicians and government personnel were implicated in a pervasive corruption network that was revealed as part of a major crackdown against the Sicilian Mafia between 1992 and 1993 (Italy in Furore as 'Mata Hari' Talks of Military Plot, *New York Times*, 19 October 1993).

Money Laundering

Because heroin and cocaine profits derive from an illegal source, producers and traffickers need to launder their proceeds to make them appear clean. Only then can they be re-invested (either in legal or illegal activities) without leaving a paper trail. Money laundering thus has three basic stages: accumulation, transformation, and re-investment. The process typically involves corrupt accountants, bankers and lawyers whose job is to invest drug-related funds in companies, banks and financial safe havens known for their prestige and integrity (Jamieson 1990: 24).

These money-laundering schemes can be extremely large. In one notable Australian case, for instance, it was discovered that $US16.5 million which had been invested in Sydney real estate operations originated from a $US1 billion heroin trade between Thailand and New York. Estimates by the Australian Transaction Reports and Analysis Centre (AUSTRAC) put the total illegal proceeds generated by drug-related money laundering in Australia alone (most of which is connected to heroin from the Golden Triangle) between $A1 billion and $A4.5 billion. This is significant, since Australia is believed to have financial reporting laws which are among the tightest of any state in the world (John Walker Consulting Services 1995: 39; World class crime, *Australian*, 18 December 1995). According to Peter Quirk (Chief of the Exchange Regime and Economic Operations Division of the International Monetary Fund (IMF), FATF Plenary Meeting, January 1995), in 1995 the United Nations estimated that at least $US500 billion is laundered each year (much of it related to illicit drugs), roughly equivalent to 2 per cent of global GDP.

The banking system remains one of the most important vehicles for laundering money. A variety of methods are used, typically involving the physical transformation of cash through banking bearer instruments such as money drafts, cheques, telegraphic transfers and the establishment of loan back schemes (McDonald 1997: 3). Nonetheless, the banking system is not the only means by which drug-related profits are laundered. Other favoured means include (US Department of Justice 1995: 34–5; Jamieson 1990: 24–6):

- the exchange of small-denomination bank notes for gambling chips or winning lottery tickets;
- transfer payments through the use of company trade accounts in more than one country;
- bulk smuggling of cash in courier-carried luggage, and its investment in offshore bank accounts;
- investment of money in front/shell companies;
- invoice manipulation, which involves the falsification of shipping documents and invoices through the overvaluing or undervaluing of imports and exports.

An additional method that is principally used to launder heroin profits from South-East and South-West Asia is the underground banking system. This procedure relies entirely on trust between families, secret societies or close knit ethnic groups who are often located many thousands of miles apart. The system has two main advantages. First, as it completely bypasses conventional financial channels, it is extremely hard to detect. Second, it is faster than that used by official banks—hundreds of thousands dollars can be transferred to another country in a matter of hours (US Department of Justice 1995: 34–5; and Jamieson 1990: 24–6). Allen Nugent (personal interview, Bangkok, February 1998), explains how the system works:

> Suppose a heroin dealer ('A') in Hong Kong wants to wire some of his proceeds to Bangkok. 'A' goes into a pawnbroker in Hong Kong (usually run by a family member) and informs the owner of his intentions. The pawnbroker notifies a sister company in Bangkok and issues 'A' with a chit authorising him to collect the funds on arrival. 'A' then leaves the equivalent sum with the pawnbroker in Hong Kong which is deposited into a bank account nominated by the sister company in Bangkok. 'A' travels to Bangkok, shows his chit, and receives his money.

Money laundering poses a major global problem. Not only does this form of white-collar crime directly enhance the economic and political power of drug syndicates; it also works to undermine the stability of local and international financial systems.

The Bank of Credit and Commerce International (BCCI) scandal provides a good example of the type of macro-economic damage that can be caused by such illicit financial activities. Following a two-year undercover operation codenamed C-CHASE, it was revealed that the BCCI had been involved in a variety of money-laundering schemes, including those of the Abu Nidal Organisation (a radical Palestinian terror group), the Colombian Medellin cartel and Manuel Noriega (the 'drug-tainted' former leader of Panama). The scandal led directly to the demise of the world's seventh largest private bank, an event which had significant repercussions in both the developed and developing world. By the time of its closure, the BCCI had assets in excess of $US23 billion, conducting operations in seventy-three countries. The affair also raised serious questions concerning the responsibilities and role of auditors and bank regulators, revealing a stream of endemic corruption in many countries where the bank had operated (Kumar 1996: 216–17; McDonald 1997: 9–10).

Narco-Terrorism

A final dimension of the illicit trade in heroin and cocaine that is eliciting growing concern is the use of terrorism by drug lords for specific political purposes. Terrorism here is regarded as the use, or threat to use, indiscriminate violence against noncombatant victims as a means to achieve specific political objectives. Generally, such violence is deployed in an attempt to force advantageous (or curtail disadvantageous) changes in the law. To date, most narco-terrorism has taken place in Colombia, where both the Medellin and Cali cartels have resorted to acts of random violence in response to Government anti-narcotic efforts. By the end of 1993, drug-related violence had cost the country the lives of an Attorney General, a Justice Minister, three Presidential candidates, more than two hundred judges, thirty kidnap victims, at least one thousand policemen and countless civilians (McFarlane 1997: 24).

Some of the acts of terrorism carried out by the Colombian cartels have been particularly destructive. In 1989, the Medellin cartel took responsibility (under the name of the 'Extraditables') for the mid-air destruction of a Colombian Aviancia jet, which resulted in the deaths of all 107 people aboard. The attack was intended to dissuade the government from extraditing the country's twelve most wanted drug lords to the USA. In February 1993, the late Pablo Escobar publicly announced a campaign of violence to pressure the government into granting immunity to drug traffickers. Immediately following the declaration, a series of attacks were carried out in several Colombian cities (claimed by the Antioquia Rebel Movement—another flag of convenience for the Medellin cartel), including three car bombings in Bogotá and Medellin which left twenty people dead (including five children) and sixty others seriously wounded (Newsweek Investigation, *Bulletin*, 14 December 1993; The ten worst acts of aircraft sabotage, *Terrorism* VI(4)

1991: 2–3 Bombs explode in Colombia cities, *New York Times*, 1 February 1993).

Russia and Italy have also been seriously afflicted by narco-terrorism in recent years. In Russia, the *Mafiya* have been implicated in numerous acts of terrorism since 1992, including several civilian bombings and at least sixteen killings of high-profile businessmen, politicians and journalists. The *Mafiya* have also been tied to a significant proportion of the 1009 police deaths that have occurred since 1994, many of which were carried out with a specific political rationale in mind (Galeotti 1998a:17; Allan 1993: 16; Top echelon of mobsters pose threat, *New York Times*, 23 August 1994). Drug-related political violence in Italy has been just as problematic, with major bomb attacks being the typical response to increased government anti-narcotic efforts. Following the introduction of tough crime legislation in 1992, for instance, a wave of Mafia-instigated terrorism swept the country. Included in the group's attacks were the assassination of the country's two leading anti-Mafia prosecutors, Giovanni Falcone and Paolo Borsellino, as well as the bombings of several historic sites and galleries in Rome, Florence and Milan (Bombers target Italy's reforms, *Daily Telegraph*, 29 July 1993).

One particularly disturbing feature of the narco-terrorism carried out in Italy and Russia is its apparent interconnectedness. Authorities in Rome have long suspected that drug-related political violence in the country has been aided by certain 'outside' forces, with such claims being especially prominent following the Rome, Florence and Milan bombings. More ominous are suggestions about a possible joint Russian/Italian narcotics death squad made up of ex-KGB agents and equipped with the latest weapons of the former USSR (Galeotti 1998a: 18; Medd and Goldstein 1997: 284–5; Sterling 1994: 16–65, 94). While such allegations have yet to be conclusively proven, they should not be dismissed lightly. Compared to the meagre salaries currently paid by the Russian state (estimated at approximately $US136 a month), employment in the service of the drug trade doubtless represents a highly tempting and lucrative alternative for many ex-members of the Russian security services. Such a development would not only qualitatively increase the geopolitical spread of violence available to drug cartels in both Italy and Russia; if left unchecked, it could also mushroom into a security threat of pandemic proportions.

There are fears that South-East Asia, too, may go down the narco-terrorist path already followed by Colombia, Italy and Russia. Largely as a result of increased USA pressure on Indo-Chinese states to strengthen their anti-narcotic efforts, opportunities for taking advantage of official corruption in the region are being curtailed, or at least reduced. The governments of Thailand, Laos, Cambodia and even Burma have all stated their willingness to work in conjunction with US Drug Enforcement Agency (DEA) crop eradication, alternative development and production interception programs, as well as to participate in DEA-organised workshops designed to enhance up-to-date anti-drug techniques and procedures. It should be noted, however, that the US Government remains somewhat ambiguous over Burma's overall commitment to eradicating heroin production in its borders.

Despite the obvious value of such international initiatives, the concern is that they could very well spark the type of violent reaction already seen in states such as Colombia and Italy. A spate of terrorist attacks carried out in the southern Thai border districts between August and December 1997, for example, are believed by a number of analysts to be the work of drug racketeers who are beginning to feel the pressures of increased government narcotics suppression efforts over the past two years. Since 1995, Cambodia has also seen a surge of assassination attempts and grenade attacks—including the August 1997 bombing of a packed night club in Phnom Penh—as local heroin syndicates have attempted to derail plans to introduce more effective narcotics and money-laundering measures (Alexander 1995: 429; Anti-drugs chief flees into exile, *Australian*, 17 March 1998; Scope of narcoterrorism link with Khun Sa viewed, *Bangkok Post*, 12 June 1995; Medellin on the Mekong, *Far Eastern Economic Review*, 23 November 1995). It is in Burma, however, that the real danger of South-East Asian narco-terrorism lies. Virtually all of the Golden Triangle's heroin production takes place in this country. Moreover, the syndicates that exist in the region (such as the Wa) have all been able to build up fairly substantial private militias over the years on the back of lucrative drug-running operations. Given these factors, any moves by the Burmese Government to crack down on opium production activities would almost certainly be met with a violent reaction (personal interview with Allen Nugent, Bangkok, February 1998).

Conclusion

There can be little doubt that the global trade in heroin and cocaine remains one of the most significant threats to national and international stability in the modern era. Production and trafficking of these two narcotic substances can be linked to the spread of AIDS and HIV, social instability, a lack of economic performance, official corruption, political violence and the growing force of organised international crime. These insidious and corrosive effects have been felt, in one form or another, in cities as far apart as Moscow, Sydney, Bogotá, New York, London and Cape Town.

In confronting the political threat posed by the illicit trade in cocaine and heroin, it is vital that the international community approach the issue in a comprehensive fashion, concentrating on the whole ambit of counter-narcotics options available. Certainly, viewing the problem as simply a matter of 'supply control and interdiction' would seem to miss the mark. Dealing effectively with the heroin and cocaine trade requires an inclusive strategy that emphasises both supply disruption and demand reduction. In other words, it necessitates social, political, judicial and educational action in source, transit and user-end countries. Of particular importance will be:

- preventative drug education, aimed at creating heightened individual, group and community awareness of the cause and effect of drug abuse;
- treatment and rehabilitation, aimed at severing the dependence on illicit narcotics and assisting with the social re-integration of recovering drug dependents;
- law enforcement, aimed at reducing the supply of illicit narcotics and rendering their procurement, sale and consumption highly risky.

If such initiatives are to work they will require a greater degree of political will than most nation states in the international community have so far demonstrated. While certain states have pledged to augment their efforts to control the cocaine and heroin trade in this direction, official apathy is widespread and continues to work against effective counter-measures. Only when there is a global appreciation of the true causes and effects of drug abuse will substantial progress be made against this highly distinctive sociopolitical, economic and security problem.

2

Drug Trafficking in South-East Asia: Security Issues

John McFarlane

THE GLOBAL DEMAND for illicit drugs has created a market estimated at some $US400 billion per year (United Nations International Drug Control Programme 1997b: 124). This market is largely controlled by criminal syndicates which have thrived on the untaxed proceeds of illegal endeavours and corrupted significant sections of the societies in which they have operated. If we add to that the loss of thousands of young lives and the effect which this has had on families and friends, the spread of HIV/ AIDS, and the distortion of the health and criminal justice sectors, it is apparent that illicit drug use and abuse is a problem which affects all levels of society in many countries.

Consider the following figures for the USA provided by the United States Office of Drug Control Policy. Each year Americans spend $US49 billion on illegal drugs; American governments (federal and state) spend $US30 billion on supply and demand reduction efforts; the social cost of drug-related crime is $US67 billion; there are 25 000 drug-related deaths; and thousands of US babies are exposed to illegal drugs *in vitro* (Mendal and Munder 1997). No nation, not even one as wealthy as the USA, can afford to lose $US146 billion from its economy as a result of illicit drug abuse. It is little wonder, therefore that the US Government has launched a 'War on Drugs', in which up to 10 000 armed services personnel, major surveillance platforms and intelligence resources, and about $US1 billion of defence funding are devoted to supporting the enforcement efforts in intercepting illicit drugs smuggled into the

USA. Nevertheless, it is a 'war' which cannot be won by tackling the *supply* side alone; if there was less *demand* by illicit drug users, the supply problem would be largely irrelevant. This is a 'war' which needs to be fought on at least two fronts if it is to be won. The recent 'Tough on Drugs' policy has recognised this fact and allocated funds both to supply and demand reduction strategies (Howard 1997).

This chapter will examine a number of aspects of the problem of illicit drug production and trafficking from South-East Asia. It will also consider some of the international and regional initiatives taken to encourage joint strategies and cooperation between governments and law enforcement agencies. These strategies have the objectives of dealing with both the demand and supply side of drug abuse, tackling the transnational crime syndicates involved in the drug trade, and attacking the proceeds of their criminal activities.

Regional Security and Stability Issues

Generally, issues of international security and stability have been analysed in terms of military or strategic threats. Whilst external military threats still exist, it is increasingly agreed that states must now consider a wider variety of security threats, both internal and external. In addition to military threats, the security of the nation state can be menaced by threats to its economic well-being, political stability, social harmony, environment and even the health of its citizens (Evans 1993: 6). Emerging from this perspective, Buzan (1991: 19–20) argues that in the post-Cold-War period 'the security of human collectives' is affected in five major areas:

- *military security* (i.e. 'the two-level interplay of the armed offensive and defensive capabilities of states, and states' perceptions of each other's intentions');
- *political security* (i.e. 'the organisational stability of states, systems of government and the ideologies that give them legitimacy');
- *economic security* (i.e. 'access to the resources, finance and markets necessary to sustain acceptable levels of welfare and state power');

- *societal security* (i.e. 'the sustainability, within acceptable conditions for evolution, of traditional patterns of language, culture and religious and national identity and customs');
- *environmental security* (i.e. 'the maintenance of the local and planetary biosphere as the essential support system on which all other human enterprises depend').

Transnational crime has a very significant impact across each of these areas.

Military security

In relation to military security, criminality can have at least three consequences. First, where a state is governed by a regime which has a symbiotic relationship with organised crime, the military and law enforcement authorities controlled by the regime can obviously be used for criminal purposes, or to protect criminal enterprises. In this category might be included the relationship between the former Soviet *nomenklatura* and organised crime, which was structurally embedded within the political and economic system of the nation. With the fragmentation of the former Soviet Union, the criminal groups which had been involved with the *nomenklatura* fragmented into predatory gangs, involving themselves in extortion and *mafiya* capitalism. The former Noriega regime in Panama and the Marcos regime in the Philippines had a generally similar relationship with criminal organisations. Lupsha (1996: 32) describes these criminal groups as 'consolidated or corporatised'.

In the second category, the organised crime groups have a number of symbiotic ties to the state, but still appear to be subject to the political will and institutions of the state. In many senses they appear to be either employees or franchised by dominant state institutions (including the police and military) which use them to their own ends. Countries where this appears to occur include Cambodia, Taiwan, Albania, Mexico, Nigeria, Rwanda, Liberia, Sierra Leone, Pakistan, Syria and Lebanon. Some critics would say that the heavy involvement of the military in business activities in a number of countries represents significant opportunities for corruption and symbiotic relationships with organised crime groups. Lupsha (1996: 33) describes these groups as 'transitional or linked organisations'.

A third set of transnational crime groups have emerged out of the absence of properly established civil society, as in the former Soviet Union and Eastern Europe; or out of insurgency and conflict, as in Sri Lanka, Burma, Afghanistan, Turkey, Somalia and Bosnia; or out of both sets of conditions. Often these organised criminal groups are linked to the former institutions of the state, such as the former organs of intelligence, the military or former totalitarian bureaucracy and economy. Lupsha (1996: 33–4) describes these groups as 'in-flux or emergent'.

Finally, military security is also affected in some countries (such as Burma, Colombia, Peru and Afghanistan) in which the drug traffickers either have their own military capacity or are able to use related insurgent groups to engage government forces in guerrilla warfare to protect their interests. Examples in this category include some of the Somalian factions, the Liberation Tigers of Tamil Eelam (LTTE) in Sri Lanka, the Kurdish Workers' Party in Turkey and some of the Caucasian separatist groups in Russia (Turbiville 1994). The reliance of a number of insurgent groups on narcotics production and trafficking to finance their campaigns gives rise to the problem of narco-terrorism (Ciccarelli 1995: 49–57). Lupsha (cited in Interpol 1987:2) defines narco-terrorism as 'acts of terror and violence against civilian populations and authority aimed at intimidation, and to thwart law enforcement and to maintain the drug traffickers' control over a given area of drug cultivation and/or production'.

One of the main difficulties in dealing with the concept of narco-terrorism is in reaching agreement on what activities we understand to be terrorism, as distinct from insurgency or merely the demonstration of political opposition. Wardlaw (1982), for example, defines terrorism as 'the use, or threat of use, of violence by an individual or group, whether acting for or in opposition to established authority, when such action is designed to create extreme anxiety and/or fear inducing effects in a target group larger than the immediate victims, with the purpose of coercing that group into acceding to the political demands of the perpetrators'. Nevertheless, official opinion on these issues varies widely throughout the South-East Asian region.

There is no real evidence that terrorist groups in the region are deliberately using drugs to encourage widespread addiction or attack the moral fibre of the people they are targeting. It is reported, however, that the Taliban militia has banned the use of opiates and other narcotics in the areas they control in Afghanistan, but that they are quite happy to export heroin to the West. While this is a good foreign currency earner, the Taliban has offered to stop this trade if the West recognises their fundamentalist regime (Rashid 1997: 15). It is clear, nonetheless, that a number of terrorist or insurgent groups in Burma, Cambodia, Indonesia, Colombia and Peru, and possibly elsewhere, are cultivating or trafficking in illicit drugs to provide the funding to sustain their political campaigns. There is also some evidence that the Government of the Democratic People's Republic of Korea (DPRK) is either trafficking in heroin or turning a blind eye to opiate cultivation, production and trafficking, in order to obtain much-needed foreign currency (Drug funding, *Canberra Times,* 12 November 1996: 6; When North Korea collapses, *Janes' Foreign Report,* No. 2397, 25/96: 3–5).

Some terrorist groups are used to protect the interests of drug syndicates. The best-established relationship of this type is in Colombia, where the militant wing of the Colombian Communist Party (Fuerzas Armadas Revolucionarias Colombias–FARC) and M-19 (the 19th April Movement, whose name derives from the date of a disputed presidential election in 1970) terrorist groups are said to be used to protect various cocaine syndicates in Colombia (Dobson and Payne 1986: 209–10).

Political security

Political security can be radically affected by crime, particularly drug-related corruption. For example, in Bolivia in 1980, a major cocaine-producing group sponsored a coup that installed General Luis Garcia Meza in what has been described as the world's first 'narco-democracy'. Violence and the drug industry flourished, even to the point of having a 'Minister of Cocaine' in the Cabinet. During his time in office, Garcia Meza reputedly converted the apparatus of government into a national protection and extortion racket for the purpose of profiting from the cocaine trade (Dziedzic 1989). General Noriega achieved something similar in Panama.

More recently, the former Salinas administration in Mexico (*Australian*, 26 September 1995: 8) and the Samper Government in Colombia (*Washington Post*, 27 August 1995: A23; *European*, 31 August 1995–6 September 1995: 5; *Canberra Times*, 6 September 1995: 18; *Money Laundering Bulletin*, 18 (September) 1995: 6) have been severely criticised as a result of alleged funding by or links with the various cocaine producers. Similar links with heroin trafficking syndicates have impacted on the political stability of Thailand (*Bangkok Post*, 20 May 1994; *Far Eastern Economic Review*, 26 May 1994: 17; *Economist*, 28 May 1994; *Conflict International*, (June) 1994: 5; *Narcotics Enforcement and Prevention Digest*, 3 August 1995: 8). This issue has led to diplomatic tensions between Thailand and the USA (*Washington Post*, 30 July 1994; *Australian*, 27 September 1995: L1).

The demise of the Cold War has coincided with the resurgence of religious extremism and an increase in ethnic disputes throughout the world. There has been a dramatic increase in civil wars. Over eighty conflicts have flared up since 1990, but only three involve disputes between states. In these conflicts it is difficult to identify the combatants, impossible to enforce rules of behaviour. In a significant number of these civil wars, the combatants have obtained substantial funds by cultivating or trafficking in illicit drugs.

Economic security

Of all the issues affecting the post-Cold-War era, perhaps the maintenance of economic security is of the greatest importance. Crime comprises a serious threat to economic security, if only due to the enormous amounts of money involved in criminal activities. The United Nations has estimated that organised crime earns $US1.1 trillion per year (Mosely 1995: 4). As previously stated, according to the best estimates currently available the annual value of the international illicit drugs trade may be as high as

$US400 billion per year. The United Nations International Drug Control Programme has commented that $US400 billion 'would be equivalent to approximately eight percent of total international trade' (1997: 124). In any event, the value of the international drugs trade is reported to exceed that of the international oil trade, and is exceeded only by the value of the international arms trade (Money Laundering: That infernal washing machine, *Economist*, 26 July 1997: 19–21; Kraar 1988: 27–38). According to Thomas A. Constantine, the Director of the US Drug Enforcement Agency, the drug-trafficking wealth of one Mexican drug trafficker, until his death in July 1997, was estimated at $US10 billion per year, or $US200 million per week. To save himself from arrest and prosecution, this man, Amado Carillo Fuentes, reportedly paid up to $US800 million per year in bribes. Constantine (1997: 8) concludes: 'Financial leverage of this magnitude dwarfs all previous notions of criminal influence'.

In 1995, Peter Quirk, Chief of the Exchange Regime and Economic Operations Division of the International Monetary Fund (IMF), assessed international money laundering at some $US500 billion, which represents 2 per cent of global GDP (Financial Action Task Force, Plenary Meeting, January 1995). In some cases the actual volume of banknotes to be laundered is so huge that the problem for the criminal entrepreneur is not so much laundering the money as physically transporting and securing it. Much of this money was generated by the illicit drugs trade. The immensity of the profits of such crimes are as threatening to the social fabric of society as are the underlying crimes themselves.

A 1997 study by the Chulalongkorn University in Bangkok put the economic value of crime in Thailand between 1993 and 1995 at $US24–32 billion, equivalent to 14 to 19 per cent of Thailand's GDP (Thailand: where the value of crime equals the state budget, *Money Laundering Bulletin* 35, February 1997:3; Phongpaichit and Piriarangsan 1994). A significant part of this amount arises from the illicit drug industry. The size of profits from illicit drugs has had direct implications for national and international politics. In South America in 1983, the Bolivian drug baron Roberto ('Papito') Suárez Gómez offered to pay Bolivia's foreign debt in exchange for the release of his son, who was at that time incarcerated in the USA on drug trafficking charges (Cable from the Australian Embassy, Santiago de Chile, 27 July 1988). In the late 1980s, the Colombian cocaine cartels offered to pay off Colombia's foreign debt of over $US10 billion, in exchange for the repeal of the extradition agreement with the USA (Dziedzic 1989: 534).

Societal security

Societal security has been severely affected in situations where crime, particularly drug trafficking, has affected the very core of society. In Colombia there were over 28 000 killings per year, at least 40 per cent of which were drug-related, before the death of Pablo Escobar, the former head of the Medellin cartel (*Wall Street Journal*, 3 December 1993: A1). Continuing violence threatens the stability of the Republic of South Africa, where well over 15 000 people have died in political or criminal incidents since 1990 (Jennings 1994: 5); much of this violence is said to be the result of drug-related gang wars and appears to be more criminal than political, particularly in Natal and on the commuter trains (Chappell 1993: 2–8; Gilmore 1994; Laurence 1993: 14). In the Asian region, crime and drug-related corruption has become a serious destabilising factor in a number of developing countries, such as Cambodia, Vietnam and Pakistan. Instability in society encourages more crime, thus perpetuating the problem. Furthermore, with increasing crime, the freedom of the press and civil rights tend to be ignored both by the criminals and by the hard-pressed law enforcement agencies.

In Brazil, it is the drug traffickers who control the ghettos, where social divisions have become so extreme that the shanty towns in Rio de Janeiro are effectively outside government control and protected by the 'drug barons'. Because they provide some services and hope to the residents, the drug barons provide the only effective order in that area. Official government authority is eroded and can only be maintained by increasingly oppressive means. The wealthy live in walled and guarded prison-like enclaves and become increasingly alienated from others less fortunate than themselves. Corruption is widespread. The police become persecutors, not protectors, and the agents of the state are commonly seen as assassins. The state becomes the enemy, and the ghettos become states within a state, characterised by misery, extreme violence and death. Sadly, there are countries in the Asia–Pacific region where the Brazilian scenario is already developing, such as Papua New Guinea, where violent crime and corruption, particularly in Port Moresby, has become a way of life.

Environmental security

Finally, crime can have a very significant impact in the area of environmental security. According to Ciccarelli (1995), environmental threats arising from the drug trade arise from two sources: damage to the ecosystem and the degradation of the individual's living environment. Some of these environmental effects are obvious, especially for those who live in areas of high drug addict populations. 'Drug parks' are a common occurrence in most major cities, where used needles and the discarded refuse of the drug culture are clearly evident. In some areas, the gangs that control street-level distribution hold the resident population under a reign of terror, creating an environment of lawlessness, apathy and despair.

Less visible threats to the environment occur in the drug production centres, sometimes thousands of kilometres away from the user. Most of the precursor chemicals used in the refinement of heroin and cocaine are toxic, and the drug producers show little evidence of being concerned with environmentally sound production practices. As a result, waste chemicals are often dumped into rivers, killing wildlife and slowly poisoning the downstream population. According to MacDonald (1989: 65–6):

> *Narcotraficantes* operating in the Upper Huallaga Valley [in Peru] have routinely polluted the valley's waterways with kerosene, sulfuric acid, quicklime, carbide and acetone used in cocaine processing. This situation has resulted in widespread deforestation, land erosion, and poisoning of rivers.

The activities of organised crime groups are geared to immediate profits. As a consequence, their actions often result in serious environmental damage.

Human security

In earlier writings, I have used the term *criminal security* to mean: 'the threat or perceived threat of crime to the individual citizen, and therefore to his/her perception of the security of the state'. On reflection, a better term to describe this concept may be *human security*, a new term which focuses on community, development, gender, and other non-state-security issues of stability and predictability. There is obviously a close linkage between human security and societal security issues, but in this case, the emphasis is more on the impact on the individual than on society.

Human security applies not only at the community level, but also in states where governance has broken down due to the activities of 'warlords', powerful drug gangs, inter-ethnic violence, serious abuses of human rights, and endemic corruption at the political, official and business levels. In some states, the situation has deteriorated to the extent that external intervention by international aid bodies and peacekeeping forces may be required. One of the consequences of these transnational threats is a blurring of the traditional lines of demarcation between the diplomatic, military, law enforcement and intelligence roles of nations, particularly the USA.

The Scale and Significance of Organised Crime

There is no internationally accepted definition of 'organised crime', although many authorities and writers have attempted to describe its attributes. Indeed, when writing its *Organised Crime Control Act 1986*, the New York State legislature concluded that due to its 'highly diverse nature, it is impossible to precisely define what organised crime is' (Ryan 1995: 4). There is a tendency now to introduce new terms to describe organised crime such as 'enterprise crime', 'continuing criminal enterprise', 'transnational criminal organisation' and so on. Organised or enterprise crime groups are active throughout the South-East Asian region and are involved in drug trafficking, money laundering, illegal immigration, transnational prostitution, credit card fraud, counterfeit documentation and corruption.* Although some of the groups such as the Chinese Triads and Japanese Yakuza are organised along traditional hierarchical lines, many of the other groups have a more informal organisation and readily form tactical alliances with other groups, as the need or opportunity arises.

The largest and most criminal groups in the Asia–Pacific region are probably the various Chinese organised crime groups including the Triads. The activities of these groups are diverse. It is estimated that internationally, some 170 000 people are active in Triads such as the Sun Yee On, 14K and Wo groups (all based in Hong Kong); the United Bamboo Gang (Taiwan-based); and the Four Seas Band and Great Circle Gang (based in mainland China). All of these Triads have extensive overseas contacts, especially in South-East Asia, Europe and the USA. There are also a number of other groups in Burma and Thailand (Chiu Chow groups), Singapore (Tiger Dragon Secret Society) and Malaysia (18 Gang and the Wah Kee) which do not appear to operate as Triads, as such, but are, nevertheless, very actively and successfully involved in transnational crime, particularly the heroin trade.

The Chinese Triads, based mainly in Hong Kong, play a crucial role in the heroin trafficking industry. Although there has been some debate amongst law enforcement officials about whether the Triads formally control the heroin trade from South-East Asia—as opposed to individual members using the Triad networks and contacts for trafficking—it is clear that Hong Kong provides an excellent distribution centre, from which the heroin can be sent to the United States, Western Europe and Australia (Williams and Black 1994: 135).

The Japanese Yakuza is said to comprise some 87 000 members in 2300 clans. According to the Japanese National Police Agency, the Yakuza generates about ¥1.4 trillion annually from its criminal and business activities. Prior to 1992, membership of the Yakuza was not a crime. The Yakuza is organised on traditional

---

* The information in this section is based on unclassified information provided by various Australian, Canadian, Japanese and USA law enforcement agencies. See also Harnischmacher (1996) and Mosquera (1993).

hierarchical lines, with strict discipline being imposed on its members. The three major Yakuza groups are the Yamaguchi-gumi (26 000 members), the Shimiyoshi-Kai (8000 members) and the Inagawa-Kai (8000 members).

The main activities of the Yakuza groups are in small businesses (especially construction), real estate and finance companies, drug trafficking (particularly crystal methamphetamine or 'ice'), protection and extortion rackets against corporate businesses (using Sokaiya i.e. 'special racketeers'), usury, corruption of public officials and businessmen, prostitution, the gambling, film and entertainment industry and importing illegal workers into Japan. Externally, the various Yakuza groups are active in the USA and its dependencies (particularly in the Marianas and Hawaii), the Philippines, South-East Asia and Australia, where they generally target members of the local Japanese community or Japanese tourists.

Vietnamese gangs, both based in Vietnam and emerging from Vietnamese refugee communities overseas, have become a significant new transnational crime problem. Originally, many Vietnamese gang members (particularly Sino-Vietnamese, known as 'Viet-ching') were employed for protection and as 'street enforcers' for Chinese Triad groups abroad. Since the early 1990s, however, Vietnamese criminal groups have been operating internationally in their own right, and have become increasingly involved in heroin trafficking (Hanoi's New Scourge, *Far Eastern Economic Review*, 6 February 1997: 26) and money laundering.

Little is known about the international infrastructure of Vietnamese crime organisations. The main Vietnamese gangs operating in the USA, Canada and Australia appear to be the 5T and BTK, along with a number of less formally organised gangs. These gangs are noted for their mobility and readiness to use violence. They are mainly involved in murder, extortion, armed robbery, drug trafficking, street crime, fraud, illegal gambling, prostitution and home invasion robberies. In addition to the groups considered above, there are Australian, European, Korean, Nigerian, Pakistani, Russian, South American and US and other regional criminal groups or entrepreneurs operating in South-East Asia, particularly in transnational drug trafficking and money laundering (Global Mafia: A Newsweek Investigation, *Bulletin*, 14 December 1993).

Drug Trafficking in South-East Asia

In brief, the drug production and trafficking situation in the South-East Asian region could be summarised as follows:

Heroin

Global opium production in 1996 was estimated at about 4300 tonnes, with the main areas of cultivation being South-East Asia and South-West Asia, with Central and South America (Mexico and Colombia) also producing significant volumes. In March 1997, it was estimated that the Golden Triangle (Burma, Thailand and Laos) produced 60 per cent of global opium production and 60 per cent of estimated global opium gum yield (or 2790 tonnes) (US State Department 1988). The US State Department estimates that Burma's production of opium gum increased 9 per cent in 1996 to 2560 tonnes, or 90 per cent of regional production and more than half of global production.

Most of the refining of opium product into heroin is undertaken in Burma by ethnic Chinese. The heroin is then trafficked predominantly through southern China or South-East Asia to overseas markets, again mainly by ethnic Chinese. The Chinese familial, cultural and ethnic links facilitate a trafficking chain from the growing areas into overseas markets, including Australia. It is estimated that probably 80 per cent of the heroin coming into Australia comes from the Golden Triangle, mainly through Sydney. Although ethnic Chinese are the most prominent traffickers into Australia, trafficking is also undertaken by Vietnamese and other ethnic groups, but generally in much smaller quantities. Within South-East Asia, Cambodia, Vietnam and Laos are becoming of increasing concern as drug trafficking or drug transit countries. The major entrepreneurial and money-laundering centres associated with the heroin trade are Hong Kong and Bangkok.

Cannabis

According to the United Nations International Drug Control Program cannabis is the most widely used drug, with about 140 million users, or 2.5 per cent of the world's population (Australian

Bureau of Criminal Intelligence 1997: 31). Afghanistan and Pakistan are the world's major producers of cannabis. Most of Australia's supply of cannabis resin is imported from Afghanistan and Pakistan (up to fifteen tonnes at a time). High quality cannabis is also grown in Thailand, Burma and Cambodia, with a lower quality grown in the Philippines. The trade in cannabis is often entreprencured by expatriates (including Australians) in the Philippines and Thailand. High quality cannabis (sometimes known as Niugini gold) is cultivated in PNG and is frequently imported into Australia, sometimes in bartering arrangements for firearms from Australia.

Amphetamines and other synthetic drugs

The United Nations International Drug Control Program estimates that about 30 million people world-wide use synthetic drugs. The drug syndicates of the Golden Triangle are turning increasingly to amphetamine production to feed the large and growing amphetamine habits of Asian countries such as Thailand, Japan, Korea, China and the Philippines. There is, however, little evidence of major importations of amphetamines manufactured in South-East Asia into Australia. Almost all the amphetamines consumed locally are manufactured in Australia. Given the well-established heroin trafficking routes from South-East Asia to Australia, and the fact that the people involved in heroin production and trafficking are often also involved in amphetamine production and trafficking, the possibility of amphetamine importations from South-East Asia cannot be entirely discounted. A number of Asian countries, particularly Korea, Japan and the Philippines have a significant problem with crystal amphetamine ('Ice' or 'shabu'), but this particular drug has yet to become a significant problem in Australia.

Ecstasy

MDMA or Ecstasy abuse appears to be a growing problem in Australia, as the drug of choice at 'dance parties' or 'raves'. Some Ecstasy (sourced from Europe) has been trafficked into Australia through Indonesia, but most is brought in directly from either

Holland or the United Kingdom. Singapore, Malaysia and Indonesia also face growing problems as a result of Ecstasy abuse, but again this product is sourced mainly from Europe.

Cocaine

There is little evidence that Australia is being specifically targeted by the South American cocaine cartels, although the potential for that to happen remains. Whilst there does not appear to be a flood of cocaine on the Australian market, there has been a steady growth in cocaine seizures in Australia. There have also been some reports of the existence of 'crack cocaine' in Australia, but not at any significant level. Hong Kong is reported to be a transit point for cocaine trafficking into North-East and South-East Asia. Bali has been used as a transit point for cocaine distribution into Australia, and there is evidence of cocaine having been exchanged for heroin in Thailand. Otherwise there is little evidence of significant South-East Asian involvement with cocaine importation into Australia.

These trends in supply need to be assessed against national and international laws and agreements intended to regulate the supply of illicit drugs.

Public Policy

Whereas drug laws lay down the rules—prohibitions and punishments—for personal conduct, drug policy lays out a program for public action which supports and facilitates implementation of the law. Like any legislation which touches on the domain of personal behaviour, drug control laws are problematic and often controversial.* In two major respects, drug policy resembles many other domains of public policy. First, it represents a compromise, a series of decisions involving priorities, resources, costs and likely returns,

---

* This and the following section of this paper have drawn heavily on a report by the United Nations International Drug Control Programme (1997b).

which must take into account a variety of objective circumstances and subjective approaches. Second, it is an area in which international agreements provide guidelines and core legislative framework whose obligations must be met by parties to them, a minimum baseline of control now exists, that can be raised but not lowered. The very existence of such conventions provides the first 'pillar' of drug policy, namely, that drug control legislation has an impact extending beyond the boundaries of a single country, which governments must consider when formulating a national control system. Whereas national drug laws address an entire population and have a relatively stable foundation which undergoes modification over the years, drug policies are more volatile, and are expressions of priorities, and therefore narrower in focus. Drug policies are balanced between enforcement and persuasion. Overall, there is a growing consensus that more should be done to understand and reduce the demand for drugs and that new principles of demand reduction be elaborated.

The Role of the United Nations

International cooperation in drug control began in 1909 at a special commission in Shanghai, which was concerned about the growing problem of opium addiction and the changes in political allegiances at the international level. This led to the Hague International Opium Convention of 1912, under which the parties agreed to limit the manufacture, trade and use of opiate products to medical use; to cooperate in order to restrict use, and to enforce restrictions efficiently; to penalise possession; and to prohibit selling to unauthorised persons.

The second International Opium Convention was concluded in 1925 and came into force in 1928. This Convention established a system of import certificates and export authorisations for the licit international trade in narcotic drugs. A Convention for Limiting the Manufacture and Regulating the Distribution of Narcotic Drugs, signed in Geneva in 1931, introduced a compulsory estimates system aimed at limiting the world manufacture of drugs to the amounts needed for medical and scientific purposes.

In 1946 the United Nations assumed the drug control functions and responsibilities formerly carried out by the League of Nations, and the United Nations Commission on Narcotic Drugs (CND) was established as a functional commission of the Economic and Social Council (ECOSOC). The CND remains the central policy-making body within the United Nations system for dealing in depth with all questions related to drug control and the International Narcotics Control Board (INCB) was established as a result of the Single Convention on Narcotic Drugs signed in 1961.

In 1991 the United Nations Drug Control Program (UNDCP) was established to integrate into a single program the structures and functions of three former UN drug control units. The UNDCP, which is based in Vienna, was entrusted with exclusive responsibility for coordinating and providing leadership for all United Nations drug control activities. Ninety per cent of the funding for the UNDCP comes from voluntary contributions given by governments and other sources, such as NGOs, and is geared towards assisting developing countries in meeting their obligations in implementing provisions of the international drug control treaties. Such assistance is provided through UNDCP head-quarters, its field office network and by projects carried out for the most part by executing agencies other than the UNDCP itself.

Before World War II, the drugs subject to international control were largely limited to those derived from the opium poppy, the coca bush and the cannabis plant. Since then, many other compounds have been synthesised which also have dependence-producing effects. By 1995, the number of naturally produced drugs subject to international control had risen to thirty-seven, whereas the number of synthetic drugs numbered 245 (United Nations International Drug Control Programme 1997b: 163; Baayer and Ghodse 1996).

The major international drug control treaties currently in force are set out in the table on the next page. Importantly, the three major international drug control treaties are mutually supportive and complementary. Each builds upon and reinforces the provisions of the others. (See also Appendix I, Tables 1 and 2, for details of the various UN agencies involved in the control of illicit drugs.)

The Three UN Conventions (status as at 31 October 1996)

Single Convention on Narcotic Drugs, 1961
Signatories
- 158 (as at 31 October 1996)

Objectives
- To merge all existing multilateral treaties
- To streamline existing control bodies into the INCB
- To extend existing control system to include cultivation

Aims of Controls
- Provision of supplies of narcotic drugs for medical and scientific purposes
- Measures to prevent diversion into the illicit market
- 1972 Protocol to the Convention calls for increased efforts to prevent illicit production of, traffic in, and use of narcotics; as well as the need for treatment and rehabilitation of drug abusers

Convention on Psychotropic Substances, 1971
(Closely resembles the 1961 Convention)
Signatories
- 146 (as at 31 October 1996)

Objectives
- To extend international drug control system to include synthetic drugs including hallucinogens (e.g. LSD), stimulants (e.g. amphetamines and barbiturates), euphorics (e.g. Ecstasy and Prozac), hypnotics, sedatives and anxiolytics.

Aims of Controls
- Early identification, treatment, education, aftercare, rehabilitation and social reintegration of dependent persons

Convention against Illicit Traffic in Narcotic Drugs and Psychotropic Substances, 1988
(Complements other Conventions, but deals also with money laundering and precursor and essential chemicals used in drug production, and calls on parties to introduce these criminal offences in national legislation.)
Signatories
- 137 (as at 31 October 1996)

Objectives
- To create and consolidate international cooperation between law enforcement authorities, such as customs, police and judicial bodies, and to provide them with guidelines in relation to: interdict illicit trafficking effectively; to arrest and try drug traffickers; and deprive them of their ill-gotten gains

- To intensify efforts against illicit production and manufacture of narcotic and psychotropic drugs by calling for strict monitoring of the chemicals often used in their production
- To provide strengthened mechanisms for extradition, mutual legal assistance, the transfer of criminal proceedings and tracing, freezing and confiscating the proceeds of crime
- To encourages the use of 'controlled deliveries'

Source: United Nations International Drug Control Program

In 1985 the United Nations General Assembly took the decision to convene an international conference on drug abuse and illicit trafficking. The conference met in Vienna in 1987 and adopted a 'Comprehensive Multi-disciplinary Outline' (CMO) in which the UN's international drug strategy framework was elaborated. This CMO was to serve as a basis on which national authorities could formulate their plans to combat the illicit drug phenomenon. The CMO comprised a set of recommendations covering the following topics: prevention and reduction of illicit demand; control of supply; action against illicit traffic; and treatment and rehabilitation.

In 1990 the General Assembly adopted a 'Political Declaration and Global Program of Action' which called upon member states to give higher priority to international cooperation against illicit production, supply, demand, trafficking and distribution of narcotic drugs and psychotropic substances, and also deal with the problem of money laundering. It provides a comprehensive statement of the action that needs to be taken by individual countries and collectively through the system of international organisations. Essential for the successful application of the many recommendations contained in the Global Program of Action is a coherent and comprehensive national policy combined with well-defined strategies for implementation. In order to assist governments in this connection, the UNDCP offers guidance in the preparation of national drug control plans, which it refers to as 'Master Plans'. A United Nations General Assembly Special Session on International Drug Control was held in June 1998. Although not dealing specifically with drug matters, the UNDCP convened the 10th United Nations Congress on the Prevention of Crime and the Treatment of Offenders in Vienna in 1998. One of the main themes of the Congress was the problem of transnational organised crime. This was a follow-up of the 1994 Ministerial Conference in Naples and its Political Declaration and Global Action Plan against Organised Transnational Crime, which were subsequently endorsed by the United Nations General Assembly.

The Role of Other International and Regional Bodies

In addition to the United Nations, there are many other international bodies which play an important part in the global efforts against illicit drugs. These include: the International Criminal Police Organisation (Interpol); the World Customs Organisations (WCO); and the Financial Action Task Force (FATF) of the Group of 7 (G7) nations. (See Appendix I, Table 3 for details of these organisations and their efforts in the control of illicit drugs).

There are also a number of formal and informal drug enforcement cooperation arrangements between various regional bodies. These organisations include: the Heads of National Drug Law Enforcement Agencies (HONLEA) in Asia and the Pacific; the South Asia Association for Regional Cooperation (SAARC) Technical Committee on the Prevention of Drug Trafficking and Drug Abuse; Foreign Anti-Narcotics Community (FANC) meetings; the Association of South-East Asian National Police (ASEANPOL); the Asia–Pacific Group on Money Laundering (APG); Mini-Dublin Group Meetings; and the Council for Security Cooperation in the Asia–Pacific (CSCAP) Study Group on Transnational Crime. (See Appendix I, Table 4 for details of these organisations and their involvement in the control of illicit drugs).

Conclusion

The issues of illicit drug production and trafficking in South-East Asia have created problems of considerable significance for almost every country in the region, and every stratum of society within these countries. The impact of this threat goes far beyond the level of crime and violence which is associated with the drug trade; it distorts the economies, corrupts good governance, diverts major resources from the health services and, in some cases, challenges the very political stability of the states affected. As we have seen, national and transnational crime surrounding drug trafficking can have significant impacts upon political, military, economic, societal, environmental and human security. These impacts clearly extend to national and international security considerations and to questions of stability and predictability in relations between nation-states.

Nevertheless, in spite of the scale of the problems of transnational crime generally, and illicit drug production and trafficking in particular, substantial effort is being made at the international, regional and national levels to advise and implement co-operative strategies to combat these problems. The world community, particularly through the United Nations, has devised a range of anti-drug strategies. If adopted by all countries, these strategies would go a long way to combating not only the *supply* of illicit drugs, and the money laundering, violence and corruption associated with the drug trade, but also the *demand* problem. Those who regard transnational crime, including drug trafficking, as 'boutique' security issues will need to re-think their position. As Williams (1995: 3) says:

> Traditionally, organised crime has been seen largely as a law and order problem rather than a transnational challenge to the viability of societies, the independence of governments, the integrity of financial institutions and the functioning of democracy . . . The difficulty is that many criminologists and law enforcement authorities focus on the local or domestic scene and have been slow to recognise the increasingly transnational nature of the problems they are examining.

Illicit drug trafficking has become central to security and international foreign policy concerns in the post-Cold-War era, and extends far beyond the scope of conventional law enforcement.

3

Illicit Drugs in Australia: An Overview

*Paddy Mahony**

IN RECENT YEARS, Australian governments have dedicated considerable funding and effort towards combating the effects of alcohol and tobacco, while allocating a significant but lesser proportion to the problems of illicit drugs in society. In 1995, an estimated 18 124 people died from tobacco-related causes and 3642 from alcohol-related causes. In comparison, there were only an estimated 778 deaths attributable to illicit drugs (Australian Institute of Health and Welfare 1997). Despite this disparity, the impact of illicit drugs on society is considerable, and the effects are so diverse that they are almost immeasurable—they include mortality, morbidity, social disintegration, family upheaval, user marginalisation, productivity losses, health costs, enforcement and judicial costs, insurance costs and costs associated with crime resulting from a need to finance drug dependence. Added to these are costs related to pain and suffering, and opportunities lost. High levels of mortality are still attributable to the use of illicit drugs, and policy makers need to be aware of emerging trends and react accordingly. This chapter provides a summary of recent trends

* This chapter is based upon the paper 'Trends and Developments in Illicit Drugs in Australia: Highlights from the *Australian Illicit Drug Report 1996–97*', presented by the author at the conference 'Illicit Drugs and Australian Democracy: The Search for New Directions', held 8 December 1997, at the Custroms House, Brisbane, sponsored by Centre for Democracy, Department of Government, University of Queensland. The conference paper was compiled with major contributions from Matthew Osborn, Sandra Hoffschildt, Rodney Amery, Tony Fuller, Kenneth Kleier, Andrew Rowe, Quentin Moran and Gloria Jackson.

and developments related to illicit drugs and money laundering in Australia drawn from the *Australian Illicit Drug Report 1996–97* (Australian Bureau of Criminal Intelligence 1997).*

Cannabis

Importation

The vast majority of cannabis resin in Australia is imported, and is usually sourced from the Pakistan–Afghanistan region. Herbal cannabis imported to Australia most commonly comes from Papua New Guinea and South-East Asia, although small quantities come through the postal system from other countries. During 1996–97 a total of sixty seizures of cannabis seeds was recorded as sent from Europe, forty-seven of these from the Netherlands. (See Appendix II, Table 6 for the country or region of origin for cannabis seizures at the Customs barrier for 1996–97.)

Domestic production

Domestic production and sale of cannabis is a large-scale industry in Australia. It is extremely difficult, however, to estimate total cannabis production in Australia, for a number of reasons. Indications are that many users are growing small numbers of plants for their own use, and the extent of this is almost impossible to measure. Given the community's growing acceptance of cannabis and the large proportion of people who have used it, there is probably a large 'hidden' user population. At an average of $2000-worth of cannabis leaf and head from each plant, the attraction of producing even small quantities for sale is considerable. In Australia hydroponic and skunk cannabis are rapidly gaining popularity. The high level of demand for and the high prices commanded by hydroponic cannabis and the hybrids such as skunk are likely to continue. This may result in a reduction in the traditional varieties and importations of herbal cannabis.

* This report covers the FY 1 July 1996 to 30 June 1997.

Availability

The availability of herbal cannabis was high during 1996–97: there was no evidence of a shortage of supply. All jurisdictions reported that availability had either remained stable or increased slightly compared with previous years. This is not likely to change, considering the indications that large amounts are still being imported, and the prevalence of indoor and hydroponic crops. The availability of cannabis does not appear to fluctuate with the seasons to the same degree as it did five to ten years ago. The primary reason for this would be the proliferation of indoor hydroponic cannabis crops. Hydroponics increases the capability of crops to produce a higher yield and consistent quality, and a greater number of crops can be grown each year. The high availability and quality of cannabis in the last few years may have contributed to the increased demand for the drug.

Law enforcement concerns

Perhaps the most salient aspect of the policing of cannabis in Australia is balancing the relative harms to the community, the cost of detecting and prosecuting offenders, and the growing acceptance in the community of cannabis use. In 1996–97 cannabis offences constituted 81.3 per cent of all drug arrests in Australia, and cannabis consumer offences constituted 81.2 per cent of all consumer arrests. This absorbed a significant proportion of resources dedicated to drug law enforcement. In addition, in contrast to most other illicit drug use, there appears to be a comparatively low rate of associated crime and harm to both individuals and the community. The decriminalisation of personal cannabis use and production may greatly reduce both police and legal resource expenditure.

Legislation

Although there is little evidence of any difference in the pattern of use between the States and Territories, there are considerable differences in legislative and policy approaches. In South Australia, the Northern Territory and the Australian Capital Territory, possession or cultivation of minor amounts of cannabis can be dealt with by way of a fine, thus avoiding a criminal record. So far, there appears to be no evidence that this approach has significantly increased the use of cannabis, but it seems to have resulted in fewer court and police resources dedicated to minor cannabis offences. The differences between State and Territory legislation, however, do create criminal opportunities. The situation in South Australia is a case in point. There, some growers pool their crops for sale, yet avoid conviction for the (collective) production of commercial quantities. Comparable legislation across all jurisdictions would remove these opportunities and possibly the amount of trafficking across State and Territory borders. This would also overcome the problem of similar offences in different jurisdictions attracting widely different penalties.

Decriminalisation

It appears that more jurisdictions are prepared to consider decriminalisation for minor possession offences. Victoria Police began trialling a system of issuing caution notices for minor offences in one district in 1997. The Northern Territory Government decriminalised the minor possession of cannabis from 1 July 1996 and implemented the use of drug infringement notices. The main benefit has been a significant reduction in the administrative costs for policing minor offences, thus freeing resources to deal with the trade in 'hard' drugs. So far there has been no evidence to suggest that cannabis use has increased as a result of these limited decriminalisation regimes. Nevertheless, before decriminalisation of cannabis is introduced further, there should perhaps be a thorough evaluation of the impacts in South Australia, the Northern Territory and the Australian Capital Territory, with the aim of determining the resultant harms and benefits.

Impact on the community

One argument that is commonly put forward against the use of cannabis is that it is a 'gateway' drug and will lead to use of harder drugs. It is more likely that the link between cannabis and harder drugs is a result of the increased likelihood of cannabis users being exposed to the availability of the harder drugs through either other users or dealers. If this is correct, then preventing this exposure may reduce the number of cannabis users that progress to the more harmful drugs. The impact of law enforcement on the cannabis market is often not considered in the debate over the control of cannabis use. Restrictions on the supply of cannabis, through successful interdiction, may result in the casual, recreational user replacing the relatively benign cannabis with other, more harmful drugs. This is particularly the case if there is in fact a causal link between cannabis use and harder drugs. The dangers of driving or operating machinery while under the influence of cannabis are currently difficult to gauge, however, and any moves to legalise cannabis use should wait until there are proven methods of measuring levels of intoxication and their effects.

Heroin

Importation

Illicit heroin continued to be readily available in Australia during most of 1996–97; it is estimated by the Australian Bureau of Criminal Intelligence that 80 per cent of detections at the Customs barrier come from South-East Asia, in particular the Golden Triangle. There is as yet little evidence that there have been importations of heroin produced in Central or South America, but intelligence suggests that this cannot be ruled out in future.

Importations detected at the Customs barrier in the past five years have fluctuated: the number of seizures has remained relatively constant but the total weight seized per year has tended to rise. The incidence of seizures points to Sydney as by far the most widely used importation point in Australia. Next seems to be Melbourne, but it comes a long way behind Sydney. Nevertheless, it is not possible to estimate with any accuracy the volume of heroin entering Australia. During 1996–97 Australian authorities seized 169 kilograms of heroin at the Customs barrier and more than 67 kilograms in other parts of Australia (over 2000 seized units were not weighed). Arrests, both at the Customs barrier and domestically, also increased slightly compared with 1995–96.

Heroin is imported by a variety of individuals, groups and syndicates. Some syndicates are small and family-based, with a high degree of vertical integration between the source country and street-level distribution; others are larger, more sophisticated networks, capable of organising and integrating a range of functions to move large amounts of heroin from production and source countries into Australia for sale to large-scale distribution networks.

Numerous individuals, groups and syndicates that are not South-East Asian or South-East Asian–Australian are involved in importing heroin; some of them are capable of importing substantial quantities of heroin over time. Seizure information on heroin importation by country of birth for the past seven years, however, shows that while South-East Asian and South-East Asian–Australian offenders accounted for just over one-third of all offenders arrested, they accounted for nearly three-quarters of the heroin seized. Many heroin importers are also involved in a range of other offences, such as money laundering, people smuggling, taxation offences, the use of counterfeit credit cards, and corruption of public officials.

Distribution

Heroin arrives at a number of destinations in Australia, but it appears that the majority of it is sent to Sydney before being brokered and distributed to other centres. Today the choice of Sydney makes sense. It handles the greatest volume of passengers and freight arriving in Australia, thus posing the biggest challenge to Customs detection measures; it is the most populous city, and contains large communities of people with close links to the heroin source countries of Asia, offering importers and distributors a degree of anonymity; and it is the most developed hub of air, road and rail communications to the rest of the country.

Availability

Heroin remains generally available in Australia, and anecdotal information suggests that law enforcement efforts are having only a limited effect on the amount of heroin offered at street level.

Further, the continuing general availability of high-grade heroin suggests that dealers are usually able to match users' demands, even after large seizures by authorities. Most jurisdictions reported that there was no evidence that suppliers stockpiled heroin to exploit market opportunities, even though occasional shortages occurred.

Purity levels

The average purity of street-level samples generally declined during 1996–97, but it was still higher than was usual during the 1980s. The purity of street heroin is generally determined by where the drug is bought and how many times it has been diluted in the distribution chain. It may be that purity levels have risen most in areas where distributors have been competing strongly for market share and have sold directly onto the street without much dilution —an example is Sydney's Cabramatta—whereas in other places dealers have diluted the heroin progressively as it has passed from one dealer level to another. The dilution of heroin with other additives to increase the total weight still occurs across all levels of the distribution chain: the more the product is handled the more likely it is to be 'cut'. This increases profits. Moreover, with the increase in purity levels in recent years, the overall price for heroin per shot can be quite low.

Arrests

Preliminary data show that heroin accounted for 8.4 per cent of all reported *drug arrests* in Australia during 1996–97. Heroin-related arrests increased slightly, from 7105 arrests in 1995–96 to 7140 in 1996–97. There was a 2.9 per cent fall in consumers arrested; however, the number of providers arrested rose by 9.3 per cent. (See Appendix II, Figures 3 and 4.)

Patterns of use

There are still questions about the overall incidence of heroin use in Australia. National household surveys between 1988 and 1995 indicate a generally stable level of use, with between one and two per cent of the broad population having used the drug at some stage in their lives. Recent anecdotal accounts and some local studies of regular drug users could suggest that heroin use has increased, but without a more up-to-date national household survey it is not possible to determine whether such localised rises are reflected in the general population.

There is also anecdotal evidence of increased consumption of heroin by professionals and members of more affluent socio-economic groups, although there is little in the way of seizures or arrests to confirm this. The trend is attributed to the high levels of purity, which enable casual users to smoke the drug without the barrier and stigma of injecting. The lack of confirmation for this in arrest data could be explained by the fact that these non-dependent users are unlikely to come to the notice of police because of the private nature of their consumption. Further, these users are generally able to finance their drug use and are not likely to become involved in overt criminal activity to support their habit.

According to local studies of regular drug users in Sydney, the average age of heroin users has fallen (O'Brien et al. 1996); this is also reflected in the total arrests in Australia for possessing heroin (see Appendix II, Figures 4 and 5). If these trends were typical, however, it would suggest that current strategies have not been successful in reducing the take-up rate of heroin use (although it is possible that they may have slowed the rate of increase).

Law enforcement concerns

Since the 1980 Royal Commission of Inquiry into Drugs, Australian law enforcement agencies have espoused the aim of targeting the major drug traffickers rather than users or street dealers. Agencies' actual performance in terms of arrests has, however, sometimes been criticised. As Sutton and James (1996) pointed out, crime data 'suggest that the great majority of drug offenders taken before Australia's justice systems are more likely to be users than providers'. The 1996–97 arrest figures for these categories of offenders show some improvement. The number of provider (supplier) arrests rose by 9.3 per cent on the 1995–96 figures: rises were recorded in the Australian Capital Territory, Queensland, Victoria and Western Australia.

When heroin is seized in Australia it is often impossible to determine with certainty where it was produced. Customs can tell from documentation where the shipment began its journey, but if this was a transit country the actual source country often remains unknown. Greater knowledge of the source of heroin seizures and their composition would be very useful. It would help law enforcement agencies to identify the proportion of heroin seizures coming from each of the world's opium-producing regions and to provide early warning of any changes to importation patterns (including identifying heroin coming from Central and South America). It could also greatly improve the Australian law enforcement community's ability to track the manner in which heroin is distributed within and across jurisdictions. The scientific techniques to identify the country of origin are available, but to exploit them fully a nationally supported and resourced heroin signature program is needed, perhaps building on the limited project currently undertaken at the Australian Forensic Drug Laboratory. (The Federal Government has recently provided some additional funding.)

Amphetamines and Related Substances

The understanding of synthetic drugs is hampered by the consing, and occasionally arbitrary, terminology used. The term 'amphetamine' should be used to refer only to amphetamine and methylamphetamine, not chemicals such as MDMA, DMA or MDEA, which, although analogues of amphetamine, are not derivatives, and are generally produced via different chemical pathways. The term 'phenethylamines' include amphetamines, the amphetamine analogues, and chemicals such as MBDB.

Of the amphetamine-related drugs, only amphetamine and methylamphetamine could be classified as pure central nervous system stimulants. There are a large number of synthetic drugs that are neither purely stimulant nor hallucinogen. MDMA, or Ecstasy, is a perfect example. In moderate doses, MDMA causes a euphoric, relaxed, happy and empathic mood. If taken in larger doses, however, it can have both a stimulant and hallucinogenic effect. With small variations, the other drugs in this group have similar effects. For the purposes of this chapter the term 'amphetamine' includes both methylamphetamine and amphetamine unless otherwise specified. The term 'amphetamine analogue' includes MDMA and other ring-substituted amphetamines. 'Euphorics' is used as a descriptive term, and includes amphetamine analogues as well as the phenethylamines. (The terms 'stimulant' and 'hallucinogen' include those other chemicals shown in Appendix II, Figure 6.)

Importation

At present, the overwhelming majority of amphetamine and methylamphetamine is manufactured in Australia. This will, however, probably change in the future as a result of the impact of various law enforcement strategies, particularly the precursor legislation. Virtually all other synthetic psychotropic drugs are imported from overseas. This situation could have one of two effects on the supply of amphetamine in Australia.

The first is that precursors will be imported illicitly, or licit precursor chemicals will be diverted to syndicates manufacturing amphetamine in Australia. This effect is, however, unlikely to be realised to any significant degree, considering the conditions developing in Asia in relation to amphetamine production.

The second possibility is that importing of amphetamines will increase. As it becomes more difficult to obtain the precursor chemicals (by purchasing them from a legitimate supplier, by diverting imports or by theft) and the availability of better quality amphetamine in Asia increases, it is probable that the importation of amphetamines will increase. There are already signs of this occurring. There has been an increase in the number and size of seizures of Ice (crystalline methylamphetamine hydrochloride); amphetamines in tablet form, manufactured overseas, are starting to appear in larger quantities in Australia; and there has been an increase in the number of Customs seizures of amphetamines.

The total weight of amphetamine and euphoric drug seizures by Customs increased from approximately 38.7 kilograms in 1995–96 to 88.7 kilograms in 1996–97. The number of seizures increased from 120 to 169. Much of this increase has been in the euphoric-type drugs, but with the recent indications that imported amphetamine tablets are available in Australia there is a possibility that some seizures thought to be MDMA may, in fact, be amphetamine.

The Australian Federal Police noted that UK and German nationals continue to constitute a large proportion of those responsible for importing Ecstasy, often connecting with expatriates who distribute the drug in Australia. The low purchase prices in Europe and the relatively high prices in Australia make importing Ecstasy a lucrative business. The United Kingdom and the Netherlands account for 24.9 per cent and 39.2 per cent respectively of the volume of amphetamine and euphoric drug seizures in Australia during 1996–97. The number of Customs seizures originating in South-East Asia increased from nine in 1995–96 to seventeen in 1996–97.

Production

Despite the increase in seizures and the difficulty of obtaining precursor chemicals, fifty-eight clandestine amphetamine laboratories were detected in Australia in 1996, an increase of nine over the 1995 figure; four MDMA laboratories were detected in 1996, compared with five in 1995. There appears to be a trend for clandestine laboratories to be portable, often relocated for each stage of the production process. The Queensland Police Service Drug Squad has reported that the production and distribution of amphetamines is increasing. It also noted that there was a large network, extending from Gympie to Redcliffe, of people involved in manufacturing amphetamines. Most of the amphetamine produced in Australia is methylamphetamine hydrochloride; amphetamine sulphate is produced but is less common. One reason for this might be the relative availability of pseudoephedrine from Sudafed tablets, one of the primary precursors for methylamphetamine.

Since 1995, the *Misuse and Trafficking Act 1985* (NSW) has included pseudoephedrine as a prohibited drug. The NSW Crime Commission's investigations into the distribution of pseudoephedrine have uncovered organised diversion of chemicals used for the manufacture of amphetamines. Law enforcement initiatives to deal with this situation involve the formation of 'chemical diversion desks' in most jurisdictions, increased liaison with chemical companies, and other investigative and intelligence projects. Several agencies reported that as a result of these initiatives more illicit amphetamine laboratories were discovered during 1996–97.

Distribution

As with most illicit drugs, a common method of *distribution* is through the users' private network, and the exchange is often conducted in residential premises. Suppliers have been reported as making frequent personal deliveries to regular customers, and several successful police operations have resulted from targeting this behaviour. Several agencies reported that the distribution of amphetamines is increasingly being conducted through nightclubs and hotels. Many amphetamine distributors have been identified as having links with outlaw motor cycle gangs.

Organised crime

Because of the relatively complex nature of amphetamine production, some level of organisation is necessary. This is generally the province of a group of people, each with relatively defined roles. There are two possible implications. First, it may appear at first glance that *organised crime* groups are involved in the vast majority of amphetamine production in Australia. The reality may, however, be that it is just a group of individuals with particular skills and similar motivation who combine to produce amphetamine. This generally does not fall into the category of organised crime, although that depends on how the term is defined. Such operations are likely to be most affected by precursor legislation and similar initiatives. Second, amphetamine production may become purely an organised crime activity, mainly because the production process and access to the necessary chemicals are beyond the means of most people. This will become more probable as precursor chemicals become harder to obtain, particularly if there is some level of unmet demand in the market.

Ecstasy

The median price of an Ecstasy tablet in 1996–97 was between $A40 and $A60, showing no change from 1995–96. This price may inhibit the drug's popularity. Nevertheless, there has been an increase in the number of supposed Ecstasy tablets seized that actually contain methylamphetamine (*Police Service Weekly* 1997). There have been reports of similar tablets containing methylamphetamine overseas, which may mean that those seized in Australia were imports. This and other examples confirm the importance of analysing seizures of synthetic drugs and of more accurate recording of information to ensure that trends are identified early. It is no longer sufficient to assume that any tablet seized is MDMA, or even to use the term 'Ecstasy' as a generic description. Because so many chemicals are sold as Ecstasy, the drug's effects can vary considerably. This will tend to encourage the adoption of different terminology for the different types, so users will know precisely what they are buying. The greater variety of chemicals, particularly euphorics, available on the Australian market will probably also encourage more precise 'labelling'.

Other Amphetamines and Euphorics

Two trends that are evident overseas have been observed in Australia: the use of crystalline methylamphetamine hydrochloride (Ice), and liquid amphetamine (Ox Blood). The Australian Federal Police have stated that Ice is perhaps the most significant drug threat facing a number of Asian countries. Ice is known to be produced in China, and also in the Philippines, where it is referred to as 'shabu'. The New South Wales Crime Commission reported that Ice is prevalent in the Philippine community in Cabramatta. Most Ice available in Australia is believed to be imported from the Philippines. There is also evidence that Ice is being manufactured in the United States, but there are no indications that the United States is a major source of the drug for Australia. There have been several seizures of new or less common chemicals during the last few years—for example, N-methyl-a-phenethylamine and MBDB. Considering the large number of phenethylamines and amphetamine analogues, this probably means that a greater variety of chemicals will come onto the market. The danger is that users will be even less sure of what they are taking, greatly increasing the risks.

Availability

There are indications that a greater variety of amphetamines and phenethylamines is becoming available on the market. These substances have in the past been sold in Australia as Ecstasy. In the United Kingdom the chemical MBDB is being sold as 'Eve' or 'Eden', and there have been a number of seizures of MBDB in Australia. As these types of drug become more widely known and used, they will probably be sold as themselves and not marketed as Ecstasy. Several jurisdictions reported an apparent increase in the availability of both amphetamine and Ecstasy.

Patterns of use

According to the National Drug Strategy 1995 household survey, amphetamines are the second most widely used illicit drug in Australia after cannabis. All jurisdictions reported that amphetamine use appeared to remain stable or increased slightly during 1996–97. Hando (1996) found that regular amphetamine users tend to be a heterogenous group of young adults who prefer to inject the drug. The use of amphetamine has become more frequent, and there is an increase in polydrug use, particularly benzodiazepines, hallucinogens, euphorics and cocaine. There are several indications of a trend for injecting amphetamine users to change to heroin (Hando 1996; Hando et al. 1996). The reasons for this could be the high quality of heroin currently available, the relatively low price of heroin, and the poor quality of amphetamines. These conditions may also serve to change the dynamics of the market from domestic production to importation or from amphetamine use to cocaine or other substitutes.

Arrests and seizures

The number of amphetamine arrests and the number and weight of seizures increased steadily from 1992 to 1995–96. Between 1995–96 and 1996–97 there was, however, a slight drop in the number of arrests, from 4041 to 3907. The age of those arrested for amphetamine use has increased markedly in all States and Territories since 1994. This may be because new users are discouraged from using amphetamines because of the low quality and purity and the demand is maintained by longer term, older users. Excluding South Australia police data (not available), the total number of amphetamine seizures for 1996–97 was 3494. (See Appendix II, Figure 7 for the number of arrests, of consumers and providers, for each State and Territory for 1996–97; Figure 8 for the number of arrests per 100 000 for each State and Territory in 1996–97; and Figure 9 for the age groups of people arrested for amphetamine offences during 1996–97.)

Discussion

It is possible that there will be an increase in importations of amphetamine into Australia in the future. This would probably be the result of two main factors: the better quality and increase in the popularity of the drug in Asia; and the effect of precursor legislation in Australia. Other forms of synthetic drugs (for example, MBDB) may also become more prevalent as a result of the increase in importations. Ice appears to be increasing in popularity in some Asian countries, which may be a prelude to an increase in its availability and use in Australia. There is also a possibility that more amphetamine users will begin to use cocaine or heroin as a substitute. This may already be occurring considering the current indicators, which suggest an increase in the availability and a decrease in the price of cocaine during 1996–97 (see Cocaine below). This would expand the demand for cocaine, which may then contribute to the appearance of a major cocaine market in Australia.

Another effect of initiatives to curb the production of amphetamine could be that the trade will become dominated by organised crime groups. It will take considerable resources to obtain the chemicals and equipment to support a clandestine laboratory, and this will deter all but the most organised and resourceful. If the demand remains stable or increases, the potential for these groups to exploit the market will become greater, possibly causing a rise in associated organised crime (corruption, violence, money laundering, and so on). Conditions appear to be conducive to this scenario becoming a reality: there is already considerable involvement in the production and distribution of amphetamines by outlaw motor cycle gangs and possibly some ethnically based crime groups.

Law enforcement concerns

There needs to be greater consistency and accuracy in the reporting of amphetamine types. At present it is not possible to determine trends in synthetic drug types because often the substance (particularly tablets) seized is not analysed and is recorded in offence data as Ecstasy or put in a general 'other drugs' category. If law enforcement is to remain aware of developments and trends in the illicit drug market more accurate reporting methods are essential.

In 1996–97 several jurisdictions reported that, although an individual might possess the equipment and chemicals required for producing amphetamine, it is not possible to gain a conviction until the chemical processing is either under way or complete and it can be proved beyond reasonable doubt that a prohibited drug was manufactured. Even when the intent to produce amphetamine is obvious it can be extremely difficult to prove. This creates several problems for police. First, the timing of any intervention is critical: if it is too early a conviction may not be gained; if it is too late the drug may have already been manufactured and distributed. Second, any police intervention at the time of chemical processing can present serious health and safety risks for the investigators.

One suggestion for overcoming these difficulties has been to introduce into legislation the requirement for a person to demonstrate lawful intent if found in possession of precursor chemicals or equipment capable of producing a prohibited drug. The prosecution should still be required to prove the potential for the use of the chemicals and equipment in the production of a drug. Perhaps the legislation should be amended to ensure conviction if the intention to produce a prohibited substance can be proved and the preparations and precursors have been obtained.

Cocaine

Importation

All illicit cocaine reaching the Australian market appears to be of South American origin. To date there have been no reports of laboratories refining raw coca paste in Australia. Of all drug types seized at the Customs barrier in 1996–97, cocaine represented just 4.3 per cent. Since 1994–95 the number of cocaine seizures at the Customs barrier has increased steadily; the 1996–97 total was more than double the 1994–95 total. Nevertheless, the relatively small quantities of cocaine seized compared with other drug types, especially heroin, reduces the overall significance of the increase.

Arrests

During 1996–97 most people arrested for cocaine importation were Australian nationals; they were followed by US and South American nationals. There was a 39 per cent increase between 1995–96 and 1996–97 (330 to 460) in the Australia-wide arrest figures for cocaine (see Appendix II, Table 14). New South Wales accounted for most of the increase, with a total of 395 arrests, which exceeded the total number of cocaine arrests Australia-wide for 1995–96. Queensland and Victoria recorded a slight decline in arrests and Tasmania and the Australian Capital Territory recorded no arrests. Western Australia and South Australia both recorded slight increases.

The greatest percentage of people arrested (consumers and providers, Australia-wide) for cocaine use were aged between twenty and twenty-nine years. In New South Wales, however, arrested users ranged in age from fifteen to thirty-four years, with a significant number of consumers in their thirties and forties. Males made up 78 per cent of the total number of identified arrested cocaine consumers (see Appendix II, Figure 12). Overall, there has been a gradual increase between July 1995 and June 1997 in the number of cocaine arrests Australia-wide. In the same period there has been a gradual increase in the number of cocaine providers arrested Australia-wide (see Appendix II, Figures 13 and 14). These trends, coupled with the continued increase in the quantity of cocaine seized by Customs in the past three financial years might suggest that over time there has been a gradual increase in the availability and use of cocaine in Australia, at least among dependent users.

Patterns of use

Australian cocaine users seem to fall into two socially distinct groups: recreational users (mainly upper-middle-class professionals who use intra-nasally) and habitual drug abusers (who often use a variety of illicit drugs and favour injecting). In a report on injecting user groups in Sydney, three main trends relating to cocaine were identified for the south-west and inner city from October 1995 to February 1996: an increase in cocaine injection among some inner city injectors and an increase in intra-nasal use among inner city professionals; more cocaine-related problems including health problems and violence; and a decrease in the cocaine price and increased availability (O'Brien et al. 1996). Cocaine users are far more likely to inject more frequently because of the brevity of the effects of cocaine, and hence they are also far more likely to contract infections such as HIV and hepatitis C.

Anecdotal evidence suggests that cocaine is being marketed more at the street level. It is the street-level market that causes the most concern to law enforcement agencies because these users tend to be polydrug users. They often favour cocaine and heroin, sometimes using a mixture of both, usually referred to as 'speed balls'. Street-level markets also tend to attract lower socio-economic groups, and this in turn could eventually lead to the emergence of crack cocaine as a preferred method of use. On the basis of current trends, however, a significant rise in crack abuse in this country is not anticipated.

Patterns of supply

Anecdotal evidence suggests that the primary reason cocaine use is not more widespread in the community is its extremely high cost in most areas when compared with other drugs. In Australia, generally, the greater the distance the drug has to be transported, the higher the purchase price. It is also evident that the ready availability and cheaper prices of amphetamines and Ecstasy further erode the potential cocaine market. It is obvious from the foregoing that it is difficult to determine the exact nature of the distribution of cocaine within Australian States and Territories. It is equally difficult to determine the interrelationship between cocaine importation and distribution. For this reason alone it would be inappropriate to target South American nationals specifically as the primary group involved in cocaine distribution in Australia.

Law enforcement concerns

If cocaine were to gain a stronger foothold in the Australian market, its use could escalate quickly (given a marketing strategy that offered reduced prices and increased availability). Cocaine importers could exploit opportunities in the current cocaine market (artificially high prices and a closed market) and the current amphetamines market (increased law enforcement activity and potential health risks). Because of the addictive nature of cocaine and its intense psychological effects, users who inject regularly can become extremely abusive and have little regard for anything other than obtaining their next 'hit'. This has implications for law enforcement agencies, especially from the perspective of occupational health and safety. Since law enforcement agencies in Australia have no direct ability to reduce the cultivation and production of cocaine in source countries, strategies designed to target cocaine importations need to maintain a focus well forward of, as well as at, the Customs barrier. Moreover, the assistance of international agencies is required to ensure that there is a timely flow of information relating to cocaine importations into Australia.

Money Laundering

Money laundering has been defined as 'the process by which illicit source moneys are introduced into an economy and used for legitimate purposes' (Financial Crimes Enforcement Network, cited in Walker 1995: 1). Organised criminal activity generates massive amounts of money each year. With the exception of crimes of 'love and passion', criminal activity is usually motivated by the desire to acquire money and thus power. The accumulation of wealth without an appropriate lawful explanation can present a serious problem for criminals, particularly those in the upper echelons of criminal enterprises. These people aim to launder their illicit funds so that their assets have the appearance of being derived from legitimate sources. If this is achieved it provides the criminals not only with funds to reinvest in their criminal enterprise but also with investment capital that may be used to participate in legitimate business enterprises (AUSTRAC 1997).

In the broadest terms, there is a limit to how criminals can deal with cash that is acquired through their illegal activities. Cash can be dealt with in several ways: spent living the 'high life'; physically stored (at some risk); used to purchase assets (such as real estate); or placed in the financial sector, which is subject to scrutiny in Australia under the *Financial Transaction Reports Act 1988* reporting requirements. The aim of the money launderer is to ensure that there is not an auditable trail from the apparently legitimate assets back to the placement stage and ultimately the activity that generated the 'black' money (AUSTRAC 1997). Generally, criminal groups will use a number of laundering techniques at any time, so that if a particular technique is detected by the authorities they will still have the ability to continue their criminal activity.

There are many individual actions that can be taken or transactions that might be conducted to dispose of illicitly acquired funds. In fact, money laundering is a process rather than a single transaction—it is the process of turning 'black money into clean' (AUSTRAC 1997: 1). The process has been described as having three basic phases:

- placement—the physical disposal of the bulk of cash profits that are the result of criminal activity;
- layering—the piling on of layers of complex financial transactions to separate the proceeds from their illicit sources (this might include a series of international telegraphic transfers or the purchase of securities);
- integration—the provision of legitimate-looking explanations for the appearance of wealth by providing investments in the legitimate economy (Savona, cited in Walker 1995: 1).

Problems of law enforcement

Some criminals are becoming increasingly aware of the difficulty faced by law enforcement agencies in relation to investigating international transactions. Accordingly, significant portions of criminal proceeds are taken out of Australia and invested in overseas bank accounts and other assets. There are also indications that profits from criminal activities overseas are being invested in Australian real estate. It is difficult to proceed with a tainted property charge, however, due to the difficulty in obtaining sufficient financial evidence from foreign countries to assist the investigation.

One of the impediments facing some jurisdictions is the lack of any reverse onus, statutory forfeiture or non-conviction-based forfeiture provisions in their legislation. For example, under Victorian legislation, any forfeiture or pecuniary penalty order had to be directly linked to the conviction for an offence. Thus, in order to have a drug offender's assets forfeited, the offender had to be convicted of trafficking for the period in which the asset or benefit was acquired. This situation was rectified upon enactment of the *Proceeds of Crime Amendment Act 1996*. Effective law enforcement in this area also depends on good liaison with overseas law enforcement agencies, to obtain up-to-date information about overseas assets (such as bank accounts and properties). AUSTRAC is developing memorandums of understanding with various overseas countries in an attempt to encourage better cooperation in relation to proceeds of crime investigations.

The Australian Federal Police reports that investigators are experiencing difficulties in quantifying and qualifying the assets of suspected drug traffickers because there is no legislative provision enabling it to request from banking institutions information about customers. The banks have taken a very narrow view in relation to section 14, Principle 11(1(e)), of the *Privacy Act 1988,* and will release information only when a search warrant is provided (where the disclosure of information is reasonably necessary for the enforcement of the criminal law, or for a law imposing a pecuniary penalty, or for the protection of the public revenue).

One problem with this need to obtain a search warrant is that an offence has to have been committed or be likely to be committed within seventy-two hours and the resultant information used as evidence in a subsequent criminal prosecution. In most cases, however, the information required from a bank is needed to build a picture of the financial situation of a suspect, which will then determine whether action under the proceeds of crime legislation is appropriate. In other words, it is a problem of 'putting the cart before the horse'.

Alternatively, the Australian Federal Police may seek a production order under section 66 of the *Proceeds of Crime Act 1987,* which compels banks to release the information. Nonetheless, this also has problems, because it must be considered by a Justice of the Supreme Court, the procedure is very time-consuming and resource intensive, and it is difficult to specify what documents are required because the banks will not release the information.

Australian overview

Between $A1000 million and $A4500 million of 'dirty' money is believed to be generated in Australia every year, and either laundered in Australia or sent overseas. The most realistic figure is probably around $A3500 million. Fraud-related offences account for the largest component of this amount, followed closely by drug-related offences (Walker 1995).

AUSTRAC maintains statistics on all reports of suspect transactions, significant cash transactions, international currency transfers
and international funds transfer instructions under the *Financial
Transaction Reports Act 1988*. It seeks first to detect potential
money laundering and second to refer such matters for investigation and provide continuing assistance to investigators as they
pursue money trails. There was an increase in the number of
suspect transactions reported in 1996–97—an 11 per cent increase
on 1995–96 and a continued increase since 1993–94. Of the total
number of suspected offence types, suspected structuring and suspected money laundering represented 29 per cent and 6 per cent
respectively. It should be noted that there can be more than one
suspected offence type nominated for any given suspect transaction report; for example in 1996–97 there were 5772 such
reports with a total of 11 259 suspected offence types. It could be
assumed that a high proportion of these reports would directly
involve the disposal of moneys obtained through drug trafficking.

Suspect transaction reports relate only to the face value recorded on the report, and often a single report of a small amount
of money can lead to the uncovering of money-laundering operations worth several millions of dollars (Walker 1995). During
1996–97 AUSTRAC also reported increases in the number of international currency transfer reports (7 per cent), international funds
transfer instruction reports (8 per cent) and significant cash transaction reports (less than 1 per cent). AUSTRAC considers that the
reason for this is the increased diligence and compliance by the
various reporting institutions as a result of AUSTRAC's education
programs in connection with the reporting conditions.

In 1996 the Australian Federal Police carried out a review of
detected incidents of failure to declare currency in excess of
$A5000 (the limit at the time) while entering or leaving Australia
between 1 February and 9 August 1996; 152 incidents were
involved. An analysis of all the incidents revealed that in the
majority of cases (both in dollar terms and the number of offenders) Hong Kong was the primary country of destination. Middle
East countries such as Lebanon and Egypt were the next prominent destinations, followed by Singapore.

The National Drug Strategy

Given these empirical trends in illicit drug use, money laundering and law enforcement, can any conclusions be drawn for policy in the field? Our analysis suggests that the problem of illicit drugs is inherently multi-dimensional—even from a law enforcement perspective. Australian law enforcement agencies have obligations not only to enforce State, Territory and Commonwealth laws, but also commitments made under international treaties. In addition, initiatives on illicit drugs require effective cooperation between various organisations such as State and Commonwealth police forces, Customs, and other government and non-government agencies. The best initiatives appear to be characterised by combined efforts to reach common objectives.

These observations give support for reinforcing the National Drug Strategy with its long-term focus on harm minimisation. The National Drug Strategy (NDS) defines policies designed to coordinate the efforts of the numerous agencies and individuals involved in drug control. The NDS evolved from the National Campaign Against Drug Abuse (NCADA), which was launched in 1985 at a time when it was recognised that continued evaluation and reform of drug-control policy would be required.

The main aim of the NDS is to minimise the harm associated with the use of drugs in Australian society. The principal policy adopted to achieve this aim is *harm minimisation*, which was defined as an approach that 'aims to reduce the adverse health, social and economic consequences of alcohol and other drugs by minimising or limiting the harms and hazards of drug use for the community and the individual without necessarily eliminating use' (National Drug Strategy Committee 1993: 4). More recently, harm minimisation has been defined in broader terms, as an approach that seeks to minimise the harm that drug use causes to all society—users and the general community. Single (1995a) noted that there are three key aspects of this conceptualisation:

• that the user's decision to use drugs is accepted while not necessarily approved. It is assumed that for the present the user will continue to use drugs;

- that, although the user is to be treated with dignity as an 'Australian citizen who uses drugs', there is an expectation that he or she will behave normally, as a person with rights and obligations under the law, and will remain responsible for his or her behaviour;
- that harm minimisation remains neutral in terms of the long-term goals of intervention. This involves formulating priorities for goals and focusing on the immediate, realisable goals. This notion does not conflict with the long-term goal of abstention.

Single (1995a) proposed a definition of harm minimisation that includes any 'policy or program directed towards decreasing adverse health, social and economic consequences of drug use even though the user continues to use psychoactive drugs at the present time'. This wider definition is an acknowledgment that there is a broad spectrum of levels of drug use, from very occasional recreational use to habitual and chronic use. Accordingly, there is a broad spectrum of risks and harms. The concept embraced prevention and reduction of actual harm as well as the harm that society and drug users might experience.

Harm Minimisation and Law Enforcement

The principle of harm minimisation is not foreign to law enforcement. In fact, much law enforcement activity has for many years focused on behaviours and activities that cause harm to society and individuals. Law enforcement primarily concerns keeping the peace and protecting life and property from harm, whether inflicted on other members of society or on individuals by their own actions. Activities such as beat patrols, intervention in domestic disputes, and traffic and public event policing all concentrate on harm minimisation and the maintenance of public order.

Law enforcement agencies can select from a range of strategies designed to minimise harm. One of these is the *diversion* of minor offenders from the court system and/or custodial sentences. Such measures adopted for appropriately classified offenders would allow police to rationalise their role consistent with the harm-minimisation philosophy. Many of the potentially harmful consequences of the current methods of offender disposal, specifically the fine and custodial outcomes, could thus be avoided in a number of cases. Diversion provides an alternative to the path through the criminal justice system. Current diversionary measures used in Australia can be taken at any time between when an offender is detected by police and when he or she is disposed of by the courts. There are a number of diversionary measures that can be taken at various stages in the judicial process. The Alcohol and Other Drugs Council of Australia (1997) has identified and defined five distinct types: informal police diversion, formal police diversion, statutory diversion, prosecutorial diversion, and judicial diversion. Each of these has a role to play in the overall diversion strategy adopted.

Conclusion

For diversion programs to work effectively, however, there needs to be sufficient facilities to which offenders can be diverted. The Alcohol and Other Drugs Council's diversion study found that funding arrangements for existing programs were inadequate and that there were not enough places to accommodate the large number of offenders who might be eligible for diversion. Single and Rohl (1997) suggest that a high-quality, coordinated diversion program can be achieved only if there is continued cooperation between health, law enforcement and criminal justice agencies. Although significant achievements have been made in establishing procedures for national policy formulation, coordination and implementation, there remains much room for improvement in the field. An effective harm minimisation program can only operate with a satisfactory research base of trends in illicit drug supply and demand. In this regard, law enforcement should become a more prominent and active participant in the strategy, especially in the provision of intelligence advice and national assessments.

Illicit Drugs and
Australian
Democracy

4

The History and Politics of Prohibition

David Brereton

UNTIL THE PASSAGE of the first anti-opium laws in Australia late last century, there was little, if any, legal control over the use of drugs for non-medical purposes. The situation now, at the end of the twentieth century, is dramatically different. Scores of substances are the subject of legal prohibitions; a broad range of criminal offences has been created relating to the production, distribution and use of illicit drugs; and very substantial investigative powers and resources are available to police, Customs and other agencies to enforce these prohibitions. This chapter describes some of the key legal developments which have occurred since the first laws were passed, looks at some of the political and social factors which have contributed to these developments, and considers the prospects for—and obstacles to—liberalisation of the existing legal regime.*

Current Drug Laws

Under Australia's federal structure, criminal law—and responsibility for enforcing drug laws—is primarily the responsibility of State Governments. As discussed below, the Commonwealth, through its participation in various international treaties and

---

* The opinions expressed in this paper are those of the author and do not necessarily reflect the views of the Criminal Justice Commission.

conventions, has played a critical role in the development of the current framework of drug laws in Australia. Nevertheless, the direct legislative and enforcement responsibilities of the Commonwealth have largely been restricted to controlling the entrance of illicit drugs into the country through the medium of the *Customs Act 1901*.

The drug laws of the various States have some distinctive features, but their structure is broadly similar. Each Act creates, in one form or another, the basic offences of possession, use, cultivation, production and trafficking, supplying and selling. The Acts also contain lengthy schedules, derived from various international conventions, listing which drugs are prohibited, and defining various amounts, such as 'traffickable' and 'commercial' quantities. These quantities are used to determine maximum penalties for sentencing purposes, and are also relevant to determining the application of any statutory presumptions (see below). Similar schedules are to be found in the Commonwealth Customs Act.

Typically, maximum penalties for the more serious offences, such as trafficking in 'commercial quantities', are in the range of twenty-five years to life, although most jurisdictions apart from Queensland set lower maxima for offences involving cannabis. Most Acts provide for persons who have been found guilty of simple possession and/or use offences to receive a term of imprisonment, but it is now very uncommon for this sanction to be imposed. Particularly for the less serious offences, there is often a very substantial gap in sentencing between 'law on the books' and 'law in practice'. The most egregious example of this discrepancy is Queensland, where the offence of possession carries a notional maximum penalty of fifteen years imprisonment and a maximum fine of $A300 000, but the standard penalty applied in the Magistrates Court—where the overwhelming majority of possession charges are heard—is a fine of a few hundred dollars, often with no conviction being recorded (Criminal Justice Commission 1994: 43). Since 1987 in South Australia, 1992 in the Australian Capital Territory, and 1995 in the Northern Territory, people detected committing 'minor' cannabis offences have been able to avoid a court appearance altogether by paying a relatively modest 'on-the-spot' fine. Also, Victorian legislation provides for the imposition of pre-conviction bonds for first offenders charged with minor drug offences (*Drugs Poisons and Controlled Substances Act 1981*, s. 76) In all jurisdictions, however, the penalties imposed for commercial dealing are still very substantial, especially for offences at the upper end of the scale.

A notable feature of Australian drug laws is the use of provisions which contravene the long-established principle that the burden of proof in criminal cases should be on the prosecution to prove each element of the offence beyond reasonable doubt. For example, the *Drugs Misuse Act 1986* (Qld) contains what is known as a 'deeming provision' for the offence of possession. This means that, if a prohibited drug is found on someone's premises, this will be regarded as conclusive evidence that the drug was in the possession of the occupier, unless he or she can persuade the court that they 'neither knew nor had reason to suspect that the drug was in or on that place' (s. 57(c)). Another example of a deeming provision is the so-called 'traffickable quantity' presumption contained in s. 235 of the Commonwealth Customs Act. This provision requires a person who has more than a certain quantity of drugs in his or her possession to prove, on the balance of probabilities, that he or she did not intend to engage in commercial dealings in relation to those drugs; if the person cannot prove this, they will be sentenced on the basis that they had an intention to traffic.

The use of deeming provisions has been justified on the grounds that, firstly, the drug problem is so severe as to justify special measures and, secondly, it is too difficult to secure convictions of drug traffickers using the traditional standard of proof required for criminal matters. Nonetheless, the utility—and fairness—of such provisions has been challenged by a number of legal commentators. In many cases deeming provisions such as that contained in the Customs Act have little practical effect, because where persons have very large quantities of a drug in their possession, their intentions will be obvious from the circumstances, but as the Model Criminal Code Officers Committee (1997: 67) has noted: 'Like many deeming rules, reversal of the legal burden of proof results in the highest likelihood of error in the most dubiously marginal area of useful application for the rule'.

Another notable aspect of Australian drug laws is the wide range of powers which are available to police and other law enforcement bodies to detect and investigate drug offences. Under the Queensland Drugs Misuse Act, for example, police have had the power in relation to any quantity of any illegal drug to: stop, search, seize and remove motor vehicles; detain and search persons; order internal body searches; and, enter and search premises with or without a warrant (s. 18). In addition, for offences such as drug trafficking, Queensland police are empowered to apply to a court to have listening devices installed on private premises. It is noteworthy that, until the passage of the *Police Powers and Responsibilities Act 1997* (Qld), several of the powers granted to Queensland Police under the Drugs Misuse Act were not available for the investigation of other serious indictable offences such as rape and murder (Criminal Justice Commission 1993: 316).

For law enforcement bodies operating at the Federal level, and in most States other than Queensland, telecommunications interception powers are also available for the investigation of serious drug offences under the Commonwealth *Telecommunications (Interception) Act 1979*. The range of offences for which telecommunications interception warrants can be obtained is now quite broad, but when law enforcement bodies were first given access to these powers during the 1980s, the powers were made available primarily for the purpose of tackling the problem of organised drug trafficking.

Over the last decade, most jurisdictions have also passed confiscation of profits legislation which can be used to attack the assets of drug traffickers and producers. In most cases this action can be taken only after the person has been convicted, but in New South Wales a confiscation order can be made without requiring a conviction, where the Supreme Court is satisfied that 'it is more probable than not' that the person has engaged in drug-related activities (*Drug Trafficking (Civil Proceedings) Act 1990*). Again, concern about the magnitude of the drug problem—and the perceived need to take special measures to deal with the problem—has been cited as one of the main reasons for introducing such legislation.

Evolution of the Drug Laws

The current framework of Australian drug laws has evolved over the course of nearly a century. The history of these laws is quite complex. Those who seek a detailed account should refer to Desmond Manderson's excellent study *From Mr Sin to Mr Big* (1993). The focus of this chapter will be restricted to outlining some of the more significant factors which have influenced the development of the current legal framework. In particular, the chapter will consider the impact of the international environment, the effect of the upsurge in illicit drug use in the 1960s and into the 1970s, and the pervasive influence of the 'law enforcement paradigm' in the shaping of contemporary drug policy in Australia.

The international context

Although the initial anti-opium laws in Australia were inspired principally by local anti-Chinese sentiment (Carney 1981; Davis 1986; Lonie 1978; Manderson 1993), from 1914 through to the 1960s the major changes in drug laws were generally in response to external, rather than internal, developments. During this period, moves to expand the scope and severity of Australian drug laws were usually initiated following the signing of an international treaty, or convention, by the Australian Government, and were justified as necessary to enable Australia to fulfil its international obligations. Australian Governments generally went along willingly with what was happening in the international sphere, but other, much more powerful countries—most notably the USA—were the driving force behind developments at this level.

The first international drug treaty—the *Opium Convention 1912*—exhorted, but did not compel, the signatories to ensure that opiates and other dangerous drugs were used only for 'legitimate' purposes. The Australian Government ratified this Convention in 1914 and used it as the basis for extending import controls to a range of substances apart from opium (Manderson 1993: 513–14). The 1925 Geneva Convention (the *International Convention Adopted by the Second Opium Conference*) committed the signatories to enacting laws limiting the importation, export, sale and use of opiates, cocaine and Indian hemp exclusively to medical and scientific purposes. Australia quickly signed this Convention—an action which, according to Manderson (1993: 514), proved to be 'critical in ensuring the adoption by State Governments in Australia of a legislative scheme of detailed regulation, prohibition and severe penalties'. The 1925 Convention was followed by a series of other treaties, including the *Convention for Limiting the Manufacture of and Regulating the Distribution of Narcotic Drugs 1931*, which established an international compliance regime; the *Paris Protocol 1948*, which ceded to the World Health Organisation the power to determine which new drugs should be treated as 'dangerous drugs' for the purpose of the 1931 Convention; and the *Single Convention on Narcotic Drugs 1961*, which consolidated and further extended control over the international and domestic drug trades. The Single Convention was instrumental, in turn, in prompting a major rewriting, updating and extension of legislation at state level (Manderson 1993: 141–3). The *Convention on Psychotropic Substances 1971* further extended international controls to include a broad range of synthetic behaviour- and mood-altering drugs.

The preparedness of Australian Governments to sign these various treaties, and to modify domestic drug laws accordingly, seems largely to have been a function of the country's subordinate status on the world stage, and its desire to be seen as a good 'international citizen', rather than being driven by concern within Australia about the problems posed by illicit drugs. When Australia prohibited the importation and use of cannabis for non-medical purposes in the 1920s, in accordance with the requirements of the 1925 Geneva Convention, the drug was virtually unknown in the country (Manderson 1993: 72). The 1953 decision by the Commonwealth Government to place an absolute ban on the importation of heroin was primarily a response to international criticism of the high level of consumption of heroin in Australia for therapeutic purposes, and was taken despite opposition from significant sections of the medical profession, a general lack of enthusiasm on the part of State Governments for any change in the law, and the absence of any discernible public outcry about existing laws

(Manderson 1993: 125–31). Since the 1960s, domestic political and policy considerations have come to play a much greater role in shaping Australia's drug laws, but, as discussed below, the treaties, and the international environment more generally, continue to play a significant role as a constraint on reform.

Emergence of a domestic drug problem

Up until the latter part of the 1960s, drugs and drug laws were generally not salient issues on the political agenda at either State or Federal level, and few law enforcement resources were devoted to policing the drug laws (McAllister, Moore and Makkai 1991: 208). This was due, in large part, to there being relatively little use—or public awareness—of illicit drugs such as cannabis and heroin. By the early 1970s, however, the focal point of activity in relation to Australia's drug laws had unmistakably shifted. Drugs and their control had emerged as a political issue of considerable significance, and 'the drug problem' had become a matter of broad public concern and debate.

The increased salience of illicit drugs as an issue was, in large part, a consequence of the upsurge in usage levels. Virtually no data on consumption patterns are available prior to the 1970s, apart from police arrest statistics, but it is generally acknowledged that usage of cannabis and other illicit drugs accelerated during the 1960s. According to the Woodward Report (Royal Commission of Inquiry into Drug Trafficking 1979: 63–4):

> By 1964 the use of . . . [cannabis] was well established in some circles, in particular in groups associated with country music. It became more popular in the mid to late 1960s through country music dances, pop festivals and rock concerts, where the habit of 'passing a joint' became fashionable. By the early 1970s, the social use of cannabis was widespread. At about this time the evidence . . . indicates that 'commercial' cultivation commenced in order to meet the demands of the growing market.

Further, the Royal Commission (1979: 297) reported that the use of heroin in New South Wales increased about the same time and that 'notwithstanding the real inadequacies of official statistics, it is clear that there have been rapid and alarming increases in the non medical use of opiate narcotics, particularly heroin'. McCoy (1980: 11) reached a similar conclusion, arguing that while 'the recent upsurge in heroin abuse is a problem in the whole of Australia . . . it has been particularly acute in New South Wales, where statistical evidence reveals a consistent pattern of escalating narcotics use during the 1970s'.

The increase in heroin dependence during the early 1970s corresponded with a marked increase in property crime in several jurisdictions (Mukherjee 1981), and it was widely assumed that these two developments were linked in some way. As documented by McCoy (1980) the growth in the illicit drug market created lucrative opportunities for organised crime to become involved in the production and distribution of drugs such as cannabis and heroin. In this context, a critical event was the murder of anti-cannabis campaigner Donald Mackay in Griffith in 1977. This brought the issue of organised crime involvement in the drug business into sharp focus, led directly to the establishment in New South Wales of the Royal Commission of Inquiry into Drug Trafficking in 1979 (the 'Woodward Commission') and, at Commonwealth level, contributed to the decision to set up the Australian Royal Commission of Inquiry into Drugs (the 'Williams Inquiry') in the same year.

The emergence of an identifiable Australian 'drug problem' and the increasing political salience of this issue triggered demands for action and put pressure on politicians and policy makers to implement responses—be they symbolic or substantive—to the problem. The initiatives which found favour during the 1970s and well into the 1980s generally involved raising maximum penalties, creating additional offences, making offences easier to prove, establishing new investigative bodies such as the National Crime Authority, significantly increasing the powers and technology available to law enforcement agencies to detect drug offences, providing for the confiscation of profits, and investing more resources in drug law enforcement. These initiatives were actively supported by law enforcement bodies around the country, and were given added legitimacy and impetus by the various inquiries into illicit drugs set up by State and Federal Governments, such as the Woodward and Williams Royal Commissions, and the Stewart Royal Commission of Inquiry into Drug Trafficking (1983). With the notable exception of the South Australian Royal Commission into the Non-Medical Use of Drugs (1979), these lawyer-dominated inquiries all offered 'more and better law' and improved enforcement as the primary solutions to the problem of illicit drug use; there was little serious consideration given to alternative responses, and little critical assessment of the likely efficacy of the solutions proposed. A consistent theme was that the problem of illicit drug use could be curbed *if only* governments got serious about the problem and *if only* law enforcement agencies were given the tools and resources to be able to do the job properly. The policy of 'getting tough' was also consonant with public perceptions that the laws were too soft on drug traffickers and that strong action was required to reduce availability of illicit drugs within the community (McAllister, Moore and Makkai 1991: 175–201).

Recent trends

The 'get tough' approach reached the high watermark (or low point, depending on your perspective) with the passage of the Queensland Drugs Misuse Act in 1987. This Act gave police sweeping powers and created mandatory life penalties (since repealed) for a broad range of offences, including supply of any quantity of a drug to a minor. Since then, however, there have been some—albeit modest—changes in the approach taken by Australian governments and law enforcement bodies to the problem of illicit drug use.

As noted earlier, the criminal law as it relates to the personal use and possession of cannabis has been relaxed in three jurisdictions: South Australia, the Australian Capital Territory and the Northern Territory. At the level of practice, some police services are taking a more innovative approach to the enforcement of laws relating to the possession and use of illicit drugs, particularly cannabis. For example, in September 1998 Victoria Police implemented a state-wide cautioning scheme for minor cannabis offenders and trials of similar schemes are underway in Western Australia and Tasmania. In New South Wales there are now relatively few cases coming through the courts where the principal offence is possession of cannabis—an indication that police are now devoting fewer resources to the enforcement of this offence (unpublished data provided by the Bureau of Crime Statistics and Research, New South Wales). Several police services—at least at the upper levels—have also declared a commitment to the philosophy of harm minimisation, and some senior police are beginning to question publicly the efficacy of traditional enforcement policies (Single and Rohl 1997; although for a more sceptical view see Brown and Sutton 1997).

At the level of public discourse about the problem, there has also been some shift in the focus and tenor of debate. The issue of whether existing legal prohibitions should be eased in some way has now become a legitimate topic for discussion, and the views of those who advocate a full or partial withdrawal of the criminal law from drug policy are no longer automatically discounted as impractical or dangerous. The fact that the Premier's Drug Advisory Council in Victoria (1996) was prepared to recommend legalising cannabis use is an indicator of this shift in thinking, even if the Council's recommendation was ultimately rejected. Similarly, although the current Commonwealth Government withdrew from the Australian Capital Territory heroin trial in mid-1997, this initiative received substantial support amongst political, professional and media elites, and could well be revived at some stage in the future.

More generally, there is a growing recognition in policy circles and some parts of the political system that law and order responses have proved to be very expensive—in social as well as economic terms—and have not reduced the availability of illicit drugs within the community (as recently published research by Makkai and McAllister (1998a) confirms). This viewpoint was forcefully expressed in the report of the all-party Parliamentary Joint Committee on the National Crime Authority, *Drugs, Crime and Society* (1989: xiv), which concluded that:

> Over the last two decades in Australia we have devoted increased resources to drug law enforcement, we have increased the penalties for drug trafficking and we have accepted increasing inroads on our civil liberties as part of the battle to curb the drug trade. All

the evidence shows, however, not only that our law enforcement agencies have not succeeded in preventing the supply of illegal drugs to Australian markets, but that it is unrealistic to expect them to do so. If the present policy of prohibition is not working then it is time to give serious consideration to the alternatives, however radical they might seem.

The change in the tenor of the drug policy debate has been the result of several intersecting factors. First, the National Drug Strategy (NDS) and its predecessor, the National Campaign Against Drug Abuse (NCADA), launched by the Hawke Government in 1985, have helped to promote a more critical assessment of the efficacy of traditional approaches, and have widened the range of players involved in developing and implementing drug policy, particularly by drawing in the health and research sectors. Second, the HIV/AIDS crisis which emerged during the 1980s helped to bring issues about harm minimisation to the fore, especially where intravenous drug use was concerned, and contributed to the redefinition of illicit drug use as a health—as well as a law enforcement—issue (Hall 1992: 564). Finally, and perhaps most importantly, compared with the USA, where the 'War Against Drugs' has been pursued with unrelenting moral fervour, there has been a healthy preparedness amongst key players in Australian drug policy to question the wisdom of persisting with existing approaches, and to recognise that taking the high moral ground may not necessarily be the best policy.

Constraints on Reform

Although the tenor and focus of debate about drug laws may have changed in Australia over the last decade or so, the magnitude of the shift should not be exaggerated. As Hall (1992: 572) points out, 'the proponents of reform have been more successful in raising doubts about the effectiveness of prohibitionist policies than they have in persuading the public of the wisdom of relaxing prohibition'.

Even in relation to small-scale cannabis offences there continues to be considerable resistance to reform. The relatively modest recommendations contained in the Criminal Justice Commission's report on *Cannabis and the Law in Queensland* (1994) are unlikely to be taken up by the major Queensland political parties in the foreseeable future, despite having been broadly endorsed by the all-Party Parliamentary Criminal Justice Committee (1996). The Victorian Government, in response to strong backbench opposition, ultimately rejected the recommendation of the Premier's Drug Advisory Council (1996) that the personal use of cannabis no longer be an offence, even though this proposal was said to have the support of the Premier. Similarly, in late 1997 the New South Wales Government was blocked in the Legislative Council in its attempt to remove imprisonment as a sentencing option for small-scale cannabis offences.

A significant obstacle to the reform of existing laws is the lack of public support for such initiatives; in this area in particular, elite opinion diverges considerably from the views of the broader community. According to the 1995 NDS Household Survey, over 90 per cent of adult respondents were 'opposed' or 'strongly opposed' to personal use of heroin, amphetamines or cocaine being made legal, and similar proportions expressed support for increasing penalties for the sale and supply of these drugs (Makkai and McAllister 1998b: 36). In the face of these findings, it would clearly require a good deal of political courage (in the *Yes Minister* sense of the term) for a government to take any action which could be construed as going soft on such drugs. Indeed, a government could only contemplate measures aimed at diluting existing laws if they were introduced with bipartisan support—something which seems unlikely in our current highly competitive political environment.

Where cannabis is concerned, public opposition to reform is not as intense. According to the 1995 NDS Household Survey, 42 per cent of adult respondents said that they supported the personal use of cannabis 'being made legal' (this term was not defined further)—up from 31 per cent in 1985. Nonetheless, this is still well below a majority and, as Makkai and McAllister (1998b: 28) point out, 'the issue generates stronger feelings among those who favour continued prohibition than among those favouring reform'. A survey conducted for the Criminal Justice Commission in 1993 produced similar findings in the Queensland context (Criminal Justice Commission 1994). Overall, these findings strongly suggest that governments would risk losing electoral support if they pressed ahead with moves to make cannabis legally available in some form; probably the most that the electorate will tolerate are modest reforms aimed at keeping users and possibly small-scale producers out of the criminal justice system.

The scope for reform is further limited by the international environment and the obligations imposed by the various treaties to which Australia is a signatory. There is some divergence of legal opinion about the extent of constraints imposed by the treaties (for example, whether they permit 'civil penalty' schemes and the use of South-Australia-type expiation notices to deal with personal scale offences). Nonetheless, all commentators agree that the Conventions do not permit the formal legalisation of possession, cultivation or use of the drugs defined in the schedules to the Conventions even if this were to be done under strictly regulated conditions (Criminal Justice Commission 1994: 48–57). Technically, because only the Commonwealth is a signatory to the Conventions, it would be open for a State Government to pass laws in defiance of the Conventions, but the Commonwealth would then be able to legislate to override the State law. If the Commonwealth itself was strongly committed to repealing some existing drug laws, it could probably choose to ignore these treaties or interpret them more narrowly—as governments already do on occasions when it suits them—and it could even consider withdrawal from the Conventions. Such responses, however, would expose Australia to a good deal of international criticism, particularly from powerful allies such as the USA.

Finally, there is still considerable ambivalence amongst key players in the area of drug policy about how far reform should go, and how quickly it should proceed (Hall 1992). There has been substantial support amongst health professionals and the research community for allowing injectable heroin to be provided on medical prescription, and for the concept of legalised 'shooting galleries'. There is still a substantial divergence of expert opinion, however, about the likely impact on usage levels if the legal status of drugs such as cannabis or heroin were to be changed (although this may depend to some extent on the form which legalisation takes and the pricing regime which is adopted). Also, while law enforcement bodies have given some positive indications that they are prepared to re-visit their approach to drug law enforcement, this sector generally remains opposed to any dilution of existing laws, especially those which are seen as reducing the array of powers available to police. For example, the Queensland Police Service has consistently resisted any move to soften the provisions of the Drugs Misuse Act in relation to small-scale cannabis offences, on the grounds that to do so would tie the hands of police in the investigation of more serious offences. It can also be speculated that any proposals by the Model Criminal Code Officers Committee to remove deeming provisions from drug legislation will be strenuously opposed by the law enforcement sector, on the grounds that to do this would make the offences too difficult to prove and send the wrong signal to drug traffickers.

Prospects for Change

In summary, it seems unlikely that there will be any significant relaxation of Australian drug laws in the short to medium term, except *perhaps* in relation to personal-scale cannabis offences; even on this issue, the political obstacles to reform remain substantial. More particularly, there is little prospect of any easing of the laws as they relate to commercial-scale production and/or trafficking in illicit drugs, apart, *perhaps*, from some modest readjustments being made through the Model Criminal Code initiative. Arguably, there may be a greater prospect of changes occurring at the level of law enforcement practice, where the political spotlight is less intense. As indicated, some police organisations—at least at the upper levels—now endorse the view that enforcement efforts should be focused primarily on large-scale traffickers, rather than users and street-level dealers. Some police leaders also formally acknowledge that policing practices at the street level should be informed by the principles of harm minimisation. As Brown and Sutton (1997) have observed, however, there remains a substantial gap between what police organisations say and what individual police officers do on the ground, and there are still considerable organisational and legal barriers to implementing harm minimisation approaches. Also, police organisations are not immune from being influenced by political and media demands to 'get tough' on drugs, which may limit their capacity to sustain this shift in approach over time.

On present indications it is probable that prohibitionist sentiments will continue to dominate at the international level, at least in the sense that significant changes to the international treaty regime seem unlikely. This may not prevent some countries from experimenting with heroin trials, or relaxing their laws in relation to possession of 'soft' drugs such as cannabis, but the basic framework covering illicit drug production and trafficking seems likely to remain intact. If for some reason the USA were to lose enthusiasm for the strict prohibitionist approach, this could have very significant consequences for the future development of international drug control policy and, flowing on from that, domestic policy in Australia. Nevertheless, while the possibility of such a paradigmatic shift cannot be discounted—wars have been declared lost before—there are few signs as yet that surrender is being contemplated.

5

Balancing Individual Rights and Community Norms

Andrew Parkin

PUBLIC DEBATE IN AUSTRALIA about the appropriate governmental response to the illicit drug phenomenon is shaped by the liberal-democratic character of the Australian political system. An underlying and endemic tension between *liberal* values and *democratic* values is deeply embedded within the system. This tension manifests itself strongly in the debate about illicit drugs, just as it plays a crucial (though often unrecognised) role in many other divisive political issues. What results is a characteristic liberal-democratic pattern of fluid policy responses, a pattern which can appear to be inconsistent, indecisive or inconclusive but which represents the political judgements and political balances struck within the policy-making process.

The Nature of Liberal Democracy

A liberal democracy can be understood here as a political system in which democratically based institutions of governance coexist with strongly embedded liberal values which recognise the rights of individuals and the legitimacy of market-based mechanisms for economic production and distribution.* As an historical and philosophical construction, it embodies two distinct conceptual

* This chapter draws significantly on Parkin (1998). See also Parkin (1996; 1997).

strands, one arising from the liberal tradition and the other from the democratic tradition.

'Liberal' here refers to a conception of society which emphasises the moral autonomy of individual persons and recognises their rights and liberties, within an overall social order based on their consent. Historically, liberalism emerged in Europe as an ideology of emancipation against the aristocracy. It advocated individual rights, the rule of law and a 'negative liberty' limiting constraint upon individuals by government. In the economic sphere, liberalism has legitimised capitalism, the ownership and exploitation of private property, the accumulation of private wealth, and the market mechanism for production and exchange. The rhetoric of the classical liberal tradition can be called upon to defend private individuals, their rights and their markets, against 'the state'.

Liberals advocate constitutional documents and institutional arrangements which specify and delimit the reach of government. This is clearest in the classically liberal American system, but Westminster-style parliamentary institutions have also embodied liberal assertions about the diffusion of power away from the monarch, about the rule of law and about the protection of individual liberties. The institutions of liberal parliamentarism, themselves continuing to evolve in Britain, travelled to Australia to form the basis of the colonial legislatures, and upon Federation in 1901 were combined more explicitly with the liberal devices of a written Constitution and federalism (Galligan 1995).

Accompanying the growth of liberal institutions in nineteenth-century Australia, and remaining significant today, were liberal ideas and ideological assumptions. Australians are accustomed to framing political arguments and pursuing political claims using the liberal language of rights. All major political parties in Australia have long accepted the broadly liberal reality of the predominantly private-market-oriented mixed economy, within an overall economic, social and educational framework and infrastructure for which government takes responsibility (Maddox 1996).

This then is the liberal tradition. The emergence of 'democratic' politics in modern times occurred in liberalism's wake as state power was eased or wrested away from its established sources. Democracy as understood here involves, in contrast to liberalism, an emphasis on collective and 'public' aspects of membership of a political community rather than on the individual and 'private' domain. It envisages in some sense the cooperative participation of citizens in the making of decisions which affect the community as a whole. It valorises such notions as 'public opinion' and 'community norms', and through the electoral process it imposes, or at least threatens, periodic aggregated judgements on politicians and political parties. The democratic tradition embraces a wide range of institutional and philosophical variants, with the more collectivist assumptions of European socialism contrasting with the Anglo-American tendency to focus on the political engagement of individuals through the parliamentary franchise and parliamentary representation. Australia was one of the pioneers of democratic norms and practices in this latter sense.

What has evolved historically in Australia has been the interweaving of liberal and democratic values to infuse and legitimise what we now understand as liberal-democratic political systems. It is easy to take this amalgam for granted, but its constituent elements have had, as sketched here, conceptually and historically separable origins.

From the liberal tradition, liberal democracy asserts the significance of the rule of law, a strong private market sector of the economy, a general acceptance of basic liberties and rights accruing to individuals, and the free association of these individuals within civil society. From the democratic tradition, it asserts the legitimacy of the freedom of citizens, individually or in voluntarily organised groups, to engage in political activity (such as seeking to influence government or seeking elected public office); it legitimises a state sector overseen by representative political institutions; and it underpins the provision of public services by governments to citizens. Linking the liberal and democratic traditions in practice is a broad recognition among citizens of the legitimacy of political institutions and procedures, an acceptance of decisions reached through due process, and a commitment to peaceful and evolutionary rather than violent change. Nevertheless, this coexistence of liberal and the democratic traditions should not be taken to indicate that liberal democracy embodies a frictionless reconciliation or amalgamation. The degree to which the two traditions are compatible is a matter of longstanding scholarly contention (Graham 1992; Damico 1986; Hoffman 1991; Hindess 1993). In everyday political life, what this coexistence means is that liberal democracies are responsive to liberal claims *and* to democratic claims. Characteristic tensions flow from this. How these tensions are played out in political life depends on a range of contingent, historical, institutional and cultural factors. In broad terms, the characteristic tensions emerge in situations such as the following: balancing expectations about self-reliance with expectations about the provision of community-provided public services; recognising the autonomy of individual citizens while at the same time insisting upon contributions to collective projects; determining through the political system the appropriate portfolio of 'public goods' (understood in the technical sense as those necessarily requiring collective provision); handling the demands on collective decision-making arising from 'prisoner's dilemmas' and 'tragedies of the commons' (i.e. from the aggregated public consequences of individual private actions); settling on some form of coexistence between majority decisions and the interests of minorities; deciding whether particular issues or problems are really 'public' or 'private' business; working out how to balance or prioritise between competing claims by different individuals for the recognition of their 'rights'; and so on.

These tensions as translated into a myriad of policy options and policy debates—about the economy, about health care, about cultural policy, about schooling, about taxation, indeed about the whole policy agenda—explain much of the character of the political process in a liberal democracy such as Australia. Put simply, the characteristic politics of a liberal democracy involves the recognition and management of these tensions. Structuring political disputes and arguments—about policy directions or legislative proposals or party platforms or the acceptability of particular laws—is this much deeper phenomenon of the shifting balance between the liberal and democratic traditions.

Tensions in the Drug Debate

Crime and law enforcement as understood and managed in a country like Australia exhibit these fundamental liberal-democratic tensions. 'Crime', probably by definition, constitutes a challenge to notions of community cohesion, consensual social order and common values, notions which underpin democratic assumptions and traditions. The political system seems readily able to engage with this sense of unease; hence the readiness with which political parties seem prepared to adopt strident 'law and order' platforms and rhetoric during election campaigns (e.g. Lee 1996).

Yet liberal-democratic politics are receptive to liberal arguments as well as to these more collectively mobilised, community-focused sentiments. Citizens are suspicious of empowering the state with an unacceptable capacity for control and intervention, even if the intended use is to investigate and combat illicit activity. While there might be recognition that the effectiveness of state institutions in crime control depends to a significant extent on their capacity for information-gathering, policing and enforcement, citizens seem pervasively wary about ceding great powers to the state and seem receptive to political arguments to this effect.

These tensions are readily apparent in policy debates about illicit drugs. There is a classically 'liberal' response to the drug problem which essentially advocates the decriminalisation of the industry (or at least some sectors of it, such as in relation to the softer drugs like marijuana and/or the consumption end of the production-distribution chain) and its re-regulation in ways more akin to a normal industry. This response draws on positive and negative elements of the liberal credo. On the positive side, it reaffirms the rights of citizens to engage in activities without state interference at least up to the point before demonstrable harm is done to others. On the negative side, it is sceptical about the continuing accountability and integrity of the police and judicial apparatus which the state must mobilise to combat the drug trade.

This liberal approach to drug use, and strategies such as 'harm reduction' which draw upon it, have some prominent advocates (see McAllister, Moore and Makkai 1991: 220–4; Weatherburn 1992; Drucker 1995). It has proved less salient within the political system, however, than a contrary perspective which regards illicit drugs, and possibly the ostensible individualism of the drug user, as threatening community cohesion and commonly held values. There are conservative and progressive variants of this community-focused discomfort with drug-taking. Conservatives probably dislike its flouting of social order and discipline. Some progressives are concerned about anti-social causes and consequences. A Melbourne *Age* editorial (13 April 1996) for example argued that 'people who regularly get high on drugs are less likely to care what happens to themselves or to anyone else' and that drug dependence is associated with social, not just individual, problems such as 'socio-economic disadvantage, unemployment, disordered relationships and homelessness'.

Two prominent attempts in the mid-1990s to liberalise public policy exercised the various sides of the debate. In both of these cases, the conservative side, legitimising itself through arguments drawing upon the discourses of public opinion and community values, prevailed over liberal reform proposals.

In April 1996, a Drug Advisory Council appointed by the Victorian Government and chaired by Professor David Penington published its report. Recognising the relatively widespread consumption of marijuana and endeavouring to remove it from the criminal company of more dangerous illicit drugs, the report recommended the decriminalisation of the possession of small quantities of marijuana. The report recommended that the use and possession of other drugs such as heroin, cocaine, amphetamines and ecstasy should remain offences, but it advocated relaxed penalties, especially for first-time offenders. It proposed that drug education should be a mandatory component of the school curriculum and that drug rehabilitation programs be expanded (Brady 1996).

In establishing the Drug Advisory Council and in commenting on some of its preliminary work, Victorian Premier Jeff Kennett had seemed to foreshadow support for some liberalisation of drug laws, and after the report's publication Kennett invited public debate in advance of Parliamentary scrutiny in which Coalition members would have a conscience vote (Button 1996). Some support for the Penington recommendations was forthcoming from the Council for Civil Liberties, from spokespersons from the Catholic and Uniting churches, and from some legal and welfare groups active in drug rehabilitation programs. These voices, however, seemed to be quickly drowned out by those of conservative opponents of liberalisation. In quick succession, firm opposition to the decriminalisation of marijuana was expressed by the Victorian police leadership, the Police Association, the Royal Automobile Club, the National Party State Council, the Liberal Party State Council, Anglican bishops, the Baptist and Presbyterian churches, the head of the Australian Secondary Principals Association and—intervening from beyond the sphere of State politics— Prime Minister John Howard (Green 1996b; Green and Mesina 1996; Nolan and Brady 1996; Green and Savva 1996). Submissions to the Premier's office and to Members of Parliament were reported to have opposed the liberalisation proposals overwhelmingly. In a special Parliamentary debate at the end of June 1996, in which Kennett's Cabinet Ministers did not participate, most government MPs opposed decriminalisation of marijuana, though all Labor MPs (bound in any case by their decision to maintain caucus solidarity) supported this and other Penington recommendations (Green 1996a).

In the face of what seemed to be overwhelming opposition to his report's key proposals, Professor Penington expressed concern that what might emerge would simply be a 'political compromise' rather than a principled response (Green and Savva 1996; Nolan and Brady 1996). But in the end, the Cabinet was unmoved, rejecting the Penington Report's recommendations on the decriminalisation of marijuana. As Green (1996c) interpreted it in an *Age* front-page commentary, 'The Premier had no choice . . . Politically, it was the only option available . . . The debate has reaffirmed the deeply held conservatism on the drug issue in the coalition parties and—based on responses during the debate—most of the community'.

The Penington inquiry coincided with, and its report recommended support for, a proposal for an experimental programme, initiated by the Government of the Australian Capital Territory, for the treatment of heroin addiction through providing controlled doses of heroin for addicts via pharmaceutical prescription. Only a few States were prepared to give the proposal any support at a July 1996 meeting of Commonwealth and State Health and Police Ministers, and the proposal remained in political limbo for the next ten months. As Kingston (1997) noted, in reviewing the demise of the Penington proposals and the ongoing lack of support for the Australian Capital Territory programme, 'public opinion remains rock-solid against [liberal reforms] and politicians [have] backed the public rather than take them on'.

In May 1997, the report of the Wood Royal Commission into the police service in New South Wales (NSW) provoked some reconsideration in that pivotal State. Arguing that punitive responses to the illicit drug trade had failed, Commissioner Wood recommended a more liberal approach to the policing of drug consumption, including the consideration of the provision of 'safe, sanitary injecting rooms' for heroin addicts. These recommendations were immediately rejected by all party leaders. They were more positively received, however, by various lobby groups including the New South Wales Police Association and the New South Wales Council for Civil Liberties, and by some prominent politicians (McClymont and Riley 1997; Bearup and Papadopoulos 1997; Lagan 1997a). By the time of the July 1997 meeting of Health and Police Ministers, the New South Wales Minister was able to report that his Government would no longer oppose the Australian Capital Territory proposal. Its first stage was duly endorsed by the meeting with, importantly, indications of support and funding from the Federal Government (Lagan 1997b; Dow 1997).

In August, Prime Minister John Howard returned from a period of sick leave and, within a week, had persuaded his Cabinet to terminate the heroin trial proposal. The sincerity of Mr Howard's personal views—that he was 'profoundly sceptical of the view that the way in which you cure the problem of heroin and marijuana . . . is to legalise it' (Mitchell 1997)—was questioned by no-one, but his shift from ambivalent endorsement of the Australian Capital Territory proposal (Middleton and Boreham 1997; Tingle and Middleton 1997) to outright opposition seemed to be a response to a perceived reading of the broader public reaction. Dr Wooldridge, the Federal Health Minister, conceded that there was 'not much community support' for the Australian Capital Territory heroin trial (Brough 1997a). The McNair Anderson opinion polls showed 44 per cent support and 51 per cent opposition to the proposal (Cockburn 1997). An aggressive campaign against the proposal was waged by prominent media outlets in Sydney, notably the *Daily Telegraph* and high-rating talkback radio hosts (Millett 1997; Brough 1997b). When the Howard Cabinet announced its decision to withdraw any Federal Government support, effectively vetoing it, Australian Capital Territory Chief Minister Kate Carnell described the decision as 'gutless and lacking in leadership'. 'It was just simply public pressure', she said, leading to a decision 'based upon emotion rather than fact' (Dow and Tingle 1997; Tingle and Middleton 1997).

Looking back over several decades at the debate over drug policies, a careful analysis (predating the Penington Report and the Australian Capital Territory proposal) concluded that.

> public opinion has played an important—perhaps critical—role in determining the direction of government policy in the drugs area . . . [P]ublic opinion has been firmly opposed to the use of illegal drugs such as marijuana and heroin, and a majority have opposed any change in their legal status . . . As a consequence, the federal and state governments . . . response has been to introduce laws transferring greater powers to law enforcement agencies which often involve incursions into civil liberties. However, public opinion has increasingly distinguished between soft and hard illegal drugs (McAllister, Moore and Makkai 1991: 199–200).

Liberal-reformist initiative and democratically legitimised resistance seem to be the way in which Australia is destined to continue to handle the policy debate on illegal drugs.

The Contribution of Criminology

Examples of how the Australian political system handles controversial criminal justice issues could be multiplied beyond this case of policy towards illicit drugs (see Parkin 1998). Consider, for

example, the debates about gun control, or money laundering, or
capital punishment, or sentencing standards, or suppression orders
on court proceedings, or criminal confiscation legislation, or 'community policing', or the purpose of imprisonment, or victim impact
statements, or juvenile crime, or random breath testing, or criminal confiscation legislation, or covert intelligence organisations,
or a host of other issues in the broad criminal justice field. Each of
these stories would have its own dynamic and, like any policy nar-
rative, its own idiosyncratic elements. Nonetheless, they would
each illustrate the common and recurrent phenomena manifest in
the policy debate about illicit drugs: that is, policy responses and
strategies which oscillate between (on the one hand) liberal sensitivity to individual rights and opposition to enhanced state capacity and (on the other hand) democratic-collectivist-statist pressures
to uphold shared cultural norms through crime-control strategies.

The spectrum of responses within the liberal-democratic political system loosely corresponds to, and draws upon, an analogous
spectrum within the criminological literature. Probably more than
most academic disciplines and movements, criminology has arisen
from and informed public policy developments, and it displays the
same interplay and tension between individualistic and structuralist conceptions which characterise the policy field in political
practice.

Young (1994: 69) has loosely summarised the development of
modern criminology in terms of the recurrence of 'two images of
the criminal', namely 'the moral actor, freely choosing crime; and
the automaton, the person who has lost control and is beset by
forces within or external to him or her'. In the terms of this chapter,
the first of these caricatures is liberal and individualist, the second
a combination of medico-psychological ('forces within') determinism and structural-sociological ('external to') determinism.

Criminology's liberal wing is both longstanding and recently re-
surgent. Histories of the discipline usually locate the beginnings of
Anglo-American criminology in the great law reform movements
of the post-Enlightenment period which adopted the new liberal
understanding of individuals as rational actors whose behaviour
responded to positive and negative incentives (White and Haines
1996; Garland 1994).

Sociologists entered criminology about a century ago with an explicit critique of the prevailing liberal assumptions, proffering 'social' and 'ecological' perspectives on crime. These perspectives led in their strongest form to a 'structural criminology' which has explained criminal behaviour not through the benefit-cost calculations of rational actors but through an understanding of the social definition, creation and production of crime (Hagan 1989; Sampson 1995). In alliance with post-Freudian psychocriminology, the sociological understanding of crime has been particularly influential in the twentieth century and has underpinned many of the policy reforms aimed at explaining and combating the 'root causes' of crime located in such factors as social disadvantage or violent childhoods or dysfunctional neighbourhoods or perverse correctional systems.

The last decade or so has seen a resurgence of neo-liberal approaches which reaffirm the view that crime can be explained, and combated, through utilitarian understandings of the benefit and cost incentives experienced by individuals (Wilson and Herrstein 1985; Buchanan and Hartley 1990; O'Malley 1994; O'Malley 1996). In part, this resurgence is simply a manifestation of the increased visibility of neo-liberalism in public policy generally. In part, it has also been fuelled by the perceived failure to combat criminal behaviour of policy instruments (such as poverty alleviation, prisoner rehabilitation, slum clearance, therapeutic intervention, schooling reform and so on) inspired by the sociological understanding of crime.

This is not the place to review the history of criminology in more detail, other than to note the commonsense view held by many observers and practitioners which recognises both 'agency' and 'structure' as explanatory elements (Brown and Hogg 1992; Ericson 1996). The point is rather that the interplay between individualist and structuralist conceptions of the meaning of crime— this 'pendulum of fashion' as Young (1994: 70) has termed it —has reinforced the policy oscillations within the criminal justice systems in liberal-democratic polities.

To the extent that politicians, opinion leaders, policy-makers and ordinary citizens perceive crime in the individualistic terms of offenders' responses to the incentives which they face, they will be more predisposed to policy prescriptions which emphasise instrumentalist cost-benefit conceptions of penalties, deterrents and opportunities. They might be sympathetic to notions of 'victims' rights' as manifest in such ideas as criminal compensation funds or victim impact statements, or 'rights' to be accorded to recreational drug users. All of these approaches can be legitimised with reference to the liberal values so readily retrievable from within the discourses and practices of liberal-democratic politics.

The relationship between criminological paradigms and policy response is more complex on the 'structuralist' side of the discipline. There is a wide variety of criminological approaches which are broadly 'structuralist'. In their own ways, the broad schools of criminological thought which White and Haines (1996) have summarised as 'strain theory', 'labelling perspectives', 'Marxist criminology', 'feminist perspectives', 'left realism', 'republican theory' and 'critical criminology' can be understood as 'structuralist' or 'collectivist' in scope, each of them in contradistinction from liberal or neo-liberal paradigms. Their immediate policy prescriptions are likewise disparate. They all, however, recognise and legitimise social conceptions of crime which extend beyond the level of individualist cost-benefit or stimulus-response approaches. They all recognise and legitimise (different) notions of community or communities. In this broad sense, they encourage political actors and institutions to recognise and legitimise collective understandings of crime and its impact. They reinforce the democratic values embedded in liberal-democratic political processes and institutions, and provide an intellectual armoury to explain why a concern for individual rights should not be the beginning and end of debates about crime.

These academic disagreements and changes of fashion have paralleled the uncertainties and inconsistencies in public policy debates. As O'Malley (1997: 256) describes this pattern, 'criminology and crime prevention [both] have histories in which "death and resurrection" of strategies is the norm rather than the exception'. The academic cycle has helped to shape the policy cycle: 'criminology itself often has provided critical reference and refuelling points' for public controversy about crime prevention (O'Malley and Sutton 1997: 18).

Conclusion

A degree of continual dissatisfaction with the workings of the criminal justice system is probably endemic within liberal-democratic states like Australia. 'What we do know about crime and corruption in Australia', argues one commentator (Williams 1988: 41), 'suggests that public policies adopted by governments tend to be inconsistent, incoherent and ineffective'. This is not an unfamiliar lament about governmental approaches to the illicit drug phenomenon in particular.

It is the argument of this chapter that some degree of policy fluidity, indecisiveness and incoherence is probably inevitable within our style of politics and government. The system is an embodiment of trade-offs between, on the one hand, liberal concerns about overbearing state power and, on the other hand, collective impulses which seek to reinforce community norms and enhance public safety. There might be periodic surges in one direction or the other. But there are also inbuilt countervailing forces of reaction which seek to return the system back towards the previous equilibrium and which can claim public legitimacy when any particular surge seems to break beyond normal parameters.

The over-enthusiastic exercise of police power (such as the harassment of low-level recreational drug users) may produce renewed political efforts to hold the state's agents to account. Conversely, revelations about alleged drug 'crime waves' or slack sentencing patterns for 'drug dealers' may produce a clamour for tougher state action. Penal-oriented 'law and order' campaigns oscillate with concerns for sensitive attention to the societal circumstances which lead to offences and disorders. Community alarm about drug-related crime coexists with community concern about the establishment and operation of powerful anti-crime investigatory bodies (see Parkin 1998).

This fluctuating pattern might be dissatisfying to those with a passion for clear programmes (whether conservative or reformist) and a distaste for the liberal-democratic politics of debate, compromise, trial-and-error, and cycles of policy fashion. Nonetheless, this form of politics seems consistently to offer at least some conceptual and political space for reformers and critics who want to facilitate or retard the swings of the pendulum, and for whom the values and discourses embedded in the system itself can bolster claims for some new balance to be struck.

This notion of 'balance' probably provides the most useful guidance to practitioners and analysts who, while appreciating the uncertain nature of liberal-democratic politics, nonetheless wish to promote intelligent and worthwhile policy reform, such as in the illicit drugs area. Working with rather than against the tendencies of the system is likely to be less frustrating and more productive. Whatever the deeper social and economic forces behind the global resurgence of liberal democracy in our times (Fukuyama 1992), one of its deeper if less spectacular meanings is an appreciation of the modest virtues of 'muddling through' (Lindblom 1959). This is not to hold out liberal democracy as an unalloyed ideal: liberalism provides a ready rationalisation for private inequalities and liberal democracies are not invulnerable to extremist pressures, populist impulses, overweening corporate power, media disinformation and the like. But even drug reform advocates—notwithstanding their frustrations—might sometimes come to appreciate some of its untidiness and inconclusiveness.

6

Impacts upon Social and Political Life

John Broome

THE IMPACT OF illicit drugs in Australia can be examined from a number of different perspectives. We can examine the physical impact of the illicit drugs trade and quantify the statistics on those who die or are hospitalised each year as a result of their use of illicit drugs. We can examine the economic impact of the illicit drugs trade, and count the costs of health and welfare services devoted to harm reduction, or the loss of government and other revenue as a result of the criminality involved, or we can count the costs of crime prevention and reduction. This chapter examines the social and political impact of the illicit drugs trade, to consider how those physical and economic costs are reflected within our society and in our political life. In doing so, the trade in illicit drugs is divided into two main areas: *supply* and *demand*.

The *demand* for illicit drugs is predominantly the result of purely Australian factors and the impact of demand is predominantly felt on Australian social, political and economic life. This impact takes many forms, from the very real and personal impact the drugs trade has on users and their families, to the somewhat less personal and, at times, less tangible effect it has on the social and political life of Australia. Some dysfunctionality in family life, the need for a significant level of health, social welfare and community service infrastructure, and social and political tension over issues such as decriminalisation and other equally controversial drug-related strategies, can all be directly ascribed to the demand for illicit drugs.

Supply, on the other hand, has an additional non-domestic input, as all the heroin and cocaine, and a proportion of the amphetamines and cannabis consumed in Australia are imported. As a result, supply also impacts on Australian social, political and economic life in a variety of ways, but with the additional concern that it exposes Australian social and political institutions to international influences over which we have little, if any, control. Because of the dimensions of the problem, a large proportion of law enforcement and other resources are devoted to the interdiction or disruption of the supply of illicit drugs. These strategies provide opportunities for the corruption of officials, both in Australia and internationally, which in turn lead to high levels of community concern and a loss of public confidence in legal and political institutions. Moreover, the exposure of Australian institutions to the international drug trade has challenged the integrity of our financial and commercial institutions, particularly as a result of the laundering of the profits of the drugs trade, and posed a serious challenge to the integrity of Australia's sovereignty.

What then are the broader dimensions of the illicit drugs trade in Australia? During 1997 the Australian Bureau of Criminal Intelligence, the Australian Federal Police and the National Crime Authority conducted a joint assessment of the criminal environment in Australia, which aggregated a large amount of information about offences relating to each of the particular illicit drugs consumed in Australia. What was clear from the research collected for, and the outcomes of, that assessment is that we do not know very much at all about the demand for illicit drugs.

Official statistics can tell us how many people were arrested in the last five years for possession or trafficking in particular drugs; however, we can't determine with any degree of accuracy how many users of illicit drugs there are in Australia. While there are conflicting indicators concerning the overall incidence of heroin use in Australia, official statistics can tell us that it appears that heroin use is increasing and that users/dealers are getting younger. We do not, however, know why. Why has there been what appears to be an 'explosion' in heroin use since the 1970s? Is heroin the late twentieth-century version of the eighteenth century's cheap gin? The research conducted in Australia on the illicit drugs trade is disparate and uncoordinated. Moreover, we are groping in the dark to find answers to questions about the personal, social, economic and political factors that facilitate or create a demand for illicit drugs.

Indeed, while it would seem that it would be in everyone's interests to know about the *causes*, rather than the *symptoms*, of demand, these are answers that may not be particularly palatable to governments, here or elsewhere. It would be a very 'courageous' government that commissioned research designed to determine the causes of the demand for illicit drugs, let alone one that accepted the results of that research. Without doubt, research of this nature would be likely to turn a very harsh and bright light on various policies that most governments would rather not reveal. There are some fundamental social and economic questions at stake here, to which the answers are likely to be politically unpalatable.

If, on the other hand, this research *was* desired, who would do it? In the current economic climate, in which universities and other academic institutions are being pressured into concentrating on those areas of research and teaching that have some 'employment-related' aspect, or which can turn a dollar for these financially strapped institutions, who is going to pay for research of this kind? Where is the 'bottom line' on social research of this kind? Where is the 'benefit' that can be measured in dollar outputs?

The Social Impact

If we are unable to determine much about the causes of demand, what do we know about its manifestations? Apart from the severe health problems experienced by users, illicit drug use also affects the wider circle of the user's family and friends. For example, not only are family members touched by the physical effects of illicit drug use on the user, and the economic effects of drug use on family finances, but the deleterious health effects felt by intravenous drug users are often passed on to members of their close contact group (sexual partners, children and other family members). Ultimately, the physical and financial effects of illicit drugs at the personal/family level often leads to various forms of dysfunctionality in family life.

What is the broader social impact of demand on Australia? As governments have recognised that they have an obligation to reduce the harm associated with illicit drug use, they have established significant health, social welfare and community service infrastructures to support users and their families. These infrastructures cost an enormous amount of money. For example, 1995 estimates (Department of Human Services and Health 1995: 5; Hall 1996: 8) suggest that (at least) $A40 million to $A50 million is spent each year in funding and providing infrastructure support to methadone maintenance programs. Similarly, based on various estimates, it is likely that more than $A200 million is spent annually in the health and social welfare sectors by governments as a direct or indirect result of the illicit drugs trade.

While I am not arguing this money should not be spent, I am claiming that these are policy choices made by governments on the basis of decisions about how governments need to respond politically to the issue of illicit drugs. This is a point that I wish to explore in some depth below. From my own perspective, a significant level of resources are also devoted to the interdiction or disruption of the supply of illicit drugs. While it is difficult to estimate the extent of the cost to the criminal justice system incurred by illicit drugs, estimates suggest that as much as $A450 to $A500 million may be expended each year (Marks 1991, 1992). Again, these are significant amounts of money being spent on the symptoms, not the causes of demand.

Apart from the immediate circle of family and friends surrounding the user, the broader Australian population is often exposed to the illicit drugs trade in a very personal sense, particularly through their exposure to illicit drug-related crime. A large number of heroin and methadone users have been convicted of property offences at some stage of their lives. For example, in the case of methadone applicants, 78 per cent had one or more convictions for property theft (Hall, Bell and Carless 1995). It has been estimated that more than $A312 million is raised each year by heroin users/dealers through property crime. 'Break and enters' are a factor in everyone's life these days, and a significant proportion of these can be attributed to the need to obtain cash to purchase illicit drugs.

But we ought not over-dramatise the situation; a direct causal link between all property crime and illicit drugs has never been established. There are many other reasons why property crimes, particularly 'break and enters', occur. Opportunities have increased, for example, as a result of the greater participation of women in the workforce, resulting in a larger percentage of homes being unoccupied during the day. There are also significant social and economic changes (some for the worse) that have occurred in recent years, not the least being high levels of unemployment (particularly youth unemployment). We have to be careful to distinguish between cause and effect.

The illicit drugs trade also opens up other areas of concern: the ever-present issue of corruption, and the exposure of Australian social and political institutions to international influences over which we have little if any control. Australia's most recent exposure to the nexus between the illicit drugs trade and corruption has been as a result of the Royal Commission into the NSW Police Service in 1996–97. The final report of the Royal Commission (1997) found that there was an 'overwhelming body of evidence' to suggest that a close relationship has existed between police officers and persons involved in the supply of illicit drugs. And it is not just the police who might be corrupted: those involved in the drugs trade within Australia and overseas require the expert advice of lawyers, banks and other financial advisers to launder the profits generated by that trade successfully.

The international aspects of the illicit drugs trade also have significant consequences for Australia. Law enforcement estimates suggest that drugs generate at least $A2 billion annually within Australia (Access Economics has suggested that it may be as high as $A7 billion). In addition, it has been suggested that a significant proportion of the estimated $A3.5 billion laundered in and through Australia each year can be attributed to illicit drugs. This exposure of Australian institutions to the international drug trade poses a significant challenge to the integrity of our financial and commercial institutions.

By its very nature, the international movement of illicit drugs and illicit funds implies the violation of Australia's borders. While the increasing globalisation of economic, trade, financial and communication systems threatens the sovereignty of the nation state, national governments do have some ability to regulate these licit activities. Illicit activities, however, particularly those associated with the drugs trade, are far more difficult to regulate, relying as they do on international networking among individual criminals and criminal syndicates. As a result, the closer Australia is bound up in the international supply of illicit drugs, the weaker our ability to maintain (or even establish) some sovereignty over these transactions. The international trade in illicit drugs has now become a significant challenge to Australia's sovereignty and poses an equal challenge to our existing social and political institutions.

The Political Impact

The enormous investment of money in treating the symptoms of demand and supply could no doubt be better spent elsewhere on improving social conditions in Australia. We can see that the illicit drugs trade has a profound effect on families and on social, political and financial institutions in Australia. So, is this expenditure warranted?

I would like to offer an alternative problem for consideration. While almost one in five deaths in Australia each year are drug-related, less than five per cent of these are the result of illicit drug use (that is, illicit drugs are responsible for about one per cent of deaths each year). Tobacco and alcohol are overwhelmingly the two most widely used drugs in Australia, and it has been estimated that alcohol and tobacco together comprise 90 per cent of the costs associated with all drug use. It is clear that licit drugs have a much greater health and economic impact than do illicit drugs. So is all this media and political attention on illicit drugs warranted? Have we got the illicit drugs trade in any real perspective? In terms of the impact on our society, tobacco and alcohol clearly outweigh illicit drugs. Are illicit drugs a political rather than social issue?

In my view, the problem of illicit drugs is both political and social. There are, as we have seen, significant social costs associated with illicit drugs: not just the personal effect they have on individuals and families, but the significant levels of 'costs' that illicit drugs transfer to the broader community (e.g. health and welfare expenditure, criminal justice system expenditure, property crime, the fear and concern raised among the public). All these 'costs' represent the removal of resources from other areas. Unlike licit drugs, which form a large part of the revenue base of governments through taxes on alcohol and tobacco, illicit drugs represent a drain on the public purse which is not recompensed by any financial benefit to the state. This dichotomy between the harm caused by licit versus illicit drugs, and the revenue provided by the one and not the other, moves the policy debate over illicit drugs into areas, particularly choices, that most people are not comfortable with.

As a result, the illicit drugs trade causes all sorts of political problems, not the least being problems of 'patch-protection' and the assignment of blame between agencies and jurisdictions. Our federal structure inevitably means that there are overlaps between Commonwealth, State and Territory law enforcement agencies, that often lead to those agencies jealously guarding their 'jurisdiction' at the expense of effective law enforcement strategies. Moreover, governments of all persuasions and at all levels are very keen to find someone else to blame for their political woes; the Commonwealth will blame the States and Territories and *vice versa* if it means that they can shift the responsibility for a problem away from themselves. The illicit drugs trade also produces a number of serious political problems for governments. For example, political parties are often far from reluctant to use issues such as law and order (or 'who is tougher on drug dealers') as political footballs in election campaigns, claiming that the problem is all the other party's fault for being too 'soft' on crime.

Time and again what passes for social and political debate in Australia on issues like illicit drugs is, in fact, ill-informed populism. As the recent debate over the proposed Australian Capital Territory heroin trial has indicated, very often policy debate in Australia is not based on sound, well-informed advice or rational decision-making, but on the populist meanderings of talk-back radio and the lowest common denominator approach taken by tabloid journalism. Unfortunately, most governments are not able to receive sound policy advice on issues such as these, mainly because successive governments—Commonwealth, State and Territory—have spent the last twenty years reducing the size of policy units within their bureaucracies, reducing the ability for sound policy advice to be generated, and increasing governmental reliance on ill-informed 'opinion' rather than on well-informed research.

Moreover political parties, be they in government or opposition, are relying more on opinion polling to drive policy decisions than on analysis and more traditional forms of public policy development. This means that an analysis by Hugh Mackay of what he says the Australian population is thinking may be more influential than considered policy development from within professional bureaucracies. That is not to say that the policy advice from within the public sector does not need to be examined against what the public will accept or that it should be the sole source of advice. It should not. Such professional advice needs to be considered for its level of political realism, its practicability and its affordability. There has to be an alternative to throwing out the public sector advice or accepting without question what is often referred to in the press as 'poll driven policy'.

There has been significant criticism of the growing use of advisers by ministers at both the State and Federal levels. While the number of advisers to ministers may have increased in recent years, the phenomenon is not new. Often advice has been provided by those to whom the minister was close. At least these days you can find the names of the advisers in the Government Directory. But as someone who has spent a number of years in that environment I can say that, at least in my experience, the role of the ministerial adviser as a driver of policy, is often overrated. More generally, most ministers rely most of the time on the advice they get from their departments and other agencies.

What is indisputable is that there has been an increasing tendency in recent years to react to public opinion rather than to attempt to lead it. Policies produced in this way are not going to meet the needs of the community and will often see options reduced. Choices will be limited to deciding what is perceived to be the least worst option, rather than to that which is considered to be the best option. Until we get a more rational policy debate started on the issue of illicit drugs, and until we are prepared to ask (and seek answers to) the hard questions about the demand for and supply of illicit drugs, the illicit drugs trade will continue to have profound effects on our social and political life, well beyond those warranted by the effects of the trade itself. While not wishing to minimise the seriousness of the illicit drugs trade of itself, there are (as I have indicated) dimensions to the problem that are of our own creating. There are policy responses open to us that can reduce the impact of illicit drugs on the personal lives of fellow Australians and on their families, responses that can also reduce the financial burden imposed on us all by current policies towards illicit drugs, or at least open up those policies to a more rational determination of priorities.

Conclusion

Where to from here? Politics is the art of the achievable, and good government is about good public policy, and obviously political parties, when in government, have to find a balance between the two. Governments need to have regard to public opinion (otherwise they end up in opposition), but often they react to ill-informed or uninformed public opinion. There have been several ocasions in Australia's recent political past that have shown governments that they can lead rather than follow public opinion, that they can inform the public about the options, and that Australians can become comfortable with and accept sound public policy that previously may not have appeared politically acceptable. The emotiveness that pervades the public debate on illicit drugs is a clear indication of the need to inform the public at large about what are, and are not, rational policy alternatives. In all this, we must be careful that we take the debate forward, pausing from time to time to ensure that the public understands what the debate is about. The danger lies in going backwards, in retreating in the face of ill-informed emotive vituperation, or, worse, in closing off sensible policy options entirely and backing ourselves into a corner in which public debate is closed off.

As I have indicated, one way forward is through more research on the problem. We need to open up the policy debate on illicit drugs to the widest possible academic and other scrutiny. We need to ensure that we have better answers to those difficult questions that I articulated earlier about the *causes*, not the *symptoms*, of the illicit drugs trade. Once we have conducted the research, we can then move on to a better-informed public policy debate about the advantages and disadvantages of policy options, and the consequences of pursuing one policy over another. A better-informed public policy allows policy-makers to lead the public debate, rather than follow behind it; it gives policy-makers the capacity to educate and inform the wider public about the issues at stake and the options, so that we can develop and encourage public support for sound policy in this area.

The illicit drugs trade has had profound impacts on our social and political life. It is an issue which we cannot afford to react to out of ignorance or political expediency. We need to understand all we can about the role illicit drugs play in our society, and we need to be equipped to ask, and answer, some profound questions about how we view our society now, and how we would like to view it in the future.

Policy Responses

7

Evaluating the National Drug Strategy

Timothy Rohl

IN APRIL 1996, the Ministerial Council on Drug Strategy (MCDS) —the principal drug policy-making body in Australia—commissioned an evaluation of Australia's National Drug Strategy. This author, together with Professor Eric Single, conducted the evaluation and presented a report to the MCDS in July 1997. The rationale behind having two evaluators was to ensure balance between the interests of the key players—health and law enforcement. This chapter draws on the findings of the evaluation of the National Drug Strategy (Single and Rohl 1997), as well as information gathered after the completion of the evaluation, to highlight some of the key issues for democratic leadership related to the problem of licit and illicit drugs in Australia.

The Evaluation Process

The terms of reference contained in the brief for the evaluation of the National Drug Strategy (NDS) required that recommendations be made regarding the following issues:
- the conceptual basis of the NDS;
- how the NDS works—particularly in respect to
  its partnerships,
  the linkages to other health and law enforcement strategies,
  the roles of the various stakeholders,

the balance of effort, whereby alcohol and all drugs are addressed in an integrated national strategy,
the ability of the strategy to respond to new situations, and how it is currently managed;
• the nation's capacity to monitor and measure the short- and long-term impact of the drug harm minimisation policy.

In contrast with the earlier evaluation (Department of Human Services and Health 1992), which involved an eight-person task force and more than a year of preparation, this evaluation was conducted in less than six months. It involved five distinct, but occasionally overlapping phases. The consultation process was the most time-consuming. It was very detailed, involving a broad range of individuals and organisations, including front-line treatment and prevention specialists, law enforcement officers, State and Territory policy-makers, user groups, and non-government organisations. As part of this process we received written submissions from these individuals and organisations, as well as a number of oral submissions from private citizens who wanted to tell their personal stories. Our national consultations enabled us to develop a sense of State/Territory perspective on a range of issues. In addition, we also spoke with a number of expert informants.

Harm minimisation

As noted above, the first term of reference was to look at the conceptual basis of the NDS. Conceptually, the NDS is based on partnerships at a number of levels:
• a partnership between the Commonwealth, States and Territories;
• the partnership between health and law enforcement; and
• other partnerships involving education, non-governmental organisations and private industry.
The strategy is based on the philosophy of *harm minimisation*, and was intended from the beginning to be comprehensive and address both licit and illicit drugs.

Throughout the consultation process, it was almost unanimously agreed that harm minimisation should remain as the basis of the NDS. There is, however, a need for more refinement and clarification of the term 'harm minimisation'. For example, you can minimise harm in respect to alcohol by drinking less, promoting low-alcohol beverages, developing server training programs, introducing alcohol accords and developing drink driver programs, and so on. On the other hand, harm minimisation does not work well with tobacco as there is no minimum level that is safe. Therefore, most tobacco strategies are aimed at cessation rather than finding safer means of intake. While the term harm minimisation was originally developed to describe programmes aimed at reducing the harmful consequences of illicit drug use, it has more recently been applied to the reduction of problems associated with the use of licit drugs as well.

The philosophy of harm minimisation has posed some very real problems for law enforcement agencies, and for many people in the community. It is seen by many as the police 'going easy' on drug users. Nevertheless, police have had to come to the realisation that harm minimisation is not about going easy on people; it is about making the community a safer place in which to live. The underlying principle of harm minimisation is that drug users should be treated with dignity as normal people. For example, Netherlands police now refer to 'Dutch citizens who use drugs'. This is a far cry from the many pejorative terms previously used to describe drug users. As a consequence, the focus for law enforcement has shifted from *users* to *dealers* and *traffickers*.

It is important to note that Australia's National Drug Strategy is highly regarded internationally. It commenced in 1985 and was originally known as the National Campaign Against Drug Abuse (NCADA). It was created with strong bipartisan support and was a significant catalyst in minimising the impact of HIV/AIDS in Australia. From its inception, the NDS has been characterised by a unique combination of features that have brought it international attention and acclaim. In particular, commentators have praised the quality and the nature of the partnership achieved between health and law enforcement. In all other countries where there are national drug strategies, the senior partner in the strategy is law enforcement and the junior partner is health.

Other features that have contributed to the success of the NDS are: the balance achieved between supply and demand reduction strategies within the NDS-funded programming; the balance between treatment, prevention, research and education; and the approach of averting arrest and redirecting users to education programs. The work of the research centres and innovative harm reduction programs, such as the needle exchange, are also highly regarded. The underpinning philosophy of harm minimisation in Australia is significantly different from the US 'War on Drugs' approach, which is almost universally recognised as having failed.

The Fragility of the NDS

In spite of the many local successes and considerable international acclaim, the NDS is extremely fragile, and is held together more by good will than by good policy or effective leadership. The net result is that the NDS is in danger of sliding off the political agenda. It lacks strong political commitment from governments. It is also fragmented and lacks coordination and cohesion, and the infrastructure for managing it on a day-to-day basis has been significantly reduced over recent years.

Lack of strong political commitment

From the evidence we received, it is clear that the NDS began well, but over time lost political impetus. The Ministerial Council on Drug Strategy (MCDS)—comprising the nation's Health and Law/Justice Ministers—is constrained by various political agendas. It has also not always received the public attention it deserves. Whilst the NDS was created with strong bipartisan support, there have clearly been difficulties in gaining national support and commitment for many of its more controversial initiatives, and particularly for initiatives dealing with illicit drugs. This is an important problem for governments, because Australians consistently define the 'drug problem' as predominantly an illicit drug problem.

The leadership problem

The issue of day-to-day leadership of the NDS is more problematic and was at the core of our recommendations. It is not possible to manage, lead or direct the NDS by committee. The MCDS is very large, and there have been difficulties because it is usually held in conjunction with Health Ministers' meetings, and Police Ministers have not always attended. The agendas have often been too full and have not focused on the 'big ticket' items.

For the NDS to be a truly national strategy, it has to reflect national initiatives; it has to work to a nationally agreed plan, and someone has to be responsible for it; and a national strategy has to be developed, implemented, disseminated and reported on at regular intervals. It was for these reasons that we strongly recommended establishing a special unit which would be the principal national agency, focusing on strategic planning, coordination, and monitoring the success indicators of the NDS. Such a unit should have the capacity to scan the policy environment, to develop proactive responses to drug issues, and assist governments in anticipating and responding to emerging drug issues which receive media and public attention. It would help to organise and set agendas for the NDS and the MCDS. It would also disseminate information on NDS activities and programs, and promote the strategy nationally and internationally.

Detailed recommendations are contained in the report (Single and Rohl 1997) relating to the unit's leadership, its location, and some of its tasks. We suggested locating it in the Prime Minister's office, in order to re-establish strong political patronage and to reflect the health and law enforcement partnership arrangements as they currently are, with the possibility of including additional partners in the future. Apart from the issue of political patronage, we also recommended this option because there was considerable concern expressed during the consultation process that the proposed new arrangements for funding the health partnerships would mean that dedicated funding would no longer be specifically tied to the NDS.

The issue of leadership of the unit was also discussed at length at the consultations. A strong view was expressed that its leader should be a person with the capacity to provide high quality leadership on drug issues. There was also much comment about the need for the leader to become the 'public face' of the NDS. We also made quite a number of observations about things that a renewed NDS might do—including organising a major event such as a national drug symposium. We were careful, however, not to make this a subordinate recommendation that would detract from the main thrust of the key recommendations.

Lack of coordination and cohesion

The fragmented nature of the NDS is detailed in our report (Single and Rohl 1997). The main point of criticism is that there are many activities being conducted by both the Commonwealth and the States and Territories that could be better coordinated under the general auspices of a National Drug Strategy. We found for instance, that many initiatives relating to tobacco, HIV/AIDS, alcohol and Hepatitis C are treated as single-issue initiatives rather than issues under the broader NDS umbrella.

Loss of infrastructure

Serious concerns were raised during the consultations about the considerable 'downsizing' of the drugs unit within the Department of Health and Community Services.

Previous Evaluations

Interestingly, many of these issues could have been addressed if the recommendations of the last evaluation had been implemented. There have been two other evaluations of the NDS. The first was in 1988. The second, in 1991/92, which was subtitled 'No Quick Fix' (Department of Human Services and Health 1992), was much more detailed and made sixty-six recommendations. In particular, it recommended renaming NCADA as 'The National Drug Strategy' and it recognised the need to underpin the NDS with a sound strategic plan. It also recommended that a special National Drug Strategy Unit be established to provide leadership and administer the NDS; and that greater emphasis should be given to the participation of law enforcement in the strategy. In our evaluation we found that some recommendations were selectively implemented and others ignored. We also concluded that the scope of the report was too broad and that there were too many recommendations. For these reasons, we determined to make fewer but more strategic recommendations.

Law Enforcement

Prior to the 1992 evaluation, law enforcement's involvement with the NDS was tokenistic. There was no access to Commonwealth funding, and little if any intersectoral collaboration existed. Since 1992, however, law enforcement has directly benefited from and significantly contributed to the refocused strategy. Indeed, health practitioners and officials consistently emphasised during the consultations that the strength of the NDS lies in the quality of the partnership that exists between themselves and the law enforcement area.

There have also been significant attitudinal changes. For instance, law enforcement practitioners have shifted from viewing drugs (including alcohol) narrowly in black-and-white legal terms, to focusing much more holistically on the 'impact that alcohol and other drugs have on individuals, families, industry, and the community'. Furthermore, health practitioners and officials have recognised that they can no longer view alcohol and drugs simply as health issues. They too have begun to see drugs and alcohol from a more holistic—social, economic and legal—perspective. In this regard, one of the early goals of the NDS has been achieved.

'The Drug Problem'

The report (Single and Rohl 1997) details the nature and extent of licit and illicit drug use in Australia. It describes factual as well as popular perceptions of the drug 'problem'. For example, nearly one in five deaths in Australia is drug-related. In 1995, 18 124 Australians died from tobacco-related causes. (There is no doubt that the most insidious drug in the community is tobacco.) In the same year, 3642 died from alcohol-related causes and 778 died from illicit drug use. In 1997, it was estimated that approximately 22 500 Australians would die either directly or indirectly as a result of drug misuse and over 175 000 Australians would be hospitalised for conditions as the result of tobacco, alcohol or illicit drug misuse. Substance abuse accounts for more disease and deaths than accidental falls, homicide, HIV/AIDS, breast cancer and cervical cancer combined. The economic costs associated with prevention and treatment of drug-related illness, loss of productivity in the workplace, property crime, theft, accidents and law enforcement activities are over $A18 billion annually. The tragedy is that morbidity and mortality associated with drug use are entirely preventable. This in itself validates the need for a National Drug Strategy.

Community perceptions regarding drug-related mortality are at considerable variance from official statistics. For example, Australians have consistently defined the 'drug problem' as predominantly an illicit drug problem. Since the NCADA/NDS household surveys commenced in 1985, heroin has been identified as the most problematic drug. Marijuana is the next most frequently identified problem drug. Almost two-thirds of respondents in 1995 identified either of these two drugs as the real problem.

Cannabis has until recently been the most frequently used illicit drug in Australia. Almost one-third of Australians (31 per cent) have used marijuana at some time in their lives, and more than one in eight (13 per cent) reported using marijuana in the twelve months prior to the 1995 NDS Household Survey. But this information is now dated; we did our research in late 1996 using data collected in 1995. By mid-1997, there was strong anecdotal evidence that cannabis was being replaced by heroin—cheaper and more readily available—as many people's drug of choice. If this is accurate, it accentuates the need for timely and accurate research to underpin the strategic work of both health and law enforcement practitioners.

Recommendations

In our report (Single and Rohl 1997) we made seven recommendations which we believe all need to be implemented to ensure the survival of the NDS. Our 'Seven Point Plan' was based on a vision of a future Australia in which the vital elements of the NDS would be integrated into health and law enforcement practices. We did not believe that we had arrived at that position yet. The Plan calls for the following:

- strengthening and expanding partnerships;
- establishing a dedicated National Drug Strategy Unit to provide leadership and management for the NDS—this is at the core of the problem;
- renewing the focus on training and educating the community about drugs and particularly the need to train mainstream health, law enforcement and community officials to effectively minimise drug-related harm;
- improving the cost-effectiveness of treatment, prevention and research;
- improving accountability in monitoring the performance of the NDS;
- strengthening the involvement and effectiveness of law enforcement within the Strategy;
- deploying better the cost-shared funding used for ongoing services and the development and dissemination of new programs.

These recommendations raise a number of issues for political leadership. Indeed the consultations we undertook gave an urgency and poignancy to such issues.

Issues for Leadership

The process of evaluation of the NDS was underpinned by very broad consultation. We sought written and oral submissions from every conceivable group with an interest in drugs. We heard from governments, academics, the medical profession, the legal profession and law enforcement practitioners. We spoke with representatives from the tobacco, alcohol and pharmaceutical industries. We consulted with NGOs, church groups, welfare groups, AIDS groups, illicit drug users, prostitutes and many others. For some, drugs are primarily a social issue, for others a health issue, for others a legal issue, or a moral or a political issue or a combination of several of these. Many views are based on personal experiences. Significantly, from our wide-ranging consultation, people consistently wanted to make the point that only government could fix the problem, however it was defined.

It was not possible, however, to speak with everyone who wanted to speak with us. Since completing the evaluation I have been sought out by a number of people who have wanted to tell me their story, in the hope that I could somehow be their conduit to government. In the main, they were people who felt powerless, whose views could not be put by professional associations or organisations. I reported some of their views to the Australian Police Ministers Council (APMC) and the MCDS. Their stories were very personal, invariably expressed with considerable passion and emotion, and they inevitably fell into three main categories: fear, blame and guilt.

- *Fear* was expressed by people concerned for their personal safety and the security of their property, who invariably advocated strong legal sanctions against drug users (as well as pushers).
- *Blame* was the commonest emotion, and it was fraught with anger and frustration. These people's experiences were often associated with the realisation that their son or daughter was a drug user or addict. They would lash out at anyone they could blame for the drug problem as they saw it, often irrationally, but poignantly.
- *Guilt* was the most tragic of the emotions, expressed invariably by parents who had lost a child to drugs. More than any other group these people summed up the dilemma with the words: 'something's wrong with our current system—whatever it is that we are doing isn't working—we've got to find a better way of dealing with drugs in our community'.

Other people spoke from a broader perspective. For example, Dr James Bell, Director of the Drug and Alcohol Units at the Prince of Wales and Sydney Hospitals, who specialises in the treatment of drug dependence and whose major research area is in methadone maintenance treatment, highlighted some of the hypocrisy associated with drugs that he saw daily. He said:

People use drugs to maintain control . . . All sorts of societies use drugs—many of us start the day with caffeine—then use alcohol to wash away failure later in the day, and then use tablets to sleep at night. When this gets out of sync, and you start the day with beer, then you've lost control.

He was making the point that in developed countries drug taking in one form or another becomes the norm, and to try and distinguish between licit and illicit drugs from a user's perspective requires some very fine distinctions.

Other researchers made the point that in every society there will be a certain percentage of people who 'just like to take drugs', in much the same way that in any society there will be those who like to run, or who are workaholics. Many of these people are successful, can easily afford to buy drugs and will continue to do so irrespective of the legal status of their actions. They do not see themselves as criminals; they simply find the law irrelevant. They are exercising what John Stuart Mill described as the 'self regulating test'. They say that so long as they are not infringing the rights and liberties of others they should be allowed to do with their bodies what they choose. Many smokers use the same argument.

Police administrations have committed themselves to supporting the philosophy of harm minimisation. Nevertheless, our research showed that this is not the way many operational police officers view drug users. They are often cynical about what they described as 'do-good philosophies', because they work constantly with the 'revolving door' of drug users and pushers.

The recent dramatic increase in heroin-related deaths has made governments of all persuasions aware that they are now under much closer scrutiny about their response to 'drugs in the community'. Dr Scott Blackwell, President of the Western Australian AMA (*PM*, 25 June 1997) said: 'Death seems to be an acceptable risk amongst young heroin users'. No death, however, can be regarded as an acceptable risk for responsible members of the community.

Conclusion

How we as a community and how governments deal with the drug problem is a major and immediate issue for leadership in a democratic society. There is a perception in the community that there is now the potential for illicit drugs to overtake tobacco and alcohol as the major cause of drug-related deaths in the community. Even though the evidence does not support this proposition, it is a case of popular perception becoming a political reality.

Whatever one's personal view is about drugs, from a political perspective—and that means a public policy perspective—the issue of drug policy does not fit easily into any one political category. To satisfy one group in the community invariably means alienating another. These overlapping contexts make it almost impossible for policy-makers to develop comprehensive and inclusive public policy. There are, however, some steps that can be implemented immediately:

- *Education*—for the community in general, for high-risk groups (particularly young people), for front-line professionals (be they health, law enforcement or welfare), for user groups etc. Education is probably the most important long-term component in any 'drug strategy'. It is also the most difficult, as the target groups are never static.
- *Treatment for users.* Inevitably this requires enhanced funding commitments for health and welfare groups.
- *Continued re-direction of police priorities towards focusing on large-scale trafficking and reduction of supply of drugs from international sources.*

To implement such a program, however, will require Australian governments to re-evaluate their policies on licit and illicit drugs. This will require strong political leadership, in order to reshape popular attitudes. Only by so doing can governments hope to reshape the political agenda and deal more effectively with the problem of illicit drugs.

8

The National Drug Strategy: A Safe Set of Words?

David Crosbie

It has become fashionable these last years to be 'anti-government'.
But this won't work. We need strong, effective government. In fact,
we can expect more rather than less government in the next
decades (Drucker 1993: 143).

Debate and decision-making over drugs policy in Australia confronts at least two difficulties. The first is that drug use is often an
emotive issue. Opinions on drugs are overlaid with moral beliefs,
personal experiences and the vicarious experience of other people's
drug use gained through the mass media and other sources of
information. As a consequence, many people in the community
have entrenched views about drugs. These features make it very
difficult for major players to foster the rational debate and deliberation required by liberal-democratic principles. The second difficulty is that democratic principles also imply that governments
are accountable to the electorate for their performance in addressing issues like drug-related harm. While emotional impediments
to democratic discussion confront many policy issues, drug policy
in Australia is almost unique in its lack of accountability. While
governments increasingly use the rhetoric of improving health
outcomes within the community as a rationale for changes in public
health funding, there are few measurable or comparable outcome
indicators relating to the effectiveness of Australia's drug policy
development.

The National Drug Strategy (NDS) has made a major contribution towards supporting the efforts of a broad range of professionals and organisations working to discuss and reduce drug-related harm. At the same time, the development of alcohol and other drug policy represents a classic case of governments using closed policy development structures to avoid public scrutiny of their performance. This chapter explores the need for drug policy development to be based more upon a model of public accountability for government performance.

Development of a National Drug Policy

Whether or not the NDS is a worthwhile program is not a contentious issue. Most people would agree that the expenditure of the significant amounts of money that have been made available to community treatment and prevention organisations, police, researchers, information providers and trainers has had a positive impact on the way Australia has responded to drug problems. In the last ten years, hundreds of millions of dollars have been spent in these areas under the NDS, and many of the initiatives funded have been recognised as best practice by professionals in Australia and overseas. What may be contentious is the degree to which national drug policy development has informed or enabled this expenditure to be allocated in the most effective way.

Problems of policy

In considering this issue of national drug policy development, it is important to clarify what we are talking about. As Prasser and Starr (1997: 24) comment more generally: 'the literature on policy is frustratingly vague on what is actually meant by the term, and the question is often dismissed in the preliminary throat-clearing with poetic invocations of "swirling complexity" '. Indeed, the term 'policy' has in many instances ceased to have any real meaning in Australia. It is a term that is often applied to any set of words that a group of people has agreed to. From a government perspective, it seems good policy is a set of words that is non-specific enough to allow all the possible options to continue to be pursued. Governments often supplement a generalised 'policy document' with a slightly more specific 'strategy framework', a more specific implementation 'strategy', and perhaps an 'action plan'. Nevertheless, even the action plan may not specify fundamental prerequisites for action like funding, resources, time lines and levels of responsibility.

If we take the *Macquarie Dictionary* as our guide, the term 'policy' is defined as: 'a definite course of action . . ., a course or line of action adopted and pursued by government'. Policy is meant to be about action. In essence, policy is *not* a safe set of words that everyone can agree to. It is this concept of policy as action that needs to inform our understanding of the term policy, particularly if the focus of discussion is the connection between policy and outcomes.

These observations return us to the major weakness of the NDS policy documents. The NDS documents have been written in such broad terms that it is almost impossible to imagine *any* action addressing any drug problem that would be inconsistent with the policies outlined. Everything from abstinence to decriminalisation is consistent with the policies outlined. This form of policy document has a limited capacity to inform real decisions about expenditure or support for particular approaches. As a consequence, real policies, by which I mean actions and priorities, on drugs vary significantly across Australia. Such documents not only make accountability almost impossible, but they also bring into question how these policy documents are developed and whose needs they are meeting.

Generally, the development of policy is supposed to be a rational process that progresses through the following processes:
• problem identification;
• research;
• recommendations (possible position/strategy);
• consultation/lobbying; policy formulation;
• policy approval;
• policy implementation;
• evaluation.
As we shall see, in practice, such rational policy processes are rarely followed.

The Ministerial Council on Drug Strategy

Currently in Australia, the principle drug-policy-making body is the Ministerial Council on Drug Strategy (MCDS) which comprises:

• nine Health Ministers from each jurisdiction in Australia;
• nine Police Ministers;
• the Commonwealth Attorney General; and
• other Ministers with special responsibility for drug policies.

The MCDS meets on average for less than six hours a year, and considers a very broad-ranging agenda including all drugs and drug issues. The MCDS does not allow its agenda or its deliberations to be made public (even under Freedom of Information) and uses its own senior government officials as the principle source of advice. Attendance at these meetings is not always high, but no reports are made about who attended or what positions were adopted by individual Ministers or their advisers. By any measure, this form of policy-making committee is not designed to be an effective policy forum. The meetings are secretive and unaccountable, they only meet for a very short period of time to discuss a wide range of complex issues, and each participant is likely to be motivated by political concerns relating to their own jurisdiction or constituency.

Although the MCDS does occasionally make policy decisions, these decisions are arrived at with great difficulty and are even more difficult to implement. In recent years the main decisions have included: placing warning labels on tobacco packets; indicating the number of standard drinks on all alcohol labels; and proposing a scientific pilot trial of heroin prescription. All of these policy decisions took several years to make, and were only arrived at following significant public pressure on the MCDS to address each of the issues. The public pressure was largely a product of individuals and organisations outside of the MCDS raising the issues and campaigning for change prior to each MCDS meeting. This public pressure introduced a level of accountability that is not possible with most issues being considered by the MCDS.

Most MCDS decisions involve endorsing reports, agreeing in principle, endorsing broad frameworks, setting up task forces and committees, and commissioning more research. It seems that the majority of MCDS work is the responsibility of senior government officials. While some government officials do have substantial drug expertise, many are required to make significant decisions despite having a limited background or understanding of drug issues.

Drug policy documents

At a broader level, Australia has few if any definitive or meaningful drug policy documents. If, for instance, someone wanted to know whether they should support or oppose a new retail alcohol outlet being opened in their town, and they sought policy advice on the issue of alcohol availability from the National Health Policy on Alcohol in Australia, they would be given the following guidelines. When considering whether alcohol availability should be increased, the policy objective is:

> To ensure that current policies on availability do not aggravate the incidence and prevalence of alcohol related problems.

> To consider practical ways in which any changes to policy can be implemented without negative impact on the responsible use of alcohol (National Campaign Against Drug Abuse 1989: 6).

Presuming that people referring to this document may actually want to know what course of action to take, there are not many answers to be gleaned from this form of generalised terminology. The document seems to be saying that increased availability (a new outlet) is good as long as it does not make things worse. Such statements are, at best, self-evident and provide little guidance to practical action.

If someone wanted to know how they could judge whether a particular drug education package was likely to be an effective program and they referred to the nationally developed policy principles they would find guidelines such as:

> Effective drug education must reflect an understanding of the characteristics of the individual, the social context and the substance, and the potential for interaction of these characteristics (Ballard et al. 1994: 11).

The selection of drug education programs, activities and resources should be made on the basis of an ability to contribute to long term positive outcomes in the health curriculum and the health environment of the school (Ballard et al. 1994: 14).

Once again these statements appear to be self-evident. To suggest that drug education is about the interaction of the drug, the person and the environment, and that drug education programs should improve the health curriculum, really tells us little about the optimal drug education forms that should be pursued.

The worrying aspect of this kind of 'policy we can all agree to' is that it is usually expensive to develop and is only really meaningful to the limited group of people who participated in developing the actual words. Unfortunately, those of us reading the end product are usually left asking what it all means in practice.

In the Australian alcohol and other drugs field we use meaningful policy terms like: 'harm minimisation', 'informed decision-making', 'outcome-focused', 'alcohol misuse', 'evidence-based', 'consultation', 'partnership', 'process evaluation'. The use of such terms may make us feel more professional or informed. In practice, however, most of these terms are so open to interpretation that their meaning shifts not only from situation to situation, but also from drug to drug, and individual to individual.

Even if the theory of generalised drug policy development is sound, the reality is that the practice of policy development is often unrelated to any form of rational policy development process. The following list offers a number of actual examples of how some drug policies have been developed in Australia recently:
• heard talk-back radio—made an instant policy change;
• decided new policy around a barbecue with friends of the children;
• journalist offered very good coverage for a policy change;
• ministerial adviser decided on policy change for personal reasons;
• the family experiences of a single politician led to policy change.

This is not to suggest that all the policies developed through the above processes were any better or worse than some of the more protracted negotiated policy documents developed by senior government officials meeting in committees. It does suggest, however, that popular opinions, personal preference and political judgment may carry more weight than professional expertise. In one sense, it is quite proper for such views to be given a hearing in a democracy. The problem is the random and arbitrary nature of decision-making that may exclude a range of equally worthy ideas.

Policy Outcomes and Accountability

At some point, judgements need to be made about whether or not a given policy represents effective or ineffective drug policy. In this regard, Martin Rein (1983: 13) reminds us that social scientists do not just examine *how* policies have developed, but play a vital role in 'determining whether policies actually accomplish what they are intended to accomplish'. In recent years, the move towards policy analysis based upon outcomes has led to a diverse range of potential measurements against which policy effectiveness might be judged and instruments or 'performance' indicators by which it could be measured.

I would like to take this opportunity, therefore, to offer the following six criteria as a possible set of performance indicators which may be used to judge the effectiveness of Australian drug policy. Effective drug policy should:
• be based upon accurate research and information identifying need;
• specify goals and objectives;
• specify target group(s);
• specify strategy to achieve policy objectives;
• be costed (per outcome); and
• be evaluated in terms of objectives and outcomes.
A community service organisation seeking funding from a government department would be expected to meet all the above criteria before any funding was provided. Yet the same government departments would often be content to continue investing significant resources into nebulous policy development exercises that have no real outcomes within the broader community. It is difficult to understand the contradiction between policy development

processes that are subject to minimum accountability and service providers (both government and non-government) that are increasingly being asked to detail and justify every aspect of their operations.

At a political level, most Australian governments have usually managed to avoid real accountability for their drug policy development. They also manage to maintain their own separate approaches to prevention, treatment, law enforcement and legal issues associated with drug problems, despite all governments receiving funding through the National Drug Strategy. Consequently, it is almost impossible to say accurately how each government is performing. For example, there are few nationally comparable statistics on the extent of drug use in each jurisdiction, the extent of drug-related harm in each jurisdiction and the degree to which government policies have increased or decreased the level of drug-related harm.* Without this data, it is difficult to see how governments can be accountable for their policies.

Improving Drug Policy

To improve drug policy we need to invest more resources in identifying what has worked to reduce drug problems, and make governments more accountable for investing in areas that can and do make a difference. As part of improving accountability there is also a need to increase the policy input of those people who have significant expertise and professional knowledge about patterns of drug use and associated harms. This expertise needs to be actively sought out and brought into policy development in the initial stages, along with the various perspectives of consumers and service providers.

Longer-term planning and action should also be the primary focus of drug policy development. Successful policies are almost

---

* What information that is available suggests Australia is not doing particularly well at reducing the use of illicit drugs such as cannabis or heroin, that the level of illicit-drug-related harm seems to be increasing (as measured by factors such as heroin-related deaths), that more young women in particular are binge-drinking alcohol, and that we have managed to generally stabilise, and in some jurisdictions reduce, male drinking and tobacco use (Williams 1997).

invariably based upon long-term strategies to achieve change, yet the formulation of drug policy can, at times, be an *ad hoc* political reaction to an issue that has received overly dramatic and 'sensational' treatment in the mass media.

For the reasons outlined above, I submit that drug policy in Australia will only improve if we address the following four areas:

- active drug policy analysis based upon real outcomes;
- transparency in decision-making and funding;
- active involvement of consumers, experts and the community in policy development; and
- support for actions that can be shown to be effective.

In essence these four areas are all related to the key democratic principle that underpins our notion of government: accountability of government to the community for the decisions taken by government to address community interests.

In Australia at present, there are several key interest groups actively campaigning for policy changes, but most have little if any input into policy making at the most senior level. The closed meetings of senior officials and of the Ministerial Council on Drug Strategy exclude input from groups such as consumers, service providers, researchers, professionals and community interest groups. This exclusive approach to policy development is currently under review following an independent evaluation of the NDS. Proposed changes to decision-making structures and levels of consultation represent an improvement in drug policy making in that they will allow experts outside of senior government officials increased input into policy making, and may contribute to an increase in accountability. Proposed changes include a new National Council on Drugs drawn primarily from experts working within the community rather than senior government officials, and increased levels of consultation on national drug policy issues.

Conclusion

If those concerned about illicit drugs in Australia can increase the level of government accountability for drug policy, there is little doubt that the whole community will benefit. Government decisions directly impact on the level of drug-related harm experienced by the Australian community. A government that is accountable to the people for its performance is much more likely to achieve outcomes than one where policy is portrayed as complex or unable to be measured in terms of real effectiveness. As Osborne and Gaebler (1993: 146–52) have pointed out:

> What gets measured gets done. If you don't measure results, you can't tell success from failure. If you can demonstrate results, you can win public support. If you can't see success, you can't reward it. If you can't reward success, you are probably rewarding failure. If you can't recognise failure, you can't correct it.

We cannot afford to reward failure in the development of drug policy in Australia. For Australia to develop effective drug policy, we must ensure that governments are democratically accountable and responsible for the outcomes of their policy decisions. Drug policy must become much more than meaningless sets of words to which everyone can agree.

9

Harm Reduction

Ann Roche and Keith Evans

FOR OVER A DECADE harm minimisation has been the over-arching official drug policy within Australia. This particular philosophical stance has fostered a number of distinctive responses to illicit drug use in this country. In particular, it is frequently argued that the holding of this position as the national policy has made possible numerous initiatives which may not have been otherwise feasible. This chapter will first examine the nature of the term 'harm minimisation' and it will then review the extent to which it can and does provide an adequate drug policy umbrella. Strengths and potential weaknesses of harm minimisation will be explored. The dilemma of locating non-use within a harm minimisation perspective will be addressed, together with the question of whether it constitutes the ultimate panacea for illicit drug problems. The chapter also presents a broader, integrated model to address illicit drug use. This alternative model encapsulates both harm minimisation and additional perspectives. It offers to policy makers, planners and interventionists an approach which has the capacity to respond more effectively to a broader range of substance use problems.

It is unlikely that policy-makers and members of the community, particularly as reflected by political opinion, would want to give up the view that the eventual elimination of illicit drugs should be the primary goal for any national drug policy. Nonetheless, such a goal is becoming ever more elusive. Across Australia public support for explicit harm-reduction-oriented policy approaches has increased over the past decade. This increase in support suggests diminishing enthusiasm for, or confidence in, non-harm-reduction and abstinence-oriented policies. This chapter offers a model, the Integrated Intervention Drug Model (IIDM), which provides a platform from which the many voices in the drug policy arena can be heard and appreciated. The IIDM is unique in that it provides a comprehensive framework for policy and strategy without the trappings of professional prejudice.

Background

There is little question that the problems posed by illicit drug use represents one of the most complex global and national challenges of the twentieth century. There have been varied and substantial programs implemented to address this issue. One response that has elicited diverse views falls under the broad banner of 'harm reduction' or, as it is also known, 'harm minimisation'. The terms 'harm reduction' and 'harm minimisation' tend to be seen as synonymous, at least in the eyes of the general public. Nonetheless, they are often interpreted to mean quite different things, and this chapter attempts to unravel some of the differences between the two terms. It is important to recognise, however, that there is no commonly accepted, specific meaning or functional application of either term.

A number of countries, including Australia, have embraced the rhetoric of harm reduction in recent years as their principal philosophical and policy stance in relation to illicit drugs. Indeed, since the mid-1980s, what distinguished Australia from some of its neighbours within the international political community was its preparedness to embrace 'harm minimisation' as its official national policy position on alcohol and other drugs. From the late 1980s to 1996, there was open, widespread and official support for both the rhetoric and the application of the term. Following a change of government in early 1997 some doubt was cast over the political acceptability of the term. Similar reappraisals have also occurred in other countries (Fleming 1995). In some quarters there was growing support for abandoning the principle altogether. During the same period, there was increasing use of the opposite position, expressed in ideological terms as 'zero-tolerance'. Despite these tendencies, at the time of writing no significant shift away from harm reduction as the official policy has occurred in Australia, and a commitment to this stance has been reaffirmed through the publication of the National Drug Strategic Framework Document covering the period.

The value of harm reduction is not questioned in this chapter. Nonetheless, we do question the extent to which harm reduction offers a comprehensive policy framework that allows scope to incorporate a sufficiently broad range of policy and philosophical positions. In essence, we ask: What are the merits and what are the limitations of harm reduction? What alternative principles, if any, could better serve our needs in this complex area?

Finding workable solutions to illicit drug use in a democratic society is made more difficult by the multi-faceted nature of drug-seeking and drug-using behaviours, the diversity of environments in which drug use occurs and, the rapidly changing attitudes regarding drug use within drug-using cultures and society generally. As discussed by Geoffrey Stokes, Peter Chalk and Karen Gillen in their introduction to this volume, 'all or nothing' responses to issues of social policy are antithetical to a democratic society. Stokes, Chalk and Gillen refer to the problems inherent in King Draco's policy that all crimes shall be punished by death as a dubious model for managing the criminal justice system. Similarly, an approach to drug policy which places its primary focus on punishing users and upholding abstinence as the primary objective is increasingly failing both the user and society as a whole.

What is Harm Reduction?

Harm reduction has been the guiding principle used to identify a range of strategies that target the *consequences* of drug use, rather than focussing on drug use itself. At its simplest, to do less harm is usually considered a higher order good than doing more harm, however harm may be defined or construed. Harm reduction may be understood as an example of negative utilitarianism. Indeed, the philosopher Karl Popper (see Stokes 1998: 69–70) argues that this principle is the only defensible guide to policy formulation in liberal-democratic polities. According to Single and Lenton (1998), the central, defining characteristic of harm reduction is that it focuses on reducing harm as its primary goal rather than reduction of use *per se*. In addition, the principle also incorporates strategies that reduce the harm for those who continue to use drugs, and that demonstrate a likely net reduction in drug-related harm. Nonetheless, Saunders and Wright (1994) have pointed out that a focus on *harm reduction* rather than *use reduction* could have an overall net result of less harm but more use.

Various attempts have been made to define harm reduction more precisely. Single and Lenton (1998), for example, identified three ways in which harm reduction has been defined and categorised to date. These were: (1) narrow definitions, which emphasised the acceptance of continued drug use; (2) broad definitions, which also allowed for inclusion of abstinence orientations; and (3) hard empirical definitions, which required evidence of success of the strategies. Narrow definitions are seen as potentially too limiting and possibly excluding programs which might appropriately have non-use of drugs as a component, even where it might be time-limited. In contrast, broad definitions were potentially problematic because of what they did not exclude. Under some broad definitions almost anything could be considered a harm-reduction approach, including the creation of drug-free states or the indefinite incarceration of drug users to prevent them doing further harm to themselves or others.

Another important distinction is evident where harm reduction is interpreted either as a broad policy goal, or as a set of strategies. Where the former could incorporate abstinence-based programs and approaches, the latter would only include measures directed at continuing users. Some, but not all, of the strategies which fall under the umbrella of harm minimisation represent radical departures and include approaches that have been applied or tolerated in the past. For instance, from a harm reduction perspective, drug use is also recognised by some as being functional, or even beneficial to society (Moore 1993). That is, drug use can serve a positive role in an individual's life. This is a challenging concept for some, and totally unacceptable to others.

It has been argued by some that harm reduction is not a new concept (Berridge 1993; Casswell 1981; Velleman and Rigby 1992). Rather, it represents a new way of conceptualising and responding to illicit (and also licit) drug problems. The advantage of harm reduction is that it has allowed for a major rethinking of the range of interventions and responses to drug use. It has enabled an array of options to be implemented that would otherwise have been difficult, if not impossible, to sustain. The principle of harm reduction has also been particularly successful in terms of its contribution to the containment of the spread of HIV/AIDS in Australia (Crofts et al. 1994). It is not difficult to give clear, if not contentious, examples of harm minimisation strategies. At an operational level, typical harm reduction strategies include:

- needle and syringe availability programs;
- methadone maintenance in prison populations;
- alternative routes of administration for drugs;
- narcan for ambulance crews;
- training in safe injecting practices;
- supervised shooting galleries; and
- provision of information on low-risk using practises.

Harm reduction strategies also allow for targeted education for drug users which does not have as an end goal the reduction in drug use *per se* (Cohen and Kay 1994). For some, harm reduction also provides a banner for the decriminalisation of all drug laws, the legal prescription of heroin for addicts, retention of laws for drug providers but not for users, teaching safe drug use, and potentially the state purchase, control and allocation of illicit drugs.

Paradoxically, it has been suggested that the all-embracing nature of the term 'harm reduction' has largely contributed to its rapid adoption and widespread appeal (Single 1995b). It can literally mean all things to all people. The lack of a narrow, prescriptive definition of harm reduction has also added to its appeal and stands it in stark contrast to other more rigid, ideologically based law-enforcement positions such as 'zero tolerance'.

The General Principles of Harm Reduction

According to Single and Lenton (1998) the following are considered to represent typical features of harm reduction policies, programs and interventions:

- the avoidance of exacerbating harm caused by the misuse of drugs;
- the treatment of drug users with dignity and as normal human beings;
- the prioritising of achievable goals;
- neutrality regarding legalisation or decriminalisation.*

These principles differentiate the strategy from the 'War on Drugs' approach.

Although there is no generally agreed meaning for the term 'harm reduction', there is widespread recognition that it would be helpful to have one (Erickson 1995). Wodak and Saunders (1995) have suggested that the term suffers from a lack of terminological

---

* The terms legalisation and decriminalisation can at times tend to be used imprecisely within the context of the harm reduction debate. This lack of precision can lead to blurring of the terms so that they might be viewed as interchangeable. This is not the case. The term *legalisation* is used to describe strategies aimed at the removal of sanctions associated with the possession and personal use of certain currently illegal substances. Major national and international lobby groups and public policy advocates support such moves in relation to the legal status of cannabis and heroin, in order to reduce the social and personal negative consequences associated with the illegal status of these substances. In particular, concerns over heroin purity and heroin-related overdose deaths are currently fuelling this debate. The term *decriminalisation* is used to describe changes to the legal status of prohibited substances such that their possession for personal use falls outside the criminal code. In South Australia, for example, 'partial decriminalisation' of cannabis has resulted in law enforcement officers treating the possession of less than a certain amount of the plant as a non-criminal offence leading to the presentation of an expiation notice (payment of the fine within the legally prescribed time period is treated exactly the same as for a 'ticketable' driving offence). Possession of more than the prescribed amount, however, is treated as a criminal offence as is non-payment of the expiation notice. The Netherlands model for managing possession and consumption of cannabis is often cited as an example of state-sponsored decriminalisation.

clarity and has a bewildering array of interpretations in a field often characterised by emotional fervour. The drug and alcohol field is one in which there is often more heat than light applied to the search for mechanisms most likely to bring about long-term change to levels of use and any associated harms (Roche et al. 1997). Over several decades there have been numerous causal models promoted for explaining the underlying cause of drug problems. Each model offers preferred or implied solutions. These models have included such diverse factors as moral weakness, lack of legal constraint, and disease states (Hester and Miller 1995). The research literature, and in particular the policy literature, is replete with opposing points of view. Indeed, contrasting positions are often held with such a degree of commitment that legal cases have ensued where deviations from prescribed paths have been detected.

Despite such conflicts of opinion, researchers have shown increasing interest in empirically assessing the impact of harm reduction strategies. The difficulty here, however, is that reduction of harm is often harder to measure than abstention, in much the same way that it is difficult to measure the tangible success of prevention efforts (Single and Lenton 1998). A key question with which we are still grappling is: What is the best way to measure the impact of harm reduction strategies so that we know which strategies yield the greatest benefit (Caulkins 1996)?

The drug and alcohol field is recognised internationally as one in which the key figures and many of the players are strongly wedded to a particular view of human behaviour and a vision of how to best address problems associated with drug use. Yet effective strategies are often the least preferred by members of the general public or politicians. Largely unproven strategies, such as school-based drug education, are perennial favourites among politicians and some influential public figures. Considerable funds are often directed to areas and activities where the least benefit is likely to be achieved, either for the individuals or the community. There is growing pressure for all policy and program providers to demonstrate efficacy. This is equally true for harm reduction efforts.

Distinguishing Harm Reduction from Harm Minimisation

The widespread adoption of the term 'harm minimisation' in Australia (if not the concepts and underpinning assumptions) comes in large part from the Federal Government's promulgation of the concept as the official government policy. Individuals, agencies and organisations seeking government funding and support have been under pressure to pay at least lip service to the rhetoric of harm minimisation. We argue, however, that it was always the intention of the architects of Australia's National Drug Strategy that the term 'harm minimisation' be inclusive rather than exclusive.

Although the terms 'harm reduction' and 'harm minimisation' are often used interchangeably, questions have arisen over whether there is any significant difference between these terms. Where the term 'minimise' has been defined by the *Concise Oxford Dictionary* as 'the smallest possible amount or degree' the term 'reduction' entails simply 'reducing or being reduced'. We suggest that these definitional distinctions provide a basis for somewhat different policy orientations. The term 'harm minimisation', for example, fits more comfortably with the notion of non-drug use as a legitimate goal in that it is consistent with reducing problems to their smallest or lowest possible level. This approach then accommodates the inclusion of abstinence, since abstinence is logically the lowest possible level of use. The term harm minimisation also carries less threatening connotations than does harm reduction. Harm reduction was originally captured as a policy term for the drug field by protagonists in Europe and Britain where there was often strong support for legalising illicit drugs.

Harm Reduction versus Use Reduction

Over the past decade, there has simultaneously been a growth in both support for and dissension over harm reduction approaches. Some of the key strategies employed as harm reduction strategies, such as needle exchange (or, as they are more commonly now known, needle availability programs) and methadone treatment programs generate considerable community disquiet. This is not to argue that they are not highly effective forms of interventions and represent some of the few primary prevention strategies in this area which are demonstrably successful when assessed against a wide range of criteria (Ward et al. 1998).

Even though there is difficulty in defining 'harm reduction', it is clear that the term represents a radical departure from 'use reduction'. 'Use reduction' simply means reducing the overall rates of use of illicit drugs. Use reduction strategies, however, have come under increased criticism for their narrow and often judgemental focus, and their inability to address a wide range of crucial issues. On the surface, reduced levels of use may be considered a positive and desirable outcome. Nonetheless, it has been recently realised that use reduction can often have dire consequences with enforced or unmonitored reductions in use, especially among heavily addicted individuals. For instance, a substantial proportion of opioid overdose deaths occur among users who have reduced their regular level of use, for whatever reason, and who thus have a much lowered level of tolerance and greater susceptibility of overdose if they return to use at their previous level.

Factors influencing reduced use may include a prison sentence, a treatment program, or involuntary reduction due to reduced supply or an excessive increase in cost of the drug. Tolerance drops quickly when intake is reduced, and the risk of overdose increases correspondingly. This phenomenon was evident in parts of South-East Asia where eradication of the opium crops resulted in a major crisis and considerable suffering for thousands of heavily addicted opioid addicts. Many of these individuals have been placed in life-threatening situations as a result of the removal of their drug of addiction. Use reduction in such circumstances can have the opposite effect to that which was originally intended.

The rise in opioid overdose deaths in Australia during the 1990s has given added impetus to harm reduction strategies. It has also drawn into sharper focus the hierarchy of needs for individual users, their families and the community at large. Maintaining the health and well-being of users until such time that their drug use abates has now become axiomatic in light of the growing death rate among users. Drug control policies are usually seen to be inconsistent, but not necessarily incompatible, with harm reduction.

Harm reduction, however, allows attention to be focussed not only on dependent or addicted individuals but also on the full gamut of drug-using behaviours and associated problems. For instance, occasional or recreational injecting drug users, especially very young users, are at substantially elevated risk of acquiring infections such as hepatitis C. Such health problems are increasingly acknowledged as having major long-term consequences and are seen as warranting immediate intervention. Hence, specific episodes of use and the context and setting of use have become a particular focus of some harm reduction efforts. Again, the primary policy goal here is not to achieve a cessation of use, although this is not precluded as a longer-term objective. The policy is more concerned with the shorter-term concerns surrounding issues of safety, morbidity and mortality.

In terms of defining harm reduction by way of what it is not, it is useful to compare Australia's official policy position with the USA's 'War on Drugs'. These two policy and philosophical positions stand diametrically opposed to each other. One represents a focus on the consequences of use, with support and care for users, and the other has been described as being literally a 'war on drug users', as it is people who are jailed, not the drugs they use (Single and Lenton 1998). Moreover, there is little evidence to suggest that a 'War on Drugs' approach, which is heavily punitive and involves incarceration of thousands of individuals, has achieved substantial inroads into successfully managing drug use and its associated problems.

The Limitations of Harm Reduction

As indicated above, the term harm reduction originally referred only to those policies and programs which attempted to reduce the risk of harm among people who continued to use drugs (Single and Rohl 1997). One of the limitations and indeed criticisms of harm reduction is the extent to which it may exclude a range of alternative legitimate policy positions. It has also been argued that to define a single preferred approach or orientation as *primus inter pares* has the potential to alienate and even exclude large sections of the field (Roche et al. 1997). Such exclusion is seen to be potentially damaging and disruptive. The limitations of a harm reduction framework in isolation from other models has become increasingly evident in recent years. Commentators such as Reuter and Caulkins (1995) have recommended support for models which could accommodate the complementary and compatible roles of both harm reduction *and* use reduction approaches.

Accepting the need for various policy positions and approaches confronts the persistent cry that harm reduction requires abstinence. At present, those aligned with abstentionist and other non-drug-use positions are forced to frame their views within a harm reduction perspective. It seems more realistic, however, to acknowledge that harm reduction does not necessarily mean abstinence or use reduction. Indeed, as noted above, use reduction clearly does not lead to harm reduction in all instances.

Towards an Integrated Intervention Model

Although there is considerable merit in harm reduction policies there remains a need for a more unified and unifying policy model. A broader, more comprehensive model may go some way to alleviate the ideological tensions within the field and would allow for accommodation of the divergent range of approaches which are currently taken toward drug use and its associated harms (Mugford 1993). In the drug policy arena it is not uncommon to observe apparently conflicting sets of policies and programs in train. For instance, we may simultaneously have a governmental policy which is use-reduction in orientation operating alongside an extensive range of programs based on a harm reduction philosophy.

Together, harm reduction and use reduction can provide a framework of principles that is broad enough to encompass various policy and program initiatives across the full spectrum of primary, secondary and tertiary interventions. Nevertheless, we suggest that neither of these sets of strategies are sufficiently in-clusive to capture the complexity of the drug field. To date, no countries have successfully evolved a comprehensive policy frame-work which can readily incorporate both use reduction and harm reduction, nor a range of other important and legitimate stances.

In an earlier paper, Roche et al. (1997) have offered a possible alternative normative model to resolve the currently unsatisfac-tory situation. The model proposed is an Integrated Intervention Drug Model (IIDM). This model would operate out of a public health perspective and would focus primarily on the overall health and well being of individuals and the community. This model comprises two levels or components. The first level represents the current principal operational approaches to drug issues. These include:

- harm reduction;
- use reduction;
- non-use; and
- abstinence.

It is envisaged that these approaches be seen as four intersecting rings which would provide tacit acknowledgment that none would hold a superior position, nor would the different approaches be merged or homogenised. Recognition is given to the distinctly dif-ferent perspectives, but with some scope for overlap where there is commonality of purpose or perspective. The strengths of the pro-posed model are seen to rest in its identification of common ground, while simultaneously accommodating opposed views, but without exacerbating such differences.

The second level or component part of the model is the contex-tual layer in which the above operational approaches are located. These are meta-level or contextual factors and include: equity; culture; gender; and socio-economic status. This list is not exhaus-tive, but illustrative of the types of considerations that need to be included. These meta-level issues are seen as essential for any gen-eral policy framework. It has not been uncommon in the past for such elements to be ignored or overlooked. It is maintained that it is the capacity of any model to address these types of factors which will determine its ultimate success or failure. Hence, con-siderable emphasis is placed on recognition of cultural context and cultural norms, gender issues, and wider social and economic factors.

It may be helpful to readers at this stage to provide an example of how the proposed model might operate in practice: A 23-year-old client of an inner city drug program is an injecting drug user who uses alcohol at a problematic level and who also smokes tobacco. The application of the Integrated Intervention Drug Model (IIDM) may well see the management of this client include the following :

- use of sterile needles on occasions of intravenous drug use (harm reduction);
- reducing excessive alcohol consumption (use reduction);
- attempting to quit smoking (abstinence).

Further factors which would need to be addressed from the perspective of the model are those referred to as meta-level factors. In this instance, the person's gender and cultural background would be considered to determine an appropriate course of action. Similar examples can be developed from a criminal justice perspective. Such a model would apply to groups and the community at large, not just individuals.

A key to the success of the IIDM is that it requires consideration be given to the four pillars of the model namely: harm reduction, use reduction, abstinence and non-use. Whilst it is possible that at any point in time, one of these approaches will be seen as best meeting the individual needs of the individual drug user, it will ensure that there has not been premature closure in terms of the other options available.

A unique strength of the IIDM is its applicability across the drug policy spectrum. In developing illicit-drug-prevention strategies we are often faced with the problems associated with official bias in favour of either a harm reduction or a zero tolerance to drugs approach. This is particularly true in the case of school-based drug-prevention approaches. The IIDM sets a framework for considering approaches to drug prevention which permits discussion of harm reduction and abstinence without requiring adoption of any particular strategy. The model's strength lies in its pragmatic approach to drug policy as opposed to policy driven by ideological prejudice.

The model may also add much to the development of coherent, comprehensive and sustainable local, regional and national drug policies. Drug policies inevitably require a diverse range of inputs. These sources of input include politicians, policy advisers, and vested interest groups from the prevention, treatment and research arenas. Other powerful influencers of drug policy include police, judiciary, user groups and the families of users. This list is not exhaustive but provides some insight into the range of influences upon the policy-making process. The IIDM sets the parameters around which to articulate and develop effective drug policy. It also acts as a constant reminder that all four pillars of drug policy must be considered and included if the final product is to meet the needs of a democratic society that values pluralism and respect for difference.

Conclusion

This chapter has provided an overview of the strengths and weaknesses of harm reduction, or as it is sometimes known, harm minimisation, as one of the major policy and philosophical responses to drug use over the past decade in Australia and a number of other countries. It has been acknowledged that harm reduction, either as an end goal or as a set of strategies, has been found to be a successful approach to dealing with drug issues. Nonetheless, we argue that to focus exclusively on abstinence or on harm reduction and the consequences of use limits opportunities to recognise and address the contribution of other significant factors. A narrow approach also curtails scope for prevention efforts. What is recommended is a broader model to guide the formulation of drug policies and intervention strategies. The advantage of such a model is that it can encompass a range of positions, some of which are antithetical to each other. In this integrated model no single approach is given priority over another. Harm reduction is therefore essential, but is only one among a range of other justifiable approaches.

10

Law Enforcement and Accountability

Adam Sutton and Stephen James

IN 1989, IT WAS ESTIMATED that costs to the Commonwealth, States and Territories of enforcing laws against illicit drugs was $A123 million each year (Parliamentary Joint Committee on the National Crime Authority 1989). In 1992, it was argued that $A320 million would be a more accurate figure (Marks 1992). More recently, in 1997, unnamed 'experts' consulted for an article in the *Bulletin* raised the estimate to $A404 million per annum. What returns does Australia receive from these massive, and apparently ever-increasing, investments? What public order, health and other social outcomes do bodies such as the National Crime Authority, the Federal Police, Customs Australia, the State and Territory drug squads and the myriad regional detective units scattered throughout Australia see themselves as achieving, when they infiltrate drug syndicates, 'seize major shipments', and 'bust' traffickers and users? Should we adhere to current law enforcement policies and strategies? If we do, what are the likely consequences for Australian society and Australian democracy? If change is necessary, how is it to be achieved? These are the types of questions this chapter will try to address.

The first section of this chapter summarises a major two-year review of drug law enforcement throughout Australia, completed in 1995 for Australia's National Police Research Unit (James and Sutton 1996). The aim of this research was to take stock of work by all specialist drug enforcement units and assess whether, and how, they could be deemed to be achieving 'success'. The next section summarises the key recommendations of the review: ideas for making the work of drug squads and similar bodies more 'rational' and accountable, and rendering them more capable of serving what we perceived as the general public interest rather than simply alleviating political pressures or satisfying the professional and bureaucratic interests of people who were engaged in this type of work. The third and fourth sections focus on longer-term consequences from the study. Australia's police commissioners, who constitute the governing board of the National Police Research Unit, endorsed many of the findings and recommendations, and have begun implementing them in local trials in Victoria, New South Wales and Western Australia. The authors are part of a team monitoring these trials over an eighteen-month period. In addition to summarising how the assessment will be carried out, this chapter also offers some views on difficulties these pilot programs are likely to encounter. It is argued that it is in the interests of a democratic, multicultural society such as Australia's that drug law enforcement undergo a fundamental shift in philosophy and direction. At the same time, we are under no illusions about the likelihood that such change can be achieved easily. For all their problems and inefficiencies, there is immense stability in Australia's drug law enforcement regimes. Moreover, blame for resistance to change cannot just be allocated to police and other enforcement bureaucracies. To be sustainable, the 'rational' drug law enforcement regimes we propose depend on the societies within which they are located being able to demonstrate reasonably high degrees of pragmatism and tolerance toward drug users and other 'deviants'.

The National Review of Drug Law Enforcement

The national drug law enforcement study was commissioned by the National Police Research Unit and was supervised by the Commissioners of Police. Extending over two years, the study involved semi-structured interviews with just under 100 individuals occupying management, operational and senior policy positions in dedicated drug law enforcement bodies, such as the state drug squads, and with representatives of key national authorities such as the Australian Federal Police, the National Crime Authority and Customs Australia. We also reviewed corporate plans, annual reports and other documentation, and assessed published and unpublished data on amounts and types of drugs seized and on arrests, charges and prosecutions under relevant legislation. To balance information received from law enforcement sources we also, wherever possible, made a point of consulting health authorities and relevant user groups in each jurisdiction visited.

What did this data collection reveals about drug law enforcement in Australia? First, and perhaps most important, it was apparent that there were marked disparities between the official or declared aims of most relevant bodies and what actually was being achieved. Officially, the overriding objective for all the drug law enforcement agencies was to target and arrest 'Mr Bigs', understood as major figures involved in the production, importation, warehousing and distribution of illicit drugs, or in financing large-scale operations (see Manderson 1993). In line with the stated policy of most agencies, most of the respondents felt that the best strategy for disrupting chains of supply lay in removing such high-level figures or, at the very least making their lives difficult. Most were adamant that lower-level distributors should only be targeted if this would assist in efforts to identify and successfully target high-fliers. Nevertheless, there was little or no evidence that these goals actually were being achieved. When challenged, few specialist agencies could provide statistical or other evidence which demonstrated that most of the people they arrested had been at comparatively high levels in crime syndicates—indeed, few agencies had even been able to develop systematic techniques for modelling drug markets and assessing the status of people within them (Green and Purnell 1996). User and health representatives were adamant that it was minor dealers and users, rather than major traffickers, who were bearing the brunt of arrests under Australia's drug laws, and all available statistics seemed to support them. A comprehensive review of published and unpublished data suggests that the great majority of people caught up with criminal justice systems throughout Australia for drug-related offences are better classified as 'users' than 'providers', and that only a very small fraction could be classified as high-level operators.

How can this vast discrepancy between what drug law enforcement saw itself as trying to do, and outcomes actually generated be explained? Our research suggested at least three reasons. The first was that the term 'high-level' is relative, and was being interpreted differently in various parts of Australia. In the Northern Territory and Tasmania a high-level figure might be a local user who, to sustain his or her habit, also supplies others on a regular basis. In New South Wales, Victoria and for most Commonwealth agencies, on the other hand, the term is more likely to be reserved for individuals regularly financing and organising multi-million-dollar productions or importations.

The second major reason for apparent failure to capture the 'Mr Bigs' was that successfully targeting a genuine high-level figure invariably presented formidable problems. Almost all experienced investigators readily conceded that it would be possible for large-scale financiers—particularly those based off shore—to invest in and profit from the illicit drug trade while having little or no direct contact with, or even knowledge of, specific operations. Such individuals undoubtedly were 'major figures', but obtaining sufficient evidence for a successful prosecution would be almost impossible. Even for financiers, producers and distributors who operated within Australia and who had significant exposure to operations, successful targeting and apprehension could be extremely difficult. Standard techniques for penetrating higher levels of drug operations—such as electronic surveillance, telephone intercepts and deep undercover operations—tended to be complex, drawn out, expensive and sometimes dangerous for the personnel involved (Goodsir 1995). 'Buy busts', the routine tactic used at the State and Territory levels, had inherent limitations. Efforts to 'move up the chain' of distributors by purchasing successively larger quantities could be frustrated by well-resourced operators if they put the opening price for substantial buys at amounts well beyond the funds available to agencies for purchases.

The third, and probably most important, reason for major disparities between the sector's stated goals and actual achievements had to do with structural factors, arising out of the way drug law enforcement had evolved in Australia's Federal system. Over time, every State and Territory has established a dedicated drug squad, and some also have Commissions with special powers (e.g. New South Wales Crimes Commission and Queensland's Criminal Justice Commission). The Commonwealth also has its specialist agencies (the National Crime Authority, Customs Australia, the Federal Police). All of these groups have been advised to concentrate on the high-level operators within their relevant spheres of jurisdiction. Despite, or more accurately *because,* of this proliferation of specialist units, the vast majority of apprehensions for drug offences were carried out by more generalist local detectives and uniformed police. Instead of being bound by specific goals and policies (i.e. to pursue high-level figures), these officers are often driven by much more diffuse forces such as the need to respond to community pressures, or to avoid complaints from local traders, or to maintain public order. It is arguable that most street-level drug enforcement was occurring in a 'policy vacuum'. Much drug enforcement activity was not carried out by the specialist agencies, because relevant offenders were mere 'minor figures', and was instead made the responsibility of non-specialists who were interpreting and applying laws in ways that often had little regard for broader Federal or State drug policy goals.

Despite the best efforts of individual drug squads and commissions, it appeared that drug law enforcement as a totality in Australia was falling well short of being a *rational system.* A rational drug enforcement system is one: 'which bases its practices on best knowledge of illegal drug supply and consumption patterns, and which continuously monitors the impacts of its interventions in order to ensure their on-going effectiveness and to minimise unintended consequences' (Sutton and James 1996: vii). Most of the specialists in drug law enforcement acknowledged that more often than not they had little or no idea about the impacts that their operations might be having on the price, purity and availability of various types of illicit drugs 'on the street'. Most did not see it as their business to be concerned about the impacts of enforcement operations on patterns of consumer behaviour. For example, police were unconcerned about whether a local 'blitz' on cannabis might simply be making some young people more inclined to experiment with Ecstasy or even heroin. Overall, the system of drug law enforcement was comparatively unreflective about its specific impacts, particularly at the 'grassroots' street level, where our health colleagues tell us that most drug-related harm actually occurs. Our recommendations aimed to rectify this problem, with the goal of making the system less 'tunnel-visioned' and more capable of taking stock of its overall operations and effects.

Recommendations from the National Review

The most important suggestion from our review was that there be comprehensive reassessment of the goals and procedures of Australian drug law enforcement, to make the idea of *harm reduction* just as important as the objective of targeting and apprehending high-level figures. For more than a decade Commonwealth, State and Territory Governments have formally endorsed harm reduction principles which give priority to reducing adverse health, economic and social consequences of drug use for individuals and communities (National Drug Strategy 1993). Prohibition has been endorsed as part of harm reduction philosophy, but only to the extent that it can be shown to contribute to the overall aim of reducing harms associated with drug use (see Premier's Drug Advisory Council 1996: 59). Unlike the United States, Australia has never committed itself unequivocally to 'War on Drugs' philosophies, nor has it seen any initiative which restricts availability of a prohibited drug as an unqualified good, regardless of its impacts on other issues such as users' health. Nevertheless, despite this endorsement in principle, the law enforcement sector was struggling to orient its day-to-day efforts to a harm reduction framework. The great majority of study respondents, for example, could not see any role for law enforcers in harm reduction, other than the relatively straightforward one of reducing supplies, or perhaps, obeying directives not to arrest people at needle exchanges. Our recommendations therefore concentrated on setting up administrative frameworks which would allow law enforcers to relate to harm minimisation in far more sophisticated ways.

It was recommended that, particularly at the State and Territory levels, attempts should be made to break down the rigid organisational demarcations which had developed between specialist investigators and more generalist drug law enforcers. Under the proposed restructuring, police specialists in the drug field were encouraged to accept a new set of responsibilities: to work in collaboration with regional detectives, non-specialist police, health personnel and relevant community-based groups to develop and implement local drug control plans, and to monitor local impacts of law enforcement and other relevant policies. While priorities may vary from region to region according to problems encountered and the characteristics of relevant populations (both user and non-user), each local plan should be premised on an understanding that law enforcement always would be more likely to *reshape*, rather than *totally suppress*, illicit drug distribution and consumption. The overriding objective was to ensure that laws were enforced in ways that kept health, welfare and other relevant harms (including drug-related crimes) to a minimum.

It was envisaged that achieving these outcomes would require that enforcement should become oriented more towards partnerships, problems and harm reduction, rather than being driven solely by intelligence data on local trafficking networks, or the conspicuous availability of particular substances. The critical task was to set up local committees, based on good working partnerships between enforcement, health and user representatives, and for such committees to establish and maintain a range of relevant indicators. For example, such indicators include the availability of illicit drugs (price, purity and the 'search time' an average user would require to make a purchase), and on associated problems (e.g. overdoses and offences which might be drug-related). Police then were to use these data, both as a basis for setting priorities for local operations, and also to decide when it would be better to exercise discretion—not, for example, directing substantial resources at enforcing laws against cannabis use and small-scale cultivation, if local indicators did not indicate that this was a priority problem.

Australia's Police Ministers and Commissioners have accepted the thrust of the report, and taken the first steps toward restructuring of drug-law enforcement along the lines suggested. Broad detail on how pilot programs are to be implemented, how they will be evaluated and possible obstacles that will be encountered are discussed below.

The National Community-Based Approach to Drug Law Enforcement (NCBADLE) Pilots

Following the national review of drug law enforcement described above, and several other initiatives, including work by the New South Wales Bureau of Crime Statistics and Research into the impacts of enforcement on heroin markets (Weatherburn and Lind 1995),* and the Police Research Unit's own policy document *Directions in Australasian Policing (1993–1997)*, Australia's Police Commissioners established and funded a National Community-Based Approaches to Drug Law Enforcement (NCBADLE) project, to implement localised drug law enforcement initiatives along the lines suggested. It should be noted that rather than following the blueprint set out in the report of the national review of drug law enforcement—which would have totally restructured the State and Territory drug squads and given them key roles in coordinating drug law enforcement at the local level—the Commissioners decided to accept a New South Wales proposal (itself inspired by a British model) to implement regional Drug Reference Groups (DRGs) and Drug Action Teams (DATs).

NCBADLE intends to trial this model in two sites in Western Australia (Geraldton and Mirrabooka), one in Victoria (the Morwell region) and one in New South Wales (Cabramatta). Pilot programs will be based on the general and specific goals of the Drug Action Team/Drug Reference Group model. DATs are supposed to work at the 'grassroots' level, bringing together operational police and other local service providers in the drug- and alcohol-related areas to apply harm reduction strategies to areas of identified concern. DATs are designed to provide feedback to local police concerning the impacts of drug law enforcement

---

* Weatherburn and Lind (1995: 33) demonstrated that 'there is no detectable relationship between the price, purity or perceived availability of heroin at street level in Cabramatta and average amount of heroin seized, either (a) across Australia or (b) within New South Wales'. This study has been influential in encouraging police managers across Australia to consider alternatives to exclusive supply reduction priorities.

activities on levels of drug harm in the community. The purpose of DRGs is to bring together senior managers from the agencies whose personnel are involved with the DATs in order to provide advice, advocacy and organisational support for DAT strategies.

The pilot programs will be evaluated in two stages. Stage One involves the development of generic evaluation methodologies, utilising a mixture of qualitative and quantitative indicators, which can be applied across different project sites. Stage Two will require implementation of those methodologies in the specific pilot locations selected following feasibility studies conducted by host police departments. The project specifies that Stage One will require two to three months' work. Stage Two will require twelve months, with three data collections during that period. The final report will be required at fifteen months—that is, after twelve months of the actual trials. Each trial site will be managed by a project coordinator, who will play a central role in collecting data relevant to the evaluation. Any training necessary for ensuring adequate data collection will be conducted by the evaluation consultants during Stage One. Data collections will comprise qualitative and quantitative material. Quantitative data will be collected, *inter alia*, from drug service agencies, the community and police. Where applicable, direct measures of drug-related harm will be applied. The evaluation will include process, output and outcome indicators.

What are the basic philosophies informing the assessment? What is critical to the success or otherwise of the projects? What specific types of information will be collected? As already emphasised, in order to make significant improvements in drug law enforcement at the community level—to make it more rational and cost effective—police departments need to commit themselves to quite significant structural and organisational changes. Our view has not been shaken—indeed it has been strengthened—by work subsequent to the national review with the New South Wales Drug Enforcement Agency, with operational police based at Cabramatta (Sydney), and with the Victoria Police Drug Squad (see Brown, James and Sutton 1997; Brown and Sutton 1997). Experience in these contexts has confirmed that health and other non-police agencies *also* will need to make major adjustments if they are to develop reciprocal trust and understanding with law enforcement personnel. Inter-agency data sharing and the development of appropriate policy setting and organisational decision making at the local level—the keys to success for each of these pilots—will be critically dependent upon the fostering of reciprocal trust and understanding between enforcement and non-enforcement groups.

The heart of the projects will be the development of processes that bring drug law enforcement into effective partnership with non-police service providers and the community in the context of problem identification and problem solving. As noted above, these processes will be complex and challenging, and will require time to mature. In particular, the relationships between partnership development, the generation of relevant and meaningful impact data, and the structural conditions under which policy and practice are informed by those data, will need to be fully understood by all parties. In this context there should be two primary and interrelated emphases in a viable and appropriate evaluation of the projects: first, the close monitoring of process development; second, the on-going development and implementation of relevant data sets to enable comprehensive long-term evaluation of impact. Variations between sites in partnership and practice development are expected and indeed will be essential outcomes from these local community-based strategies. If the trial projects are to produce generalisable outcomes, however, it is vital that differential developments be monitored closely in order to determine the parameters of success (or, of course, failure). Identifying effective and ineffective process will be crucial, and will require that substantial attention be paid to intra-organisational and inter-organisational decision making and structuring. If processes fail, practices will falter. The availability of four separate project sites offers an unusual opportunity to monitor and compare the constituent features of process development under different conditions.

Collection at the local level of reliable, relevant and timely information about illicit drug availability and harms will be critical to the success of each pilot project. While data collections must be compatible with State and Federal frameworks, at the same time, each project site will generate its own specific needs for evaluation data, arising out of the goals mutually agreed by the local police service and local community stakeholders. In the long term, some of these needs will be met by the standard quantitative sets, but others will be served by particular kinds of localised quantitative and qualitative information. It is clear, for example, that each site will need to develop local indicators on the price, purity and availability of illicit drugs. These data sets will need to be complemented with more qualitative intelligence on trends in use among key groups (e.g. young people). From the outset, it will be essential that evaluation teams monitor issues relevant to the process of interagency cooperation within a harm reduction framework. Data regularly collated in this framework could relate to such issues as: how representatives of various agencies understand the concept of harm reduction; what they perceive as the main problems or obstacles to achieving cooperation with other agencies; and the extent to which health officials and user group representatives feel confident about exchanging information with counterparts in law enforcement (and, of course, vice versa).

In summary, it is absolutely critical to monitor ways in which the DATs, DRGs and operational drug law enforcement personnel make use of data in decision making and in setting strategic priorities. The mere collection of data is necessary but by no means sufficient to generate appropriate and effective harm-reduction drug law enforcement practices (see Brown and Sutton 1997). One of the evaluation's major contributions will be its comprehensive assessment of the ways in which the DAT and DRG structure has enabled drug law enforcement to operate rationally, on the basis of best knowledge, and in the context of community partnerships. At the end of the evaluation period partnership processes and specific project practices will have developed and be clearly understood and monitored across the project sites. Development and implementation of relevant quantitative and qualitative evaluation measures will also have been completed. By this time, on-going collection of meaningful and reliable impact data which can extend beyond the evaluation period will be in place, and processes for integrating impact data with drug law enforcement policy-setting and decision-making will be in place, understood by all parties, and closely and continuously monitored.

Challenges for the Pilot Programs

It is easier to recommend the adoption of community-based strategies than it is to implement them. This is due, in part, to the difficulties of transforming traditional police structures and practices to accommodate community-based approaches (see Brown and Sutton 1997). It is also due to our understanding of the concept of 'community'. Both of these types of problems—internal and external to policing systems—are likely to have impacts on the community-based drug law enforcement pilots.

Internal problems

Law enforcement initiatives which lie outside the domain of traditional reactive criminal investigation and order maintenance tasks, and especially those which require proactive work in the community and through intersectoral partnerships, typically face resistance from peer and management cultures within policing. Grafted onto this generalised scepticism or contempt for 'unorthodox' approaches is the difficulty many police have with integrating harm reduction into their traditional law enforcement roles in the drug-using and drug-moving environments. This is a problem particularly for criminal investigators.

There are at least two significant problems here. First, cultural stereotyping and enforcement experience has taught many police to despise drug users, especially dependent, 'hopeless' users, who are seen as complicit in the criminal forces of the drug market. In particular, their personal degradation is complemented by their alleged involvement in property crime to support their dependencies. This is not the clientele that traditional police choose to be 'lenient' towards: hence the surveillance and harassment of the user population, and the resulting high charge rate for use and possession. Use and possession charges represent in many circumstances the modern equivalent of the old public order maintenance statutes such as 'drunk and disorderly', which for many decades were used for dealing with problematic street populations.

Second, even for those police who recognise the need for some alternatives to 'street cleaning' approaches to use, possession and minor street dealing, the discretionary environment can be complex. While prohibition remains on the books, police may well continue to feel vulnerable when they choose not to enforce laws against even minor drug offences. Police have always been expected to exercise discretion, but it is difficult to develop appropriate accountability structures and clearly specify all the conditions where discretion is legitimate and preferable. Younger and more inexperienced police in particular may fall back on strict law enforcement simply to 'cover themselves' in the face of possible criticism.

Solutions to these problems are not going to be simple. The trivialisation and marginalisation of non-traditional policing endeavours is a chronic problem, but they can be eroded through the provision of adequate status and rewards within the organisation for personnel who choose to engage and excel in these endeavours. Traditional indicators of police performance—arrests, seizures, etc.—have always been poor measures, but they are embedded in police culture and police organisational structures. So too is the idea of rewarding specialised detective work rather than more generalised 'community-based' duties. The challenge here is to devise new and innovative ways to measure effectiveness, and to create organisational structures which will reward effectiveness measured on these new bases.

Negative cultural stereotyping of and experiences with the drug-using population are also stubborn obstacles to re-orienting practice towards harm reduction. The full practice of community-based harm reduction offers the best chance to overcome them. By engaging with non-enforcement agencies and personnel (needle-exchanges, treatment centres, user groups, educational personnel and so forth), police can balance their selective law enforcement experiences and data with other perspectives, information and worlds. The discretionary dilemmas are subject to the same kinds of moderation. Discretion is best defended when its reasons can be articulated and its outcomes are both measurable and accountable. In the field of harm reduction, all this is achievable. The harm reduction approach is coherent and organisationally approved, and with the kinds of knowledge and expertise gained by those working within its practices, the benefits of exercising discretion in certain ways can be propagated.

One should never be naive about the difficulties of 'main-streaming' harm reduction approaches within policing. The considerable structural problems that confront police departments in efforts to shift from traditional reactive models of policing are intimidating (Brown and Sutton 1997). Nevertheless, the organisational diffusion process of having well-rewarded, experienced, authoritative and management-endorsed harm minimisers within police ranks is both necessary and possible in a way that was inconceivable a decade ago. At the same time, we need to note that even successful mainstreaming within policing will not overcome all of the obstacles confronting the progressive engagement of law enforcement in community drug harm minimisation.

External problems

In saying that dedicated drug law enforcement should be shifted away from centralised bureaucracies—at the State and Territory levels at least—and that police specialists in the illicit drug field should be encouraged and required to work more with non-police groups who have knowledge about local drug and harm minimisation issues, we have been reiterating classical arguments for community-based policing (Moore 1992). We have been suggesting, in a sense, that law enforcement 'put itself in the hands of the community' in terms of its needs and demands. Such rhetorical arguments for community policing have dominated reform discourse for twenty years. But their familiarity and its logic should not blind us to the problems that underpin any community-based approach. One of the crucial problems associated with police trying to move away from hierarchical, bureaucratic models towards locally-based partnerships is that they have tended to take for granted the notion of 'community'.

Underpinning the community-based policing literature put out both by police departments and by external proponents of such policing is a consistent assumption: that there is a law-abiding majority 'out there' waiting to embrace law enforcers if and when they snap out of their absorption with internal procedures and routines, and ready to work with them to produce the social order which best conforms with local values and priorities. This assumption has always been more of a convenient fiction than reality. The practical experiences of the police reveal intense divisions within the community along lines of class, age, gender, race, ethnicity and so forth. These divisions demand different kinds of policing, and it was at least in part due to the political expressions of these demands that police in the USA began to retreat from intimate community contact during the 'reform' era (Kelling and Moore 1988) and to move toward the remote, centralised, 'paramilitary' models we now find so unsatisfactory (e.g. Beyer 1992; Goldstein 1979; Hogg and Findlay 1988; James and Sutton 1993; McIntyre and Prenzler 1997). The connections between intimate community contact (or contact with particular sections of the community) and police corruption were obvious then, and they remain so today. Close engagement with certain kinds of community interests and values have a high corruption potential for police. The paradox is that such engagement fulfils at least some of the criteria for community policing: an intimate knowledge of and preparedness to work with 'relevant local interests'. In the national drug law enforcement study, one police officer interviewed, on a later admission before the Wood Royal Commission, was thoroughly corrupt. Yet he had a deep knowledge of the drug problems and issues in the locality he was policing. Compared with most other informants, this corrupt interviewee demonstrated a remarkable understanding of local patterns of illicit drug availability and use.

It is clear, then, that the notion of 'community' in community policing is problematic. Law enforcement agencies, however, continue to oversimplify the entity that they wish to police with: which in the main, is the abstracted middle-class (or 'respectable' working-class) families and businesses. Since the 1960s, the advent of feminism, multiculturalism and other social movements has forced some adaptations to this definition of community, but the assumption of a vast and implicitly supportive constituency with affiliation to 'core values' and mainstream institutions remains a key reference and anchor point for community policing.

This assumption is now unsustainable, and its unsustainability is increasingly obvious as society undergoes substantial change within the evolving conditions of postmodern capitalism. This may mean that as Australia enters the third millennium, notions of community policing will become less and less achievable. To understand this concern, it is necessary first to reflect upon what it was about the 1960s and 1970s that made notions of community (and community policing as a corollary) appear relatively unproblematic. In Australia, and a number of other Western countries, this was the height of the Keynesian era, during which governments had key roles in 'steering' and stabilising capitalist economies: promising near full employment, 'buying off' workers through wage fixing systems, and providing universal access to health, welfare and education. In many ways it was these activities by governments which helped bring about those 'core values' and majority investments in social stability which have been crucial assumptions of community policing.

As the 1980s and 1990s progressed, however, we have seen increasing evidence that high levels of state intervention in the economy and in the provision of social infrastructure simply cannot be sustained. As theorists such as Habermas (1976) and O'Connor (1973) argue, reasons for the decline in state intervention are partly internal to the capitalist state itself. Political demands in a democracy have meant that modern economies have become increasingly overloaded by the need to service education, health, welfare and, of course, law and order. This servicing has resulted in the state scooping too much off the economy, and as a consequence, over time, capital has declined to invest. Major commitments to investment in physical and social infrastructure have also tended to deprive the modern state of its capacity to be flexible. The state is less able to increase expenditure (and hence boost demand) during times of recession, and then to reduce it when the economy is buoyant.

In addition to these internal factors, making it hard for governments to sustain the institutions essential for a (comparatively homogeneous) 'community', we also have seen external pressures. Capital is increasingly more mobile and global. It no longer needs or depends upon the government or labour force of Australia, or any other specific Western state. Business can, and does, shift elsewhere, wherever labour is cheapest and government least burdensome.

All of these changes have quite profound effects. Zigmunt Bauman (1988) argues that as far as global capital is concerned, populations in many Western countries are no longer needed for their labour power; they are only now needed as consumers. He suggests that in time this will lead to a kind of bifurcation in modes of social control. On the one hand, we will have affluent consumers who are 'seduced' into surrendering freedom. On the other hand, we will have non-affluent (non-working, non-consuming) outsiders, who in effect can only be 'repressed'. It would be easy to dismiss Bauman as engaging in some sort of futurist fantasy if he were to be alone in predicting these kinds of outcomes. But others are echoing his arguments. In particular, policy analyst Bill Jordan (1996) has written on the social implications of economic rationalism. As in most Western countries, governments in Australia have been embarking for some years now on a program of successively decreasing government intervention into the marketplace, and allowing market forces determine the shape of social outcomes. Whether the issue is education, housing, welfare, health, or employment programs, governments are encouraging communities to become more 'enterprising' and to make their own choices. Such choices are to be driven by rational self-interest and by the economic resources available to them.

Faced with the need to make major decisions about these matters, many individuals, groups and families are making what Jordan (1996) has called the decision to join a 'club' with others who share similar values and expectations. This makes a considerable amount of self-interested sense; by joining with others say in a local chamber of commerce, or a housing estate, or a private school, one can share the infrastructure costs and the values of these institutions. But these clubs only work if their members can exclude those who cannot make the necessary contributions, or who are going to become an unusually large drain upon resources, or whose behaviour violates shared values. Jordan argues that as with other businesses, associations formed through market choices have an innate tendency both to exclude 'problem' people, and to deny responsibility for their wellbeing. In other words, people who miss out on our club memberships, because they cannot afford to join, or are unemployed, or are drug users, or are all of the above, are not our problem. It is not in our self-interest to let them join, and it is not in our interests to be responsible for them.

This process of exclusion is somewhat different from other forms that are based upon moral grounds. That is, people are not necessarily excluded because we think they are morally delinquent or bad or mad. They are not tolerated in our clubs—our housing estates, our schools, our shopping centres—simply because they are not our business, and they don't contribute to our business. The 'communities' generated by the processes underpinned by such economic rationalist philosophies are likely to be a far cry from the all-inclusive, consensus-based models that the 'community policing' literature often seems to imply.

The central problem is that police have rarely found one homogeneous, consensual and united community 'out there'. They have found many communities with different values, experiences and expectations. These differences always have been hard to balance, and perhaps nowhere more so than in community-based drug control.

The essential issue is that such drug control demands tolerance, and tolerance is a commodity which is both unevenly distributed across communities, and which, if the analysis above is correct, is likely to become even shorter in supply. Tolerance does not mean liking, or enjoying, or rewarding. It *does* mean acceptance of certain social realities, such as the fact that illicit drug use exists, and will continue to exist despite prohibition. It means accepting that some forms of drug use, and some means of drug consumption, such as sharing intravenous needles, are more dangerous than others. It means accepting that not all drug users are the same, and that there are no simple solutions to the harms that drug use may generate. Nonetheless, this tolerance or acceptance is often at odds with community understandings of drug use.

Conclusion

Australians have been encouraged for many decades to view the illicit drug user and the legal drug abuser as deviants, and to view all illicit drug use and wider drug abuse as physically dangerous and often morally wrong. We have been taught to exclude the drug user, particularly through law enforcement and the criminal justice system. It is no surprise then that some communities have difficulty in abandoning those perspectives. For them, harm reduction means a reversal of all they have come to believe. The provision of needle exchanges, the provision of health and welfare services to users rather than the strict application of the criminal law, the tolerance of drug use that these approaches imply, all represent a retreat from 'normal' standards. It is not easy to persuade communities to abandon their long-held beliefs and to become tolerant.

Police engagement in harm minimisation will require that they attempt this persuasion. Police are still considered authoritative and experienced within many community settings, and people are bound to be influenced by police endorsement of harm minimisation. But at the very time that a strategy has been crafted which calls for the toleration and inclusion of once-excluded people in order to stop them harming themselves and their communities, the emergence of the new forms of social exclusion generated by postmodern society is occurring.

On this analysis, the problems for community-based drug control are significant. Even if communities, however defined, can be persuaded about the logic of harm minimisation, they may well resist its practice, because they do not want it in their backyard. This would appear to be the most plausible explanation for much of the resistance to such harm minimisation strategies as needle exchanges, resistance which has been evident for instance recently in Cabramatta in Sydney and Footscray in Melbourne. In many such cases, the resistance is not necessarily based upon an outright hostility to the concept, but rather to the fact that the needle exchange is to be located here, and not there, in some other suburb or town centre. If the resistance was only due to conceptual ignorance or misunderstanding, then perhaps it could be dealt with. But when it is based upon self-interest, then it is based upon a sentiment that governments increasingly are urging on populations as a necessary and useful social force.

One of the dilemmas for police engaged in the pilot programs will be how to deal with self-interest, or more particularly with competing self-interests. It is difficult not to be sympathetic to retailers suffering a drop in sales because of the reputation their shopping precinct has developed for attracting drug users, or members of a residential area who are sick of discarded syringes. Equally, we need to understand the need for users to have clean and cheap syringes and to be free of harassment so they take drugs in ways that reduce the harm as much as possible. So, the question becomes, to which expressions of community self-interest will police listen when it comes to implementing community-based drug control?

Clearly, some expressions of self-interest—especially those with commercial arguments on their side—speak considerably louder than others. This is arguably the biggest challenge facing community-based drug control, and one which will most test the resolve and commitment of police organisations wanting to be involved in effective harm minimisation practices. In essence, it requires police to propose and argue a case for the wellbeing of a whole community which quite simply subordinates the interests of local groups that traditionally support, and have in turn been supported by, law enforcement. Only when Australian law enforcement organisations consistently take this position, argue and win consequent debates *and* successfully implement relevant programs, will harm reduction become a reality in policing. It is unlikely that the pilot programs, on their own, will be able to achieve such a significant turn of events.

11

Developing More
Effective Responses

Alex Wodak

FOR THE LAST quarter century, a royal commission or other major official inquiry has taken place on the subject of illicit drugs somewhere around Australia almost every year (Australian Parliamentary Group for Drug Law Reform 1997). Scarcely a day passes without the subject of illicit drugs being discussed extensively on radio, television, or in the print media. Surveys of public opinion document the salience of illicit drugs among the various issues which generate anxiety in the community.

This depth of community concern about illicit drugs exists in many other industrialised countries, in which public debates about drug policy are also taking place. During the 1980s and 1990s, illicit drug problems have also become evident in an increasing number of developing countries. Injecting drug use is now a major concern in Asia and South America, where HIV infection has begun to spread among and from drug injectors, threatening both public health and the economic gains of recent decades.

The extent of global illicit drug problems, the alarming trends in global drug use, and adverse consequences of illicit drug use led to the United Nations General Assembly Special Session On Drugs (UNGASS) in New York in June 1998. At this meeting, the international community committed itself to the goal of eradicating consumption of heroin and cocaine within a decade. This implausible objective was set at a time when global heroin production had trebled and global cocaine production doubled in the previous decade (United Nations International Drug Control Programme

1997b). This denial of reality is also reflected in national legislation. In 1988, the United States Congress passed laws declaring that the United States of America would become drug-free by 1995 (US Office of National Drug Control Policy 1998).

This chapter argues that Australia must move beyond its preoccupation with law enforcement to adopt more effective responses based upon public health priorities and social concerns. The chapter is organised according to the following questions:

- How does Australia respond to illicit drugs like heroin and cocaine?
- How did Australia develop its drug policy?
- What have been the outcomes of the drug policy?
- Are Australia's drug policies effective?
- Have any other countries made better progress?
- How can Australia achieve better outcomes?

How Does Australia Respond to Illicit Drugs Like Heroin and Cocaine?

In financial terms, Commonwealth and State Government expenditure in response to illicit drugs in 1992 was estimated at $US393 million ($A620 million) (United Nations International Drug Control Programme 1997b). Of this not inconsiderable sum, 84 per cent was allocated to law enforcement, 6 per cent to treatment and 10 per cent to prevention and research. Although these figures are somewhat imprecise, they represent the best indication available of the uneven proportions of government expenditure allocated to supply reduction and demand reduction. Commonwealth and state expenditure on methadone programs has been estimated at $A30 million per year (Commonwealth Department of Human Services and Health 1995). In 1991, Australian expenditure on needle syringe programs was estimated at $A10 million. It is likely that expenditure on needle syringe programs in Australia doubled between 1991 and the turn of the century.

Australia officially adopted a national policy of 'harm minimisation' at the Special Premiers' Conference held in Canberra on

2 April 1985. The meeting was convened by the then Prime Minister and attended by all State Premiers and both Chief Ministers. The term 'harm minimisation' was not defined at that time. A national commitment to harm minimisation has been endorsed on several subsequent occasions by the Ministerial Council on Drug Strategy (MCDS), Australia's paramount drug policy making body.

During the 1990s, it was common practice for Australian government officials to refer to national drug policy as 'the balanced approach'. In 1998, however, Prime Minister John Howard strongly endorsed a 'zero tolerance' approach and commended this policy on several occasions. He borrowed this unfamiliar rhetoric and philosophy, with all its connotations of intolerance and moral dogma, from the USA.

Following the evaluation of the third national drug strategy in 1998, the MCDS again endorsed a national policy of harm minimisation, but this was defined to include the three goals of *supply reduction, demand reduction* and *harm reduction*. Harm reduction was now air brushed with zero tolerance. But by this time, a harm reduction approach to illicit drug problems had become well entrenched among health department and law enforcement officials across the nation. The primary focus taken by health department and law enforcement officials was to reduce the health, social and economic adverse consequences of illicit drugs without necessarily reducing consumption. Abstinence was promoted but not at the expense or risk of exacerbating adverse outcomes. Harm reduction interventions such as needle syringe programs and methadone treatment programs have been strongly supported in community opinion polls (Schwartzkopf et al. 1990). Nonetheless, the vociferous opposition of a critical minority attracts considerable attention.

How can Australia's response to illicit drugs best be understood at the end of the twentieth century? The allocation of substantial resources to illicit drug law enforcement and minimal resources to treatment, prevention, research and harm reduction indicates that the core of the national drug policy is supply reduction, while demand reduction and harm reduction are but subsidiary objectives.

How Did Australia Develop Its Drug Policy?

In the 1890s, prior to Federation, several Australian states prohibited the smoking of opium. At the time, the practice of smoking opium was confined to Chinese, many of whom were working on Australia's goldfields (Manderson 1993: 20). The drug laws were expanded in the first decade after Federation, although the Commonwealth Comptroller-General of Customs, H. N .P. Wollaston, stated in his report to the Commonwealth Parliament in 1908 that 'it is very doubtful if such prohibition has lessened to an extent the amount which is brought in to Australia' (cited in Manderson 1993: 61). He added:

> owing to total prohibition, the price of opium has risen enormously ... the Commonwealth gladly gave up about £60 000 revenue with a view to a suppression of the evil, but the result has not been what has been hoped for. What now appears to be the effect of total prohibition is that, while we have lost the duty, the opium is still imported pretty freely (H. N. P. Wollaston cited in Manderson 1993: 61).

At the 1925 Geneva Convention, Australia agreed to enact laws to 'limit exclusively to medical and scientific purposes the manufacture, import, sale, distribution, export and use of medicinal opium, cocaine, morphine, Indian hemp and heroin' (Manderson 1993: 71). Although the use of 'Indian hemp' (or cannabis) was virtually unheard of in Australia at that time, authorities responded to the call for conformity to the new international legal framework. The under-secretary of the Colonial Secretaries Department concluded that 'the omission of that drug from the operation of the Act would possibly be of small moment' (cited in Manderson 1993: 72). Nevertheless, it was decided that since Indian hemp had 'been considered by the conference as requiring to be included, it might perhaps be as well, if practicable, to bring it within the purview of the dangerous drugs laws' (Manderson 1993: 72). On this shaky foundation, the mighty edifice of cannabis prohibition was constructed.

During the first half of the twentieth century in Australia, the occasional cases of heroin dependence were managed by the medical profession under the supervision of state or territory health departments (Manderson 1993: 105–8) much as similar cases of dependence to other opioids such as morphine are managed today. Doctors would try to encourage their heroin-dependant patients to become abstinent. After several unsuccessful attempts, the doctors would contact their state (or territory) health department. Further prescription was authorised if all were agreed that every possible, reasonable attempt had been exhausted. Australia was required by international treaty obligations to report per capita legal heroin consumption. Heroin consumption in Australia in 1951 was reported to be the highest in the world and appeared to be increasing. Australia came under increasing international pressure to prohibit the use of heroin even though problems consequent on consumption of the drug were not evident. The Director-General of Health in New South Wales said, for example: 'Heroin . . . is quite effectively controlled in this state and . . . I see no justification to enforce absolute prohibition' (cited in Manderson 1993: 126). The Australian Federal Council of the British Medical Association (BMA), later to become the Australian Medical Association (AMA), argued that there 'should be no curtailment of availability'. Although the Royal Australasian College of Physicians and the Royal College of Obstetricians and Gynaecologists both declared in 1953 that 'the use of heroin should not be prohibited', the Commonwealth advised State Premiers in May 1953 that the importation of heroin was to be absolutely prohibited. Prohibition of importation and production of heroin was gazetted on 25 June 1953.

In the following years, the states exhausted their stocks of heroin. Thereafter, doctors prescribed other drugs than heroin when managing painful conditions. Initially, there was little evidence that the prohibition of heroin production or importation in 1953 had resulted in significant negative consequences. This assessment began to change in the late 1960s when US servicemen on rest and recreation leave from the Vietnam war began visiting capital cities in Australia. Some US servicemen brought heroin with them and introduced young Australian men and women to the drug and the practice of injection. The Bourbon and Beefsteak bar in Sydney's Kings Cross became the first centre of Australia's heroin trade. Over the following years, heroin injecting spread to all Australian states and territories. The number of young men and women injecting heroin appeared to increase inexorably. New illicit drugs appeared on the scene with monotonous regularity.

What Have Been the Outcomes of the Drug Policy?

In 1997, using the Delphi technique,* a diverse group of clinicians, researchers, law enforcement officers, government officials and drug users estimated that there were currently 100 000 regular injecting drug users with an additional 175 000 occasional injecting drug users (Australian National Council on AIDS and Related Diseases 1998). This group estimated that the number of injecting drug users had increased at a rate of 7 per cent per annum from the 1960s. This rate represents a doubling time of just ten years.

There are a number of indications, however, that the rate of increase of injecting drug use in Australia during the last years of the twentieth century was occurring at an even faster pace. This perception is based on an increase in the number of drug seizures, the amounts of drugs seized, deaths from drug overdose, demand for drug treatment and a rapid increase in the demand for sterile needles and syringes. In addition, there was a steady decrease in the age of persons arrested for drug-related offences; age of persons presenting on the first occasion for drug treatment; age of persons attending needle syringe programs; and the reported age of initiation. This suggests a long-term increase in illicit drug use with a particularly rapid growth phase during the closing years of the twentieth century.

Drug overdose deaths in Australia have also increased significantly during the last thirty years. Opioid overdose deaths

---

* The Delphi technique was developed by the Rand Corporation. It is a method of forecasting using groups of experts, and usually involves anonymity of responses, feedback to the group as a whole of individual and collective views, and the opportunity for any respondent to modify an earlier judgement.

increased in Australia from six in 1964 (1.3 per million population aged 15–44 years) to six hundred in 1997 (71.5 per million population aged 15–44 years) (Hall et al. 1999). This represents a 55-fold increase in the rate of opioid overdose deaths over this thirty-three year period. The proportion of all deaths attributed to opioid overdose increased from 0.08 per cent in 1964 to 7.26 per cent in 1997 (Hall et al. 1999). Between 1991 and 1997, the number of overdose deaths in Australia doubled. By 1999, more drug overdose deaths were reported in the state of Victoria than all road crash deaths in that state. The number of drug overdose deaths in Australia at the end of the twentieth century was running at half the number of deaths from youth suicide, widely recognised for some time to have become a major public health concern.

Although attempts to attribute criminal offences to illicit drug use has its difficulties, there can be can little doubt that drug-related property crime in Australia was exceedingly common and growing rapidly at the end of the twentieth century. There was an increase of 69 per cent in armed robbery offences nationally from 1996 (34.1/100 000) to 1998 (57.9/100 000), while there was a 25 per cent increase in unarmed robbery from 1996 (55.3/100 000) to 1998 (69/100 000) (Australian Bureau of Statistics 1998). In New South Wales between 1995 and 1998, robberies committed with a firearm increased 29.7 per cent, robberies with a weapon (which was not a firearm) increased 188.3 per cent and robberies without a weapon increased 37.8 per cent. Interviews with 267 inmates convicted of burglary offences in New South Wales indicated a higher median rate of burglary (13.7 per month) among heroin users than among burglars who did not use heroin (8.7 per month) (Stevenson and Forsythe 1999). Median weekly burglary income for heroin users ($A3000) was far greater than for non-users of heroin ($A1000). Although a substantial proportion of heroin users commit crime before commencing illicit drug use, there can be little doubt that drug use prolongs and exacerbates criminal behaviour. It is difficult to envisage that the current prohibitions are reducing drug-related crime.

High levels of official corruption have also been linked to illicit drugs. This connection was confirmed in a number of official inquiries and royal commissions. For example, both the Fitzgerald

Report (Royal Commission into Possible Illegal Activities and Associated Police Misconduct (Qld) 1989) and the Woods Report (Royal Commission into the New South Wales Police Service 1997) concluded that official corruption was widespread and linked to the enforcement of laws relating to illicit drugs.

It was widely assumed during the second half of the twentieth century in Australia that support for 'tough on drugs' policies inevitably results in growing political popularity. Nevertheless, there is now increasing national and international evidence for the view that support for draconian drug policies is becoming a political liability rather than an asset. Two thirds of respondents in a 1999 public opinion poll expressed disapproval of the Commonwealth Government's handling of illicit drug issues. This poll was held after the Prime Minister had aligned himself with a 'zero tolerance' approach. The strong political support for Victorian Premier Mr Jeff Kennett among young voters has been linked to the Premier's support for drug policy reform. In the United States, drug policy referenda were held in six states coinciding with the mid-term congressional elections in November 1998. Majorities for reform were reported in all six states. In Switzerland, 71 per cent of voters in a national referendum in September 1997 supported retaining heroin prescription, with majorities in all twenty-six cantons.

Australia did not adopt its current drug policies following a careful and thorough assessment of the effectiveness of previous policies and a rigorous evaluation of policy options. The prohibition of cannabis and the prohibition of heroin were both historical accidents. Once adopted, however, they have been automatically defended whenever questioned. The commitment to these policies has become increasingly entrenched, at the same time as community support for them appears to be eroding.

After many years of high levels of youth unemployment in Australia, large numbers of young people now face a choice between high income from illegal employment in the drug trafficking industry and low income at the end of a long dole queue. Decades of globalisation have provided efficient means to transport capital, labour, goods and services around the world. Rapid improvement in transport and telecommunications facilitates trade in legal commodities, and also inevitably illegal commodities. With a 37 000 kilometre coastline, and with seven million air passengers and two million containers arriving each year, detection of illicit drugs entering Australia is a formidable task. The price of a kilogram of heroin increases more than 1000-fold between the processing laboratories in Asia and Australia's drug markets. As more imported illicit drugs are intercepted, the traffickers move from plant-based drugs (with a long supply line) to chemical-based drugs (with a shorter supply chain). Sooner or later authorities and communities must have the wisdom to choose between what can and cannot be achieved and the courage to tackle what can be accomplished.

Are the Drug Policies Effective?

During the 1990s, an increasing number of community leaders began to express anxiety about the relative ineffectiveness of Australia's drug policy. Police commissioners at a national meeting in 1998 expressed the need to 'almost wipe the slate clean' by moving from 'punishment to rehabilitation' (*Australian* 25 April 1998: 9). In 1998, capital city mayors unanimously supported drug law reform and a scientific evaluation of heroin prescription. Even the West Australian branch of the National Party supported cannabis reform and a heroin trial. The growth in support for drug law reform followed a collapse of confidence in the effectiveness of a drug policy based on law enforcement.

If our national drug policy was designed fundamentally to decrease drug use, decrease deaths, decrease crime and decrease corruption, Australia's drug policy in the latter decades of the twentieth century was clearly not achieving these objectives (Wodak and Owens 1996). It is important to recognise not only the failure of drug policy, but the magnitude of this failure. Failure to this extent in the corporate world would inevitably result in bankruptcy. Military failure on this scale would almost certainly result in the court martial of those responsible. Corrections may also occur in politics, but more slowly. Governments are often very concerned to emphasise the importance of drug users accepting responsibility for their own individual actions. But governments seem less inclined to accept direct responsibility for the consequences of their own policies.

Despite the comprehensive and resounding failure of a law-enforcement-based drug policy in relation to drug use, deaths, crime and corruption, some significant public health gains have been achieved. Establishing and maintaining control of HIV infection among and from injecting drug users in Australia has been a major public health achievement (Feachem 1995; Wodak and Lurie 1997). HIV control has been maintained among injecting drug users (MacDonald 1997). Evidence to support this conclusion is consistent, substantial, and derived from multiple diverse sources (National Centre in HIV Epidemiology and Clinical Research 1998). HIV prevalence was 0.2 per cent among inmates received into Australian prisons between 1991 and 1997 (McDonald et al. 1999). This is about three times higher than HIV prevalence in the general community. As at least 50 per cent of inmates in Australian prisons are serving sentences for drug-related offences, the sustained low prevalence of HIV among inmates is a very strong indicator that HIV prevalence (and incidence) remains very low among injecting drug-users in the community (National Centre in HIV Epidemiology and Clinical Research 1998)

Similarly, there is growing evidence to suggest substantial reduction in new infections of Hepatitis C among injecting drug users (MacDonald et al., unpublished paper). The prevalence of Hepatitis C among drug users with a history of injecting less than three years appears to be declining, suggesting that the number of new infections in this population is falling. Nevertheless, these achievements were gained despite, and not because of, supply control. In fact, these achievements only took place because law enforcement officials had the wisdom to identify correctly the importance of these public health threats to the community. Following recognition of the magnitude of the HIV threat to Australia in the early 1980s, law enforcement officials have generally been very discriminating when policing in the vicinity of needle exchange and methadone programs.

One of the supposed indicators of the effectiveness of the law enforcement approach is the level of drug seizures. From time to time, State and Commonwealth ministers and even the Prime

Minister have expressed great pride in announcements of successful major seizures. These announcements have been accompanied by overly optimistic estimates of the impact of major seizures on the availability of illicit drugs. Alas, subsequent data have indicated that these major seizures were not followed by detectable changes in the price and availability of illicit drugs. Even the Australian Bureau of Criminal Intelligence (1998: 89) reported that 'heroin is a serious concern and it is obvious that current policies are not working'. The same report noted that 'heroin remains generally available in Australia and anecdotal information suggests that law enforcement efforts are having only a limited effect on the amount of heroin offered at street level.' (Australian Bureau of Criminal Intelligence 1998: 41).

Have Any Other Countries Made Better Progress?

Faced with the poor outcomes from Australia's drug policy in recent decades, it would not be surprising if some were to conclude that illicit drug policy was too difficult and progress was impossible. Nevertheless, it is now clear that a number of European countries have made substantial progress recently, even though most other developed countries have reported unacceptable and deteriorating outcomes during the same period. In Switzerland, health problems, public nuisance, and crime related to drugs all increased steadily during the 1980s and early 1990. HIV was poorly controlled among injecting drug users. Authorities in many cities appeared to have lost control of public order due to widespread drug injecting in public places. Following a vigorous national debate, Swiss policy changed in the early 1990s and improvement soon followed. Drug overdose deaths in Switzerland halved from 419 in 1992 to 209 in 1998. Public nuisance related to drug injecting in public places declined steadily during the 1990s. Drug-related crime has also been declining in Switzerland during the 1990s (Swiss Federal Office of Public Health 1999).

Estimated government expenditure in response to illicit drugs in Switzerland in 1994 was 1011 million SFr, of which 500 million SFr was allocated to law enforcement, 260 million SFr to care, treatment, therapy and rehabilitation, 200 million SFr to harm reduction, 35 million SFr to prevention and 16 million SFr to research and training (Swiss Federal Office of Public Health 1999). These financial commitments had a number of positive outcomes. The capacity of the methadone treatment programs throughout the country expanded from 728 in 1979 to 15 382 in 1997. The number of admissions to residential abstinence programs grew from 1900 in 1993 to 2100 in 1996. Heroin programs were established on a research base between 1994 and 1997, and by 1998, 1056 patients were receiving treatment in the form of heroin prescription provided with considerable psychosocial assistance. The capacity of detoxification and rehabilitation residential centres increased from 1250 in 1993 to 1750 in 1997. The first injecting room in Switzerland was established in the city of Bern in 1986; by 1999, there were fourteen injecting rooms spread across the German-speaking part of Switzerland. In these facilities, drug injecting takes place under supervision, with immediate assistance provided in the event of an overdose. No deaths have been reported from any Swiss injecting room to date (Swiss Federal Office of Public Health 1999). Although the heroin prescription trial and injecting rooms have captured a great deal of national attention in Australia, less emphasis has been placed on the fact that strenuous efforts have been made to expand the range, increase the capacity and improve the quality of drug treatment in Switzerland.

In the Netherlands, drug overdose deaths have been maintained at a low and stable rate of about fifty per year in a population of fifteen million. The number of sterile needles and syringes exchanged with injecting drug users in the city of Amsterdam has halved during a five-year period in the 1990s, without a change in policy. This coincided with a steady increase in the mean age of injecting drug users, suggesting that the population of injecting drug users was declining because of a decline in the number of new recruits.

The encouraging results in Switzerland and the Netherlands during the 1990s suggests that pragmatic approaches based on solid evidence can improve public health outcomes. Consequently, there has been a growing interest in Western Europe in more public-health-oriented approaches, especially as countries with a historical commitment to belief-based moralistic approaches reported unacceptable and deteriorating outcomes.

How can Australia Achieve Better Outcomes?

The following strategies are offered as means of achieving better outcomes from illicit drug policy in Australia.

Redefining the problem

The most important step is to redefine illicit drug use as primarily a health and social issue rather than a criminal justice problem. Law enforcement will always be needed to complement health and social interventions, but should no longer be allowed to dominate policy, funding allocation or public rhetoric. It should also be recalled that there are many precedents for such a reclassification. In most Australian states, the high cost, ineffectiveness, and substantial unintended negative consequences of a law enforcement approach to public drunkenness resulted in a similar reclassification. Following two decades of experience with a primarily health and social response to public drunkenness, there have been few calls for a review of this approach.

Setting appropriate penalties

Unauthorised, large-scale cultivation, production, transport, distribution, sale or possession of all mood-altering drugs should continue to attract penalties including, where appropriate, criminal charges. The magnitude of the penalties, however, should be in proportion to the quantity and type of drugs seized. It is logical that unauthorised *trade* in mood-altering drugs should attract different penalties for different drugs. It is also logical that the precise *quantities* of mood-altering drugs which attract a penalty will need to be defined separately for different drugs.

More emphasis on non-custodial sentencing options is required to divert selected offenders from the criminal justice system to drug treatment. The cost of incarceration is four to eight times higher than residential abstinence promotion treatment and twenty-five to fifty times the cost of methadone treatment. Incarceration is undoubtedly unavoidable for some drug users with deeply entrenched criminal behaviour, especially if the offences involve violence. Diversion is available in most Australian jurisdictions at present but rarely occurs because of inadequate resources. The New South Wales Drug Court established in 1999 was allocated $A12 million to manage 300 participants over two years.

Cultivation, production, transport, distribution, sale or possession of small quantities of illicit drugs consistent with personal use should not attract criminal sanctions. Quantities considered to be consistent with personal use will need to be defined for each type of drug. A system of accountable police discretion will be required to minimise the risk of corruption.

Cannabis: decriminalisation, regulation and taxation

The regulation and taxation of cannabis production and sale is inevitable. At present, the Australian cannabis industry has an estimated turnover of $A5 billion per annum. It is also estimated that current taxation revenue generated by the Australian cannabis industry is negligible. Hypothecation, or the specific dedication, of cannabis tax revenues for the purposes of illicit drug law enforcement, prevention of drug use and treatment of illicit drug users is likely to be a popular policy, although government officials, especially in Treasury, would be inclined to oppose it.

While the regulation and taxation of cannabis production and sale may well be a long-term inevitability, it is more probable that progress towards such a policy will be incremental. Expiation of cannabis charges on payment of a fine was first introduced in South Australia in 1986 and is subsequently being introduced in other states and the ACT. Although this approach appears to reduce expenditure on cannabis law enforcement, it has resulted in an increasing number of offenders (net-widening), many of whom are socially and economically disadvantaged.

Any cannabis policy which permits possession and consumption while prohibiting production and sales is unlikely to be sustainable indefinitely. Nonetheless, allowing legal consumption while maintaining supply as illegal, commonly referred to as 'decriminalisation', may be inevitable for a period and is certainly preferable to total prohibition.

Balanced allocation of funding

Effective drug policy cannot be developed without a fundamental change in allocation of funding. Under current policy, the majority of government expenditure on illicit drugs is allocated to programs with a poor return on investment. Conversely, treatment interventions which provide a very favourable return on investment are poorly funded. *Equal funding for law enforcement, prevention and treatment would provide a far better return to the community than the current allocation.* The limited resources provided to health and social interventions also condemn law enforcement to unacceptable outcomes.

Adequately funded, research-based drug education

Adequately funded, research-based drug education is required for schools and the community. Nevertheless, there are limits to this strategy. Experience with drug education suggests that modest, long-term gains are far more likely than the heroic, short-term gains assumed by most politicians and community members.

Drug treatment: improving the range, capacity and quality

Expanding the range, increasing the capacity and improving the quality of drug treatment is a fundamental requirement of any effective drug policy. Improvement in drug treatment is the most important component of a comprehensive approach designed to reduce the unacceptable number of drug overdose deaths in Australia. Expansion of drug treatment facilities and options will also decrease drug-related crime, especially if emphasis is given to attracting the most severely entrenched drug users into treatment. *As long as drug users in Australia continue to find it more difficult to enter drug treatment than to obtain illicit drugs from the trafficking industry, poor outcomes are inevitable.* In order to recruit and retain the majority of drug users in drug treatment, the target populations must be offered drug treatments which they find attractive and accessible. Therefore, drug treatment will need to be expanded to meet demand. Needle syringe programs must also meet demand, because of the high health, social and economic costs of an uncontrolled HIV epidemic among injecting drug users.

Evaluation of new treatment options

New treatment options must be evaluated, as the current range of treatments is too limited. Selection of new interventions for research evaluation should be based on strong theoretical rationales, impressive empirical data or both. Cost effectiveness should also be a consideration. Rigorous research evaluation of heroin prescription was recommended by a committee of the ACT legislative assembly in 1991 and finally approved by a six : three majority of Health and Police Ministers at the Ministerial Council on Drug Strategy on 31 July 1997. Federal Cabinet, however, declined to act on this decision less than three weeks later. Following the impressive health, social and economic gains of the 1994–97 Swiss heroin trial, a number of European countries have now commenced, committed themselves, or are strongly considering beginning a heroin trial. Injecting rooms have been established in Switzerland, Germany and the Netherlands. These facilities are more difficult to evaluate but appear to have reduced deaths from drug overdose, reduced the number of new infections of blood-borne viruses (including HIV, Hepatitis B and Hepatitis C), reduced injection of illicit drugs in public places and may also have reduced corruption of public officials.

Renewed commitment to harm reduction

Australia's commitment to harm reduction needs further clarification following the calls for zero tolerance in 1998 by the Prime Minister. It is now clear that attempts to *reduce* the adverse consequences of illicit drug use are almost always successful, while attempts to *eliminate* harm are often inadvertently counterproductive. The paramount focus of national drug policy must be a reduction in the adverse health, social and economic consequences of mood altering drugs. Reducing consumption may be a means to achieving this end, but use reduction should not be the primary goal of drug policy. The injection of street drugs of unknown concentration, possibly adulterated with unknown substances or microbial agents, is inherently unsafe. Consumption of the same drugs by non-injecting routes of administration is less hazardous.

Attempts to reduce the supply and demand of illicit drugs in Australia over the last quarter century have been unsuccessful. While a reduction in the number of persons who inject illicit drugs would be highly desirable, whether this is achievable, given the increasing global production of illicit drugs and the relative ineffectiveness of drug education, is another question. It may well be that the undermining of the illicit drug trafficking industry by recruiting and retaining drug users into a more attractive and effective drug treatment system will substantially reduce both demand and the number of new recruits to drug use.

Conclusion

Australia is currently achieving unacceptable outcomes in response to illicit drugs including increasing drug use, deaths, crime and corruption. Australia's drug policies were originally adopted for cannabis on an almost arbitrary basis, and those for heroin following international pressure. Experience with more than seven decades of cannabis prohibition and almost five decades of heroin prohibition suggests that these policies are expensive, ineffective and counterproductive. 'Fine tuning' of these policies or 'more of the same' is unlikely to achieve improved outcomes. A fundamental review of drug policies is required that redefines the problem of illicit drugs as primarily a health and social issue. Unless such a redefinition is accompanied by a major re-allocation of funding, progress will not occur. Although, the vast bulk of government funding has been allocated to law enforcement, the few successes of Australia's drug policy can be attributed to the harm reduction programs.

Australia now has the example of other more successful countries to emulate. Attracting drug users from the illicit supply system into drug treatment will improve the lives of drug users and their families as well as reducing crime for the entire community. It now appears that the reform of Australia's drug policies is more a question of 'when' than 'whether'.

Conclusion

THE ILLICIT DRUG TRADE and its control have emerged as a major concern of public debate in Australian society. The rising death toll from heroin overdoses, and the associated problems of drug-related crime, ethnic violence and official corruption, have all underscored the major negative impact of this problem on Australia. As was outlined in the introduction, this book aims to contribute to the contemporary Australian debate by providing an informed discussion on the following questions. What is the extent of the contemporary drug problem in Australia and how is it impacting on the country's liberal democratic institutions and political culture? How effective has the contemporary Australian response to its drug problem been? How might Australia's overall National Drug Strategy be improved within the confines of the country's liberal democratic values and culture? The major findings and conclusions by the contributors to this volume are summarised below.

The drug problem, liberal democratic institutions and political culture

What is the extent of Australia's drug problem and its impact on liberal democratic institutions and political culture? From the chapters in this book, it seems that there is no precise account of the extent of the drug problem in Australia. Nevertheless, it does appear to be large, covering a wide assortment of narcotics ranging from amphetamines to cannabis, hallucinogens and heroin. While many of these drugs (such as heroin, cannabis and ecstasy) are imported directly into the country through sophisticated trafficking routes, others are mainly produced domestically. Most amphetamines consumed within the country, for instance, are manufactured locally and trafficked by syndicates controlled by bikie gangs. Currently there does not appear to be a major cocaine problem, largely due to the prohibitive price of this narcotic. There is a residual concern that should this drug become more freely available (a fair amount is already being imported into the country through the post), a price reduction is likely to occur—thereby opening the way for a potential explosion in cocaine use (particularly if the quality of other synthetic drugs should decrease).

In terms of the effect of illicit narcotics on contemporary Australian life, there is a broad consensus that drug abuse undermines the country's social and political stability in the widest possible sense. Some of the main concerns raised in this regard include the following dimensions: The *negative physical and psychological effects* that are commonly associated with sustained drug taking contribute to dysfunctionality in personal and familial life, helping to undermine communities as well as weakening social cohesion more broadly. The *crime and violence* that typically surround the drug trade erode respect for the rule of law and fuels social instability. Such effects also erode the key civic values of tolerance, trust and honesty that are crucial for sustaining a democratic political culture.

The *financial costs* associated with trying to control the illicit drug trade damage economic performance by reducing the public and private funds available to stimulate growth. This is largely because resources have to be diverted towards treating addicts through detoxification, health and rehabilitation programs, financing the clinics needed for those afflicted with infectious diseases as a result of sharing needles when injecting drugs, and providing for more effective law enforcement. A number of concrete indicators illustrate the true extent of this financial cost: methadone programs are thought to cost the country between $A15 and $A49 million each year; drug-related health and social welfare schemes at least $A200 million per year; and law enforcement measures designed to disrupt the supply of illicit drugs a staggering $A450 million a year. The *enormous profits* that are associated with the illicit drug trade play a key role in undermining political stability by encouraging official (government and law enforcement) corruption and white collar crime. Money laundering in particular is emerging as a major issue of concern in this regard. Estimates by the Australian Transaction Reports and Analysis Centre (AUSTRAC), for instance, put the total illegal proceeds that have been generated by drug-related money laundering schemes in Australia (most of which involve illicit property and real estate dealings) at well over $A3 billion. This figure is even more significant given that Australia is believed to operate one of the strongest cash-reporting legal regimes in the world. The contemporary drug problem also has a serious *international dimension* in that Australia's social and political institutions are increasingly exposed to external influences over which it has little control. This represents a significant challenge to the country's territorial integrity and sovereign independence. International drug trafficking represents another aspect of globalisation that reduces Australia's capacity to make autonomous policy decisions.

Effectiveness of the Australian response

How effective has the Australian response to the drug problem been? Throughout this book, various initiatives are described that have attempted to deal with the problem of illicit drugs in Australia. Most of these initiatives have reflected a law enforcement perspective. That is, illicit drugs have been treated essentially as an issue of law and order, with their manufacture, use and distribution criminalised. For most of this century, the trend has been towards expanding the scope of this criminal law approach by:
- subjecting more substances to prohibitions and controls;
- increasing the scope and number of offences and making them easier to prove in court;
- increasing the severity of statutory penalties;
- extending the enforcement and investigative powers available to the police, Customs and other agencies.

Treating illicit drugs in this fashion can be seen as an inevitable consequence of the principal assumption that underscores liberal democratic criminal law systems in Australia. In simple terms, individual or collective action in these polities tends to be made subject to the force of this criminal code in one of two instances: either if it poses an immediate threat to society; or if, left unchecked, it would be likely to cause widespread social harm.

Given the negative effects that drug abuse has on general social stability, criminalising the use of certain drugs has traditionally been accepted as a necessary restraint on individual freedom, the main purpose of which is to safeguard society as a whole. The tendency towards treating drugs as an issue of law and order has been further encouraged by the moral proselytising of the USA, which has tended to approach the control of the international drug trade with something akin to an evangelistic fervour. Most of the chapters in this book, however, have questioned the effectiveness of this approach.

On one level, it is suggested that even the focus of criminal legislation is somewhat misplaced, given the far greater social and individual harm that the abuse of licit drugs (such as alcohol and tobacco) appears to engender (at least in terms of deaths) when compared to illicit drugs. It has also been argued that the cost effectiveness of a law enforcement approach to drug abuse is highly questionable. Relatively little impact has been achieved against the so-called 'Mr Bigs' of the drug trade. Perhaps most worrying is the admission that law enforcement measures against what is arguably the most serious (and certainly the most popularly feared) narcotic—heroin—have largely failed. Indeed, this drug is expected to become more freely available and cheaper in coming years. The fear is that this trend will encourage a shift in user patterns away from softer drugs such as cannabis.

The effectiveness of the overall National Drug Strategy (NDS) (implemented since 1993) is also questioned on the grounds that it lacks political commitment and democratic leadership, as well as coordination and cohesion. A number of strong criticisms are directed at the organisational structure currently responsible for the formulation of drug policy in Australia. Particular failings of the NDS include its exclusion of relevant expert knowledge, its lack of accountability, the absence of community and consumer input, and the infrequency of its policy meetings. Certainly, in recent years, there have been gradual moves to adopt a marginally more innovative response to drug abuse and control in Australia. This is exemplified by such reforms as a slight relaxation of the law relating to the personal use and possession of cannabis in some, but not all, states; the introduction of trial cautioning schemes for minor cannabis offenders; attempts to introduce heroin trials; and moves towards adopting a more community-oriented approach to drug law enforcement. Nonetheless, progress in this direction has been uneven at best. The contributions to this book point to some of the reasons for this. These include factors such as the negative consequences of the appeal of key political leaders to ill-informed populism—the effects of which are compounded by the lowest-common-denominator mentality of tabloid journalism and talk-back radio. The constraining effects of the international drug regulation treaties to which Australia is a party remain important. Furthermore, there is great ambivalence among key players in the area of drug policy (including health professionals, the research community and law enforcement officials) over exactly how far reforms towards decriminalisation should go.

Improving the National Drug Strategy

How might the National Drug Strategy be improved within the confines of Australia's liberal democratic culture and institutions? In looking to the future, how might Australia's response to the drug problem be improved? Given the obstacles just outlined, most would agree that there is little prospect of any dramatic shift occurring in the National Drug Strategy—at least in the short-to-medium term (with a possible exception in relation to the personal possession of cannabis). As was illustrated by the discussion in this book, however, there is considerable scope for change of a more limited nature. In particular, the current policy-making structure needs to be made more accountable and open to relevant expert knowledge. There should be a greater emphasis on initiatives that tackle drug abuse as a problem of demand as well as one of supply. Finally, a greater attention needs to be devoted to clarifying and fulfilling the objectives of harm minimisation and harm reduction through more intensive community-based drug law enforcement programs and a more integrated approach to the problem. Giving more funding to public health priorities would assist here.

Few would disagree that it remains essential for Australian governments and their agencies to continue to work together to develop new, more effective and more informed methods for dealing with and understanding the problem of illicit drugs. Governments should build upon and extend the achievements of the past. For example, there should continue to be an overall drug strategy implemented through a dedicated National Drug Strategy Unit; increased training for mainstream health, law enforcement and community officials to minimise drug-related harm through the early identification and treatment of drug-related problems; and enhanced involvement and effectiveness of law enforcement in preventing drug-related harm. Greater emphasis also needs to be placed on regional cooperation and on increasing commitment to implementing effectively the multi-disciplinary United Nations drug control programs—in source, transit and user countries.

This book has not offered detailed or comprehensive strategies for reduction in demand or supply or for minimising or reducing harm. It has pursued the more modest objective of presenting a critical review of the policy-making process on illicit drugs, its various political contexts and rationales for policy. As the chapters in this book demonstrate, the task of understanding, controlling and managing the trade in illicit drugs is a complex and multifaceted one. As in any field of social science, devising precise indicators of the success of a policy and conducting evaluations without access to all the necessary information is inherently difficult. At a minimum, however, it is envisaged that better implementation and evaluation strategies would emerge out of a policy process based upon improved research capacities, and these, in turn, would require more effective international and regional coordination.

If it is accepted that most of the traditional law enforcement strategies for reducing supply and demand have been unsuccessful, this is sufficient reason for reframing the problem and embarking on more experimental strategies oriented towards somewhat different objectives. That a number of the proposed alternatives remain untested is not sufficient grounds for rejecting them. Such comments put a premium on the need for political commitment to meet the challenges presented by the increasing use of illicit drugs. In this regard, there exist significant deficits in both commitment and accountability. Although on most assessments the policies have failed, no government or minister can be held directly responsible. This political flaw seriously impedes the search for, and implementation of, more workable policies. Where political institutions do not respond adequately to serious public problems, especially those directly involving life and death, two further consequences are possible. The institutions themselves may suffer a decline in credibility and legitimacy; and reformers may seek to achieve their objectives outside the law. Early in 1999 this is precisely what occurred in New South Wales with the decision by various community health care groups and individuals to establish a safe injecting room in the Wayside Chapel in Kings Cross. The deteriorating outcomes of illicit drugs policy and unresponsive policy making prompted a campaign of civil disobedience. That such a campaign was considered necessary is testimony to the failure of political process.

One glimmer of hope for a shift in approach is evident in New South Wales, where the State Government embarked on a new political strategy for dealing with illicit drugs. The unique centrepiece of the strategy was the holding of a major public forum called the Drug Summit.* This forum was designed to raise awareness of the drug problem among State Government ministers and the general public, and prepare the ground for reforms. The participants in the Drug Summit, held on 17–21 May 1999, in Parliament House, Sydney, heard contributions from representatives of all concerned groups in the community, including advocates and opponents of reform. Importantly, it heard compelling testimony from previous drug users and those whose lives had

* For a detailed account of the issues and outcomes of the New South Wales Drug Summit see Swain (1999).

been adversely affected by drug use. As a consequence, the State Government initiated a range of reform strategies that included the bold decision of approving the opening of a legal, medically supervised, heroin injecting room in St Vincent's Hospital, Darlinghurst for an eighteen-month trial.

Such policy-making strategies and reforms signify an important departure from the way governments have dealt previously with the problem of drugs. By trialling the injecting room, the New South Wales Government has begun to recognise, albeit cautiously, that it is defensible to treat drug addicts in a humanitarian way, and not just as criminals. By basing its reforms on the Drug Summit, the Government incorporated an element of democratic deliberation into a policy debate that has usually resisted such features. It is significant that not only did the Government exercise political leadership on a controversial topic, but it did so in a way that extended the processes of liberal democracy. From the perspective of this book, such initiatives are to be commended. They provide a model for emulation in other States and at the Federal level of government.

Appendices

Appendix I: International and Regional Control Bodies

Table 1: United Nations drug control bodies

Member States of the United Nations

United Nations General Assembly

185 member states (1996)

Principal body through which the United Nations adopts resolutions, conventions and protocols, and approves funds, and serves as the forum through which individual governments express their views.

International Narcotics Control Board (INCB)	Commission on Narcotic Drugs (CND)
13 members serving in private capacity	53 member states
independent, quasi-judicial control organ for implementation and monitoring of the UN Drug Conventions	CND is one of six ECOSOC commissions
	supervises application of international conventions and agreements
promotes government compliance	
ensures sufficient supplies for medical and scientific purposes and that leakages of licit drugs do not occur	considers any required changes
	drafts new conventions and international instruments
identifies weaknesses in national and international control systems	central policy-making body within the UN for all questions relating to drug abuse
annual report to ECOSOC	

United Nations Drug Control Board (UNDCP)

Established in 1991 to integrate three former UN drug units, its objectives are:

to coordinate and provide leadership for all UN drug control activities;

to anticipate developments which could create or aggravate illicit drug production, trafficking and abuse and to mobilise and support remedial measures;

to be a world-wide centre of expertise and information in all fields of drug control;

to assist CND and INCB in implementing treaty-based functions and promoting new instruments, as needed;

to provide technical assistance and training to help governments in setting up adequate drug control structures, strategies and programs;

to provide technical cooperation in different fields of drug control to elaborate methodologies and approaches to be shared;

to assist governments in the development of sub-regional initiatives and plans of action with the basic concept of joint operations between concerned countries.

Key: ⇊ Direct connection (administrative or constitutional)

   ↓ Reporting, cooperative and advisory relationship

Source: United Nations International Drug Control Program (1997: 170–1)

Table 2: Other UN agencies with significant involvement in drug control

World Health Organisation (WHO)	Aims to reduce the abuse of all psycho-active substances
International Labour Office (ILO)	Deals with prevention and drug-related problems in the workplace
United Nations Crime Prevention and Criminal Justice Division (CPCJD)	Deals with the linkages between crime and illicit drugs, including such areas as money laundering and judicial system reform.
Food and Agriculture Organisation of the United Nations (FAO)	Assists in projects aimed at raising income levels of farmers and reducing incentives to cultivate illicit crops
United Nations Industrial Development Organisation (UNIDO)	Assists governments and the private sector to establish and manage agro-industries in illicit crop areas

United Nations Educational, Scientific and Cultural Organisation (UNESCO)	Integrates preventive education concerning drug use.
United Nations Children's Fund (UNICEF)	Incorporates drug abuse prevention work in its activities
United Nations Joint Program on AIDS (UNIAIDS)	Addresses the linkages between intravenous drug injection and the spread of the HIV virus
United Nations Development Program (UNDP)	Promotes the inclusion of appropriate drug control elements in its developmental activities
United Nations Population Fund (UNFPA)	Integrates drug abuse prevention messages in its education programs
United Nations Interregional Crime and Justice Research Centre (UNICRI)	Undertakes research on the relationship between criminal behaviour and drug abuse

Table 3: Other international bodies involved in drug control

International Criminal Police Organisation (Interpol) 175 member states	Enhances cooperation amongst drug law enforcement services; strengthens the ability of national services to control illicit drug trafficking; coordinates requests for information; and disseminates tactical and strategic drug intelligence
	Monitors information on illicit manufacture, diversion and distribution of psychotropic substances
	Coordinates matters relating to money laundering, the confiscation of assets of illicit origin and financial investigation techniques
	Conducts seminars and circulates publications on the above matters.
World Customs Organisations (WCO) 132 member states	Develops, promotes, implements and maintains international customs and trade instruments
	Provides guidance and assistance to members to achieve optimum results in the observance of such instruments, particularly in relation to the illicit traffic in narcotic drugs and psychotropic substances.

Financial Action Task Force (FATF) of the Group of 7 (G7) Nations 26 member countries, mostly members of the OECD	Established by the G7 in 1989 due to the concern of the G7 that international money laundering (particularly from narcotics sales) had reached such proportions that it was capable of affecting the economies of some countries
	Promulgated 40 Recommendations, covering the legal, financial, regulatory and law enforcement aspects of dealing with money laundering.

Table 4: Formal and informal cooperation arrangements, at the regional level

Heads of National Drug Law Enforcement Agencies (HONLEA) in Asia and the Pacific	A subsidiary of the CND, but administered by the UNDCP
	Consists of four regional groupings covering the Asia–Pacific, the Americas, Africa and Europe
	Subject to funding, each HONLEA group meets once each year
South Asia Association for Regional Cooperation (SAARC) Technical Committee on the Prevention of Drug Trafficking and Drug Abuse	Established in 1987, and comprises membership from Bangladesh, Bhutan, India, Maldives, Nepal, Pakistan and Sri Lanka
	The Drug Office Monitoring Desk is located in Colombo
Foreign Anti-Narcotics Community (FANC) meetings	An informal but regular meeting of foreign narcotics liaison officers based in Bangkok and Islamabad, with the aim of information exchange and coordination
Association of South-East Asian National Police (ASEANPOL)	A cooperative network of ASEAN police forces, established in 1980, to facilitate cooperation on matters such as illicit drug trafficking, fraudulent travel documentation, mutual assistance in criminal matters, commercial crime and piracy
	One major objective is to ensure political, economic and cultural stability, to secure economic growth in the region
	Has stated that it plans to establish a shared computer database on criminals and criminal activities in the region

Asia–Pacific Group on Money Laundering (APG)	Established in 1995 as a regional secretariat of the FATF to promote the acceptance and adoption of the 40 recommendations in those countries in the Asia–Pacific which are not members of the FATF
Mini-Dublin Group Meetings	Arose out of a meeting of UNDCP major donor countries in Dublin some years ago, but the so-called 'Dublin Group' now meets each six months in Brussels
	Regional meetings are held periodically in centres where drug production and trafficking is of major concern, and are usually attended by diplomatic officers from foreign missions posted to those cities
	In the South-East Asian region, meetings are held periodically in Bangkok, Beijing, Dhaka, Hanoi, Rangoon and Vientiane
Council for Security Cooperation in the Asia–Pacific (CSCAP) Study Group on Transnational Crime	A 2nd Track 'think tank' supporting the ASEAN Regional Forum (ARF), whose objectives are:
	— to gain a better understanding of and reach agreement on the major transnational crime trends affecting the region as a whole;
	— to consider practical measures which might be adopted to combat transnational crime in the region;
	— to assist those countries which have recently become engaged in regional security cooperation to endorse United Nations and other protocols dealing with transnational crime, particularly in the narcotics area.

Appendix II: Selected Australian Statistics*

Table 5: Seizures of Cannabis, 1996–97

Means of entry	NSW	Vic	WA	Qld	SA	Tas	NT	Total	Average weight (g)
Air cargo	2	3	0	1	1	0	0	7	452
Air pass./crew (body)	47	16	16	19	0	0	4	102	20
Air pass./crew (baggage)	40	8	15	28	5	0	2	98	36
Aircraft search	0	0	0	1	0	0	0	1	3
Itinerant/light aircraft	0	0	0	1	0	0	0	1	20 000
Small craft	0	0	0	8	0	0	0	8	1 020 317
Parcels post	300	177	78	107	18	2	5	687	17
Sea cargo	3	0	0	2	1	0	0	6	934 087
Sea crew	0	0	1	0	0	0	0	1	11
Ship search	6	0	1	3	1	0	8	19	551 901
Total	398	204	111	170	26	2	19	930	

Source: Australian Customs Service

* The tables and figures in this appendix are reproduced from P. Mahony et al. (1997). The original data for the statistics shown in the tables and figures were supplied by Australian Bureau of Criminal Intelligence (ABCI); Australian Bureau of Statistics (ABS); Australian Customs Service; Australian Federal Police (AFP); Australian Government Analytical Laboratory (AGAL), Pymble, New South Wales; State Forensic Laboratories (in Queensland, New South Wales, South Australia, Western Australia and the Australian Capital Territory); the police forensic laboratories in Victoria and the Northern Territory; and the United States Drug Enforcement Administration (US DEA).

Table 6: Seizures of cannabis by country or region of origin, 1996–97

Country/Region	Weight (kg)	No.
United Kingdom	0.840	160
Netherlands	1.056	115
Europe (other)	5.741	123
Unknown	8 647.923	333
New Zealand	0.186	40
South-East Asia	5 004.752	35
United States	1.795	34
Canada	0.076	13
South-West Asia	10 001.403	24
Hong Kong	0.105	12
Papua New Guinea	26.225	12
South Africa	600.762	12
Jamaica	2.008	5
Fiji	0.002	2
Japan	0.012	2
Niger	0.001	2
Other	0.031	6
Total	**24 292.927**	**930**

Source: Australian Customs Service
Note: 'Other' denotes countries with only one seizure. Export seizures are excluded.

Table 7: Cannabis arrests per 100 000 population

State/Territory	1995–96	1996–97
ACT	142.53	157.47
NSW	235.21	226.70
NT	205.43	369.57
Qld	279.67	439.80
SA	1 251.83	1 088.97
Tas	531.22	227.64
Vic	417.38	199.10
WA	780.19	712.91

Source: ABS, ABCI
Note: Estimated Residential Population in June 1996

Appendices

Table 8: Seizures of heroin, Australia 1996–97

	NSW	*Vic*	*WA*	*Qld*	*SA*	*Tas*	*NT*	*ACT*	*Total*
Weight (kg)	142.1	25.61	0.004	0.77	0.20	0	0.37	0	169.0
No.	40	7	4	6	3	0	2	0	62

Source: Australian Customs Service (1997)

Note: Weights shown may be net, gross or estimated.

Figure 1: Purity level of heroin seizures, < or = to 2 grams, 1996–97

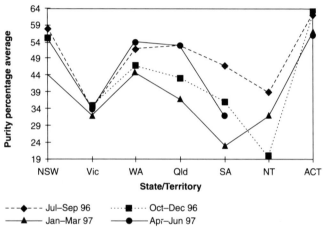

Source: AGAL and State Forensic Laboratories 1997

Figure 2: Purity level of heroin seizures, >2 grams, 1996–97

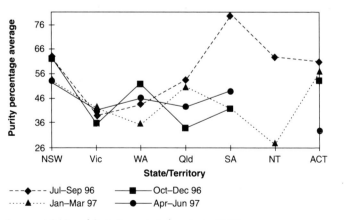

Source: AGAL and State Forensic Laboratories 1997

Figure 3: Heroin arrests, 1992 to 1996–97

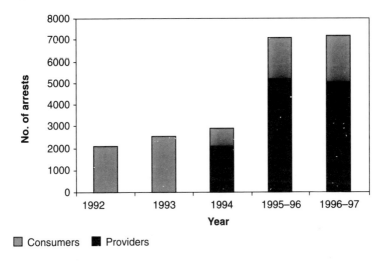

Source: ABCI
Note: Totals only available for 1992 and 1993

Figure 4: Heroin consumer and provider arrests by jurisdiction, 1996–97

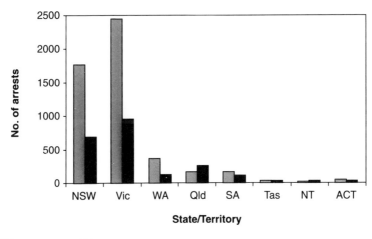

Source: ABCI

Figure 5: Mean age of offenders for heroin arrests, Jan. 1995 to June 1997

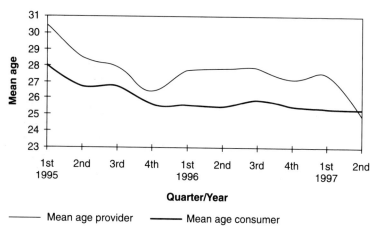

Source: ABCI

Figure 6: Classification of common synthetic psychotropic drugs

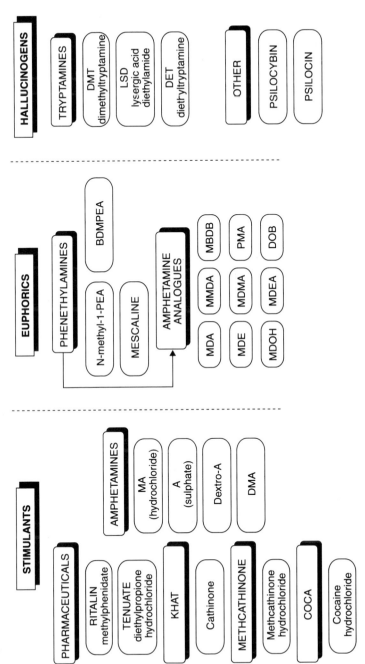

Table 9: Terms commonly used for synthetic drugs

Class	Chemical name	Common terms
Stimulant	Amphetamine	A
	Methylamphetamine, methamphetamine	MA
	Crystalline methylamphetamine hydrochloride	Ice, Euphoria
	Dexamphetamine, D-amphetamine	DA
Euphoric	Phenethylamine	PEA
	3, 4 methylenedioxy-MA	MDMA, Ecstasy
	3, 4-methylenedioxy-N-ethylamphetamine	MDEA, Eve
	3, 4-methylenedioxyamphetamine	MDA
	N-ethyl-3, 4 MDA	MDE
	N-methyl-1-(3, 4-methylenedioxyphenyl)-2-butanamine	MBDB
	3, 4-methylenedioxyphenylbutanamine	not known
	4-bromo-2, 5-DMA	DOB, Bromo
	Paramethoxyamphetamine	PMA
	3, 4-dimethoxyamphetamine	DMA
	Alpha-benzyl-n-methylphenethylamine	not known
	4-bromo-2, 5-dimethoxyphenethylamine	2CB, Nexus, Spectrum, Bromo, Herox, Synergy
	N-hydroxy-3, 4-MDA	MDOH
	N-hydroxy-3, 4-MDMA	Flea
	3-Methoxy-4, 5-MDA	MMDA
	4-bromo, 2-5 dimethoxy PEA	BDMPEA
Hallucinogen	Dimethyltryptamine	DMT
	Diethyltryptamine	DET
	Lysergic acid diethylamide	LSD
Unknown	N-methyl-1-PEA	not known

Table 10: Seizures of amphetamines and MDMA, 1996–97

Means of Entry		NSW	Vic	WA	Qld	SA	NT	Total
Air cargo	Wt (kg)	23.90	0	0.03	0.49	0	0	24.42
	No.	12	0	1	1	0	0	14
Air pass./crew	Wt (kg)	20.75	10.67	4.10	10.58	0	0.13	46.24
	No.	13	5	10	7	0	3	38
Small craft	Wt (kg)	0.01	0	0	0	0	0	0.01
	No.	1	0	0	0	0	0	1
Parcels post	Wt (kg)	6.72	9.09	0.66	0.50	0.03	1.00	18.00
	No.	70	19	19	5	1	2	116
Total	Wt (kg)	51.38	19.76	4.79	11.57	0.03	1.13	88.66
	No.	97	24	30	13	1	5	169

Source: Australian Customs Service

Note: No seizures were recorded for Tasmania. Small variations in totals are the result of the rounding of weights to two decimal places.

Figure 7: Amphetamine consumer and provider arrests, 1996–97

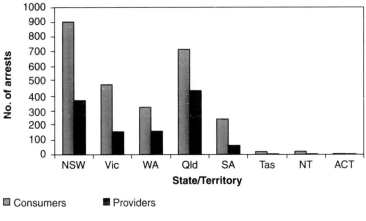

Source: ABCI

Figure 8: Amphetamine arrests per 100 000 population, 1996–97

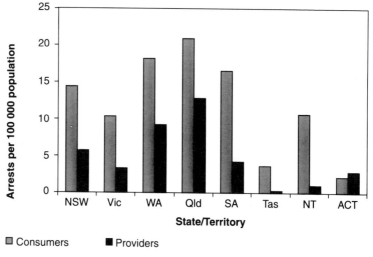

Source: ABCI and 1996 Census data.

Figure 9: Amphetamine arrests by age group, Jan. 1995–June 1997

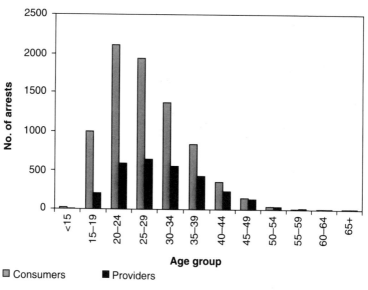

Source: ABCI

Table 11: Coca cultivation and potential leaf production, Andean region, 1995 and 1996

Net cultivation (hectares)	1995	1996
Peru	115 300	94 400
Bolivia	48 600	48 100
Colombia	50 900	67 200
Total	**214 800**	**209 700**
Potential leaf production (tonnes)		
Peru	183 600	174 700
Bolivia	85 000	75 100
Colombia	40 800	53 800
Total	**309 400**	**303 600**

Source: US Drug Enforcement Administration 1996

Figure 10: Seizures of cocaine, 1989–90 to 1996–97

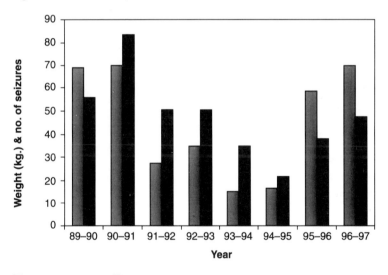

Source: ABCI

Table 12: Seizures of cocaine, by State and Territory, 1996–97

State/Territory	Weight (grams)	No.
New South Wales	51 752.68	41
Victoria	698.01	3
Western Australia	15 068.04	3
Queensland	–	–
South Australia	–	–
Tasmania	–	–
Northern Territory	0.09	1
Australian Capital Territory	0.27	1
Total	67 519.09	49

Source: Australian Customs Service

Table 13: Importation methods of significant seizures of cocaine, 1996–97

Importation method	No.
Courier—body pack	6
Courier—internal	2
International mail and express parcel	5
Personal luggage (all forms)	4
Shoes	3
On board international flights	2
Scuba tank	1
Bicycle	1
Computer equipment	1
Step (exercise) machine	1
Wine or spirit bottles	1
Total	27

Source: Adapted from AFP and Australian Customs Service seizure data

Figure 11: Importation methods of cocaine by seizure weight, 1996–97

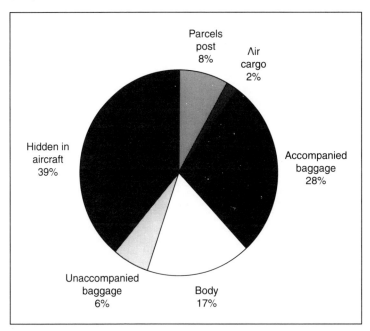

Source: Customs 1997

Table 14: Cocaine arrests, 1995–96 and 1996–97

State / Territory	1995–96	1996–97
New South Wales	269	395
Victoria	36	29
Western Australia	2	12
Queensland	19	15
South Australia	4	8
Tasmania	0	0
Northern Territory	0	1
Australian Capital Territory	0	0
Total	**330**	**460**

Source: ABCI

Figure 12: Cocaine arrests by age group, 1996–97

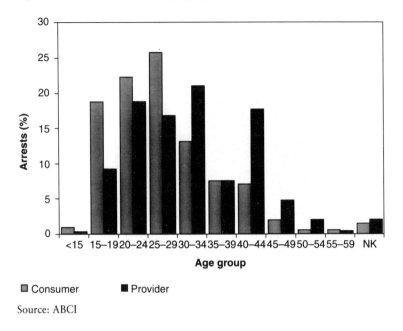

☐ Consumer   ■ Provider

Source: ABCI

Figure 13: Cocaine provider arrests, 1996–97

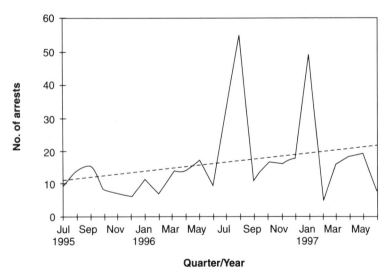

Source: ABCI

Figure 14: Cocaine arrests, 1996–97

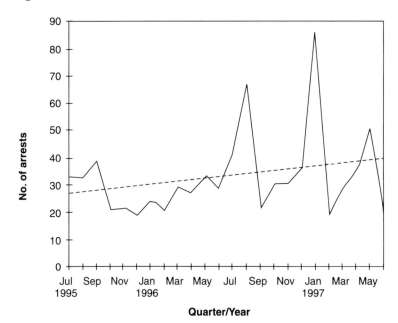

Source: ABCI

Table 15: Narcotic analgesics and their trade names

Chemical name	Trade name
Morphine sulphate	Anamorph, MS Contin—a Schedule 8 drug (highly restricted)
Codeine phosphate acetominophen paracetamol	Panadeine Forte. Endone is a similar drug.
Oxycodone hydrochloride	Endone
Pethidine	A Schedule 8 drug (highly restricted)
Methadone hydrochloride	Physeptone—a Schedule 8 drug (highly restricted)

Table 16: Benzodiazepines and their trade names

Chemical name	Trade names	Comments
Temazepam	Normison Temaze Euhypnos Nocturne Temtabs	Fluid from capsules is injectable. This route of administration can lead to gangrene.
Oxazepam	Serepax Alepam Murelax	Prescribed for short-term treatment under the PBS for anxiety and sleep disorders.
Clonazepam	Rivotril	Prescribed in the treatment of epilepsy, anti-convulsant. Known as Super Valium in the United States.
Diazepam	Valium Antenax Diazemuls Ducene Diazepam	Prescribed for short-term treatment under PBS for anxiety and sleep disorders.
Flunitrazepam	Rohypnol Hypnodorm	Not available under the PBS. The favoured drug of benzodiazepine users.
Nitrazepam	Mogadon	Prescribed for short-term treatment under the PBS for anxiety and sleep disorders.

Table 17: Significant seizures of anabolic and androgenic substances, 1996–97

Date	Quantity	Narrative
July 1996	1000 tablets	Seized at Melbourne mail exchange—sourced to Thailand
October 1996	3000 tablets	Seized at Melbourne mail exchange—sourced to Thailand
October 1996	3380 tablets	Seized in Victoria—sourced to Thailand
November 1996	1031 tablets	Seized in the Northern Territory—sourced to the UK
November 1996	1323 tablets	Seized in the Northern Territory—sourced to the UK
November 1996	1418 tablets	Seized in the Northern Territory—sourced to the UK
January 1997	963 grams	Approximately 4500 tablets seized at the Sydney mail centre
February 1997	8000 tablets	Approximately 8000 tablets and twelve vials seized in Melbourne—sourced to Thailand
April 1997	1000 tablets	Seized in Queensland—sourced to Thailand

Table 18: Number and quantity of drug seizures by State and Territory, 1996–97

DRUG	Amount	ACT	NSW	NT	Qld	SA	Tas	Vic	WA	Total
Amphetamine	Seizures	47	1 295	22	1 269	1	29	378	552	3 593
	Grams	146	68 527	316	28 105	23	6 966	41 947	9 713	155 743
	Units	0	21 932	0	2 975	0	0	0	1 368	26 275
	Missing	0	329	0	285	0	0	122	8	744
Heroin	Seizures	110	2 346	23	476	0	0	1374	467	4 796
	Grams	346	181 229	112	9 057	0	0	44 478	1 306	236 528
	Units	0	937	0	625	0	0	0	675	2 237
	Missing	0	582	0	285	0	0	777	0	1 644
Other opiates	Seizures	4	79	12	11	0	39	5	32	182
	Grams	2	808	912	7 643	0	6 178	3	320	15 866
	Units	0	46	0	0	0	0	0	199	245
	Missing	2	37	0	0	0	0	4	0	43
Cocaine	Seizures	1	352	1	56	1	0	27	17	455
	Grams	0	57 755	0	6 730	2	0	1 685	15 086	81 259
	Units	0	315	0	0	0	0	0	2	317
	Missing	0	129	0	21	0	0	2	0	152

Cannabis	Seizures	667	14 388	876	18 346	31	1 953	5 453	12 948	54 662
	Grams	486 350	16 276 406	72 248	9 171 808	1 212	112 002	2 776 526	403 839	29 300 391
	Units	0	71 056	0	151 706	0	0	0	82 395	305 157
	Missing	0	4 260	0	8 623	0	0	1 284	0	14 167
Steroids	Seizures	1	52	2	18	0	3	0	13	89
	Grams	1	8 116	24	0	0	50	0	228	8 419
	Units	0	138	0	51	0	0	0	63	252
	Missing	0	24	0	16	0	0	0	0	40
Hallucinogens	Seizures	7	177	17	151	0	5	46	148	551
	Grams	1	957	608	81	0	171	4 270	2 545	8 633
	Units	0	9 040	0	5 475	0	0	0	1 816	16 331
	Missing	0	29	0	75	0	0	23	0	127
Other drugs	Seizures	15	787	3	11 656	0	43	274	318	13 096
	Grams	137	113 170	100	2 843	0	1 956	2 006 154	5 330	2 129 660
	Units	0	5 765	0	15 151	0	0	0	1 587	22 503
	Missing	0	307	0	5 525	0	0	119	0	5 951

Note: 'Seizures' indicate the number of seizures recorded, including those where the quantity of the drug was not recorded. 'Missing' indicates the number where the quantity of the drug was not recorded. 'Units' include plants, seeds, tablets, microdots, capsules, ampoules and tabs. 'Grams' and 'units' should be combined to give the total (recorded) quantity of the drug seized.

References

Alcohol and Other Drugs Council of Australia (ADCA) 1997. Internet, http://www.adca.org.au.

Alexander, Y. 1995. Narco-terrorism: Future threats. *INTERSEC* 5(11–12): 429–31.

Allan, R. 1993. New World Order brings chaos in many countries. *Criminal Justice International* 9(3): 16–18.

Attanasio, T. 1994. The emergence of Russian organised crime. *The Narc Officer* (May/June): 91–3.

Australian Bureau of Criminal Intelligence (ABCI) 1996. *Australian Illicit Drug Report, 1995–96*. Canberra: ABCI.

—— 1997. *Australian Illicit Drug Report, 1996–97*. Canberra: ABCI.

—— 1998. *Australian Illicit Drug Report, 1997–98*. Canberra: ABCI.

Australian Bureau of Statistics 1998. *Recorded Crime in Australia*. Canberra: ABS.

Australian Institute of Health and Welfare 1997. Unpublished data in supplement to E. Single and T. Rohl, *The National Drug Strategy: Mapping the Future*. Report commissioned by the Ministerial Council on Drug Strategy. Canberra: AGPS.

Australian National Council on AIDS and Related Diseases 1998. *Estimates and Projections of the Hepatitis C Virus Epidemic in Australia*. Sydney: Hepatitis C Sub-Committee, Hepatitis C Virus Projections Working Group, National Centre in HIV Epidemiology and Clinical Research.

Australian Parliamentary Group for Drug Law Reform 1997. *Drug Lore —The Questioning of our Current Drug Law*. Canberra: Australian Drug Law Reform Foundation.

Australian Transactions Analysis Centre (AUSTRAC) 1997. Response to Australian Bureau of Criminal Intelligence questionnaire. Sydney: AUSTRAC.

Baayer, L. and Ghodse, H. 1996. The response: Evolution of international drug control 1945–1955. Draft paper for UNDCP.

Ballard, R., Gillespie, A. and Irwin, R. 1994. *Principles for Drug Education in Schools*. Belconnen, ACT: University of Canberra.

Bauman, Z. 1988. Is there a postmodern sociology? *Theory, Culture and Society* 5: 217–37.

Bearup, G. and Papadopoulos, N. 1997. Call for 'creative' approach to drugs. *Sydney Morning Herald*, 17 May.

Berridge, V. 1993. Harm minimisation and public health: An historical perspective. In N. Heather, A. Wodak, E. Nadelmann and P. O'Hare (eds), *Psychoactive Drugs and Harm Reduction. From Faith to Science*. London: Whurr Publishers.

Beyer, L. 1992. *Community Policing: Lessons from Victoria*. Canberra: Australian Institute of Criminology.

Brady, N. 1996. Revealed—radical drugs plan. *Age*, 11 April.

Broome, J. 1997. The impact of the drugs trade on social and political life in Australia. Paper presented at the conference on Illicit Drugs and Australian Democracy: The Search for New Directions, University of Queensland, Brisbane, 8 December.

Brough, J. 1997a. Coalition split as Cabinet meets on heroin. *Sydney Morning Herald*, 19 August.

—— 1997b. How the trial was fixed. *Sydney Morning Herald*, 23 August.

Brown, D. and Hogg, R. 1992. Essentialism, radical criminology and left realism. *Australian and New Zealand Journal of Criminology* 25: 195–230.

Brown, M., James, S. and Sutton, A. 1997. Law enforcement and the prevention of drug related harm. In P. O'Malley and A. Sutton (eds), *Crime Prevention in Australia: Issues in Policy and Research*, pp. 238–54. Sydney: The Federation Press.

Brown, M. and Sutton, A. 1997. Problem oriented policing and organisational form: Lessons from a Victorian experiment. *Current Issues in Criminal Justice* 9: 21–3.

Buchanan, C. and Hartley, P. 1990. Criminal choice: An economic view of life outside the law. *Policy* 6(1): 54–8.

Button, J. 1996. Drugged state. *Age*, 11 April.

Buzan, B. 1991. *People, States and Fear: An Agenda for International Security Studies in the Post-Cold War Era*. 2nd edn. London: Harvester Wheatsheaf.

Carney, T. 1981. The history of Australian drug laws: Commercialism to confusion. *Monash University Law Review* 7: 165–204.

Casswell, S. I981. A harm-reduction education programme. *Proceedings of the First Pan-Pacific Conference on Drugs and Alcohol, 1980*. Canberra: The Australian Foundation on Alcoholism and Drug Dependence.

Castillo, E. and Unsinger, P. 1998. Report on the situation in Mexico: Insurgency model applied to transnational crime. Unpublished paper.

Caulkins, J. 1996. What does mathematical modelling tell us about harm reduction? Paper presented at the 6th International Conference on Harm Reduction, Hobart, Tasmania, March.

Chalk, P. 1997. *Gray Area Phenomena in Southeast Asia: Maritime Piracy, Drug Trafficking and Political Terrorism*. Canberra Papers on Strategy and Defence No. 123. Canberra: Australian Defence Studies Centre.

Chappell, D. 1993. Violence in South Africa. *Criminology Australia* (April/May): 2–8.

Ciccarelli, J. (ed.) 1996. *Transnational Crime: A New Security Threat?* Canberra: Australian Defence Studies Centre.

Ciccarelli, J. 1995. Narcotics trafficking as an emerging security threat: A theoretical and normative examination. Master of Defence Studies thesis. University College, Australian Defence Force Academy.

Cockburn, M. 1997. Nation's voters divided over ACT drug trial. *Sydney Morning Herald*, 19 August.

Cohen, J. and Kay, J. 1994. *Taking Drugs Seriously. A Parent's Guide to Young People's Drug Use.* UK: Thorsons.

Congressional Research Service (CRS) 1997. Drug abuse: A US concern for over a century. *Global Issues* 2(3): 29–33.

Constantine, T. A. 1997. International organised crime—Today's primary law enforcement challenge. *The Police Chief* (August): 8–10.

Control Risks Group (CRG) 1997. *Business Security Outlook 1996.* London: Control Risks Group Ltd.

Criminal Justice Commission 1993. *Report on a Review of Police Powers in Queensland, Volume II: Entry, Search and Seizure.* Brisbane: CJC.

——— 1994. *Cannabis and the Law in Queensland.* Brisbane: CJC.

Crofts, N. et al. 1994. Blood-borne virus infections among Australian injecting drug users: Implications for spread of HIV. *European Journal of Epidemiology* 10: 687–94.

Damico, A. 1986. The democratic consequences of liberalism. In A. Damico (ed.), *Liberals on Liberalism*, pp. 167–84, Totowa NJ: Rowman and Littlefield.

Davis, S. 1986. *Shooting Up.* Sydney: Hale and Ironmonger.

Department of Human Services and Health 1995. *Review of Methadone Treatment in Australia—Final Report.* Commonwealth Department of Human Services and Health.

——— 1992. *No Quick Fix: An Evaluation of the National Campaign Against Drug Abuse.* Canberra: AGPS.

Dobson, C. and Payne, R. 1986. *War Without End.* London: Harrap Ltd.

Dow, S. 1997. States can back out of heroin trial deal. *Age*, 1 August.

Dow, S. and Tingle, L. 1997. Outcry as PM blocks heroin trial. *Age*, 20 August.

Drucker, E. 1995. Drug prohibition and public health: It's a crime. *Australian and New Zealand Journal of Criminology* 28 (special issue): 67–73.

Drucker, P. F. 1993. *Post Capitalist Society.* Oxford: Butterworth-Heinemann.

Dziedzic, M. 1989. The transnational drug trade and regional security. *Survival* 31(6): 533–48.

Economist Intelligence Unit 1991. *Eastern Europe's Drug Routes*. Economist Intelligence Unit Foreign Report No. 1. London: EIU.

—— 1995. *China's Own Drug Crisis*. Economist Intelligence Unit Foreign Report No. 2417. London: EIU.

Erickson, P. G. 1995. Harm reduction: What it is and is not. *Drug and Alcohol Review* 14: 283–6.

Ericson, R. 1996. Making criminology. *Current Issues in Criminal Justice* 8(1): 14–25.

Evans, G. 1993. *Cooperating for Peace: The Global Agenda for the 1990s and Beyond*. St. Leonards: Allen and Unwin.

Feachem, R. G. 1995. *Valuing the Past . . . Investing in the Future. Evaluation of the National HIV/AIDS Strategy 1993–94 to 1995–96*. Commonwealth Department of Human Services and Health, Canberra: AGPS.

Fleming, P. M. 1995. Prescribing policy in the UK: A swing away from harm reduction? *International Journal of Drug Policy* 6: 173–81.

Fukuyama, F. 1992. *The End of History and the Last Man*. London: Penguin.

Galeotti, M. 1998a. Stark choice facing Russia's police. *International Police Review* (Mar/Apr): 16–18.

—— 1998b. The *Mafiya* and the New Russia. *Australian Journal of History and Politics* 44(3). Forthcoming.

Galligan, B. 1995. *A Federal Republic*. Cambridge: Cambridge University Press.

Garland, D. 1994. Of crimes and criminals: The development of criminology in Britain. In M. Maguire, R. Morgan and R. Reiner (eds), *The Oxford Handbook of Criminology*, pp. 17–68, Oxford: Clarendon Press.

Garran, R. 1997. Corporate Hara-kiri. *Australian*, 17 March: 24.

Gilmore, I. 1994. Township killings raise doubts over ANC control. *Weekend Australian*, 9–10 July.

Goldstein, H. 1979. Improving policing: A problem-oriented approach. *Crime and Delinquency* (April): 236–58.

Goodsir, D. 1995. *Line of Fire: The Inside Story of the Shooting of Undercover Policeman Michael Drury*. Sydney: Allen and Unwin.

Graham, G. 1992. Liberalism and democracy. *Journal of Applied Philosophy* 9(2): 149–60.

Grassley, C. 1997. The US effort to fight drug abuse. *Global Issues* 2(3): 10–11.

Green, P. and Purnell, I. 1996. *Measuring the Success of Law Enforcement Agencies in Australia in Targeting Major Drug Offenders Relative to Minor Offenders*. Adelaide: National Police Research Unit.

Green, S. 1996a. Drug laws—There will be change. *Age*, 1 June.

—— 1996b. Police 'no' to drug laws. *Age*, 18 April.

—— 1996c. The Premier had no choice. *Age*, 12 June.

Green, S., and Mesina, A. 1996. Bishops express fears on drug use. *Age*, 23 May.

Green, S., and Savva, N. 1996. Howard 'no' on drugs reform. *Age*, 30 May.

Habermas, J. 1976. *Legitimation Crisis*. London: Heinemann.

Hagan, J. 1989. *Structural Criminology*. New Brunswick, NJ: Rutgers University Press.

Hall, W. 1992. The Australian debate about the legalisation of heroin and other illicit drugs, 1988–91. *Journal of Drug Issues* 22: 563–77.

—— 1996. Methadone maintenance treatment as a crime control measure. *Crime and Justice Bulletin: Contemporary Issues in Crime and Criminal Justice* 29(June): 12pp.

Hall, W., Bell, J. and Carless, J. 1993. Crime and drug use among applicants for methadone maintenance. *Drug and Alcohol Dependence* 31(2): 123–9.

Hall, W., Degenhardt, L. J. and Lynskey, M. T. 1999. Opioid overdose mortality in Australia 1964–1997: Birth-cohort trends. *Medical Journal of Australia* 171: 34–7

Hando, J. 1996. Treatment needs of regular amphetamine users in Sydney. In *Looking to the Future: a second generation of drug research*, Proceedings of the Tenth NDARC Annual Symposium, October 1996.

Hando, J., O'Brien, S., Darke, S., Maher, L. and Hall, W. 1996. *The Illicit Drug Reporting System (IDRS) Trial*. University of New South Wales, Sydney: National Drug and Alcohol Research Centre.

Harnischmacher, R. 1996. Chinese triads and Japanese Yakuza—How dangerous is the Asian Mafia? *Australian Police Journal* (June): 87–94.

Hester, R. K., and Miller, W. R. (eds) 1995. *Hand-Book of Alcoholism Treatment Approaches. Effective Alternatives*. 2nd edn. Boston: Allyn and Bacon.

Hindess, B. 1993. Liberalism, socialism and democracy: Variations on a governmental theme. *Economy and Society* 22(3): 300–13.

Hoffman, J. 1991. Capitalist democracies and democratic states: Oxymorons or coherent concepts? *Political Studies* 39(2): 342–9.

Hogg, R., and Findlay, M. 1988. Police and the community: Some issues raised by overseas research. In I. Freckelton and H. Selby (eds), *Policing in Our Society*. Sydney: Butterworths.

Howard, J. 1997. Press statement by the Prime Minister of Australia, Hon. John Howard. 2 November.

International Monetary Fund 1991. *The World Economic Outlook*. Washington, DC: IMF.

Interpol 1987. Connections between drug trafficking and terrorism. *Periodic Report II*. 19 November. Interpol.

James, S. and Sutton, A. 1993. *Review of the Barwon Police Community Consultative Committee*. Report commissioned by the Victoria Police. Melbourne: VICSafe.

—— 1996. Joining the War Against Drugs? Assessing law enforcement approaches to illicit drug control. In D. Chappell and P. Wilson (eds), *Australian Policing: Contemporary Issues*, 2nd edition. Sydney: Butterworths.

Jamieson, A. 1990. *Global Drug Trafficking*. Conflict Studies No. 234. London: RISCT.

—— 1992. *Drug Trafficking After 1992*. Conflict Studies No. 250. London: RISCT.

Jennings, J. E. 1994. Controlling political violence: Russia and South Africa. *Criminal Justice International* 10(4): 5.

John Walker Consulting Services 1995. *Estimates of the Extent of Money Laundering in Australia*. Sydney: AUSTRAC.

Jordan, B. 1996. *A Theory of Poverty and Social Exclusion*. Cambridge: Polity Press.

Kelling, G. and Moore, M. 1988. The evolving strategy of policing. *Perspectives on Policing No. 4*. National Institute of Justice, U.S. Justice Department.

Kingston, M. 1997. Experts v the public. *Sydney Morning Herald*, 4 January.

Kraar, L. 1988. The drug trade. *Fortune*, 20 June: 27–38.

Kumar, S. 1996. Drug trafficking as an international security problem. *Strategic Analysis* XIX(2): 209–29.

Lagan, B. 1997a. Heroin on trial. *Sydney Morning Herald*, 25 June.

—— 1997b. NSW boost for free heroin trial. *Sydney Morning Herald*, 31 July.

Latter, R. 1991. *Terrorism in the 1990s*. Wilton Park Papers No. 44. London: HMSO.

Laurence, P. 1993. The politics of crime in South Africa. *Canberra Times*, 8 May: 14.

Lee, M. 1996. Governance and criminality: The 1995 New South Wales election campaign and law and order. *Current Issues in Criminal Justice* 8(2): 152–62.

Lindblom, C. 1959. The science of muddling through. *Public Administration Review* 19: 79–88.

Lintner, B. 1995. *The Drug Trade in Southeast Asia*. Jane's Intelligence Review Special Report No. 5. London: JIR.

—— 1996. Narcopolitics in Burma. *Current History* 95(605): 435–6.

Lonie, J. 1978. *A Social History of Drug Control in Australia*. Royal Commission into the Non-Medical Use of Drugs. South Australia. Research Paper 8.

Lupsha, P. A. 1996. Transnational organized crime versus the nation state. *Transnational Organized Crime* 2(1): 21–48.

Lynskey, M. T., Hall, W. 1998. Cohort trends in age of initiation to heroin use. *Drug Alcohol Review* 17: 289–97.

McAllister, I., Moore, R. and Makkai, T. 1991. *Drugs in Australian Society: Patterns, Attitudes and Policies*. Melbourne: Longman Cheshire.

McCaffrey, B. 1997. Dealing with Addiction. *Global Issues* 2(3): 5–10.

McClymont, K. and Riley, M. 1997. Carr's go slow on drugs. *Sydney Morning Herald*, 16 May.

McCoy, A. W. 1980. *Drug Traffic: Narcotics and Organised Crime in Australia*. Sydney: Harper and Row.

—— 1991. *The Politics of Heroin: CIA Complicity in the Global Drug Trade*. 2nd edn. New York: Lawrence Hill Books.

McDonald, A., Ryan, J., Brown, P., Manners, C., Falconer, A., Kinnear, R., Harvey, W., Hearne, P., Banaszczyk, M. and Kaldor, J. 1999. HIV prevalence at reception into Australian prisons, 1991–1997. *Medical Journal of Australia* 171: 18–21.

MacDonald, M., Wodak, A., Ali, R., Crofts, N., Cunningham, P., Dolan, K., Kelaher, M., Loxley, W., van Beek, I. and Kaldor, J. 1997. HIV prevalence and risk behaviour in needle exchange attenders: a national study. *Medical Journal of Australia* 166: 237–40.

MacDonald, M., Wodak, A., Dolan, K., van Beek, I., Cunningham, P. and Kaldor, J. (submitted for publication). HCV antibody prevalence among injecting drug users at selected needle and syringe programs in Australia, 1995–1997.

McDonald, R. 1997. Money laundering methodologies and international and regional counter-measures. Paper presented before the 2nd Meeting of the Council for Security Cooperation in the Asia–Pacific (CSCAP) Study Group on Transnational Crime, Bangkok, 10–11 October.

MacDonald, S. 1989. *Mountain High, White Avalanche*. New York: Praeger Publishers.

McFarlane, J. (n.d.) Transnational crime and national security. Cited on p. 53 in J. R. Ciccarelli (1995).

—— 1997. Transnational crime as a security issue. Paper presented before the 2nd Meeting of the Council for Security Cooperation in the Asia–Pacific (CSCAP) Study Group on Transnational Crime, Bangkok, 10–11 October.

McFarlane, J. and McLennan, K. 1996. *Transnational Crime: The New Security Paradigm*. Strategic and Defence Studies Centre Working Paper No. 295. Canberra: Australian National University.

McIntyre, S. and Prenzler, T. 1997. Officer perspectives on community policing. *Current Issues in Criminal Justice* 9: 34–55.

Maddox, G. 1996. *Australian Democracy in Theory and Practice*. 3rd ed. Melbourne: Longman.

Mahony, P. et al. 1997. Trends and Developments in Illicit Drugs in Australia: Highlights from the *Australian Illicit Drug Report 1996–97*. Paper presented at conference on 'Illicit Drugs and Australian Democracy: The Search for New Directions', Brisbane, 8 December.

Makkai, T. and McAllister, I. 1998a. *Patterns of Drug Use in Australia*. Canberra: Commonwealth Department of Health and Family Services.

—— 1998b. *Public Opinion Towards Drug Policies in Australia*. Canberra: Commonwealth Department of Health and Family Services.

Manderson, D. 1993. *From Mr Sin to Mr Big: A History of Australian Drug Laws*. Sydney: Oxford University Press.

Manwaring, M. G. (ed.) 1993. *Gray Area Phenomena: Confronting the New World Disorder*. Colorado: Westview Press.

Marks, R. 1991. What price prohibition? An estimate of the costs of Australian drug policy. *Australian Journal of Management* (December): 202–3.

—— 1992. The costs of Australian drug policy. *Journal of Drug Issues* 22: 535–48

Medd, R. and Goldstein, F. 1997. International terrorism on the eve of a new millennium. *Studies in Conflict and Terrorism* 20: 284–5.

Mendal, W. W. and Munder, M. D. 1997. The drug threat: Getting the priorities straight. *Parameters* 27(2): 110–24.

Middleton, K. and Boreham, G. 1997. 'Sceptical' leader endorses trial supply of heroin. *Age*, 14 August.

Millett, M. 1997. PM breaks own code. *Sydney Morning Herald*, 22 August.

Mitchell, B. 1997. Howard's doubts set to stymie drug trial. *Age*, 16 August.

Model Criminal Code Officers Committee of the Standing Committee of Attorneys-General 1997. *Model Criminal Code, Chapter 6, Serious Drug Offences. Discussion Paper*. Canberra: The Committee.

Moore, D. 1993. Social controls, harm minimisation and interactive outreach: The public implications of an ethnography of drug use. *Australian Journal of Public Health* 17: 58–67.

Moore, M. 1992. Problem-solving and community policing. In M. Tonry and N. Morris (eds), *Modern Policing*. Chicago: University of Chicago Press.

Mosely, R. 1995. High-tech crime looms as major global concern. *Criminal Justice Europe* 5(4): 4.

Mosquera, R. 1993. Asian organised crime. *The Police Chief* (October): 68–9.

Mugford, S. 1993. Harm reduction: Does it lead to where its proponents imagine? In N. Heather, A. Wodak, E. Nadelmann and P. O'Hare (eds), *Psychoactive Drugs and Harm Reduction. From Faith to Science*. London: Whurr Publishers.

Mukherjee, S. 1981. *Crime Trends in Twentieth-Century Australia*. Sydney: Allen and Unwin.

National Campaign Against Drug Abuse (NCADA) 1989. *National Health Policy on Alcohol in Australia*. Canberra: Commonwealth of Australia.

National Centre in HIV Epidemiology and Clinical Research 1998. *HIV and Related Diseases in Australia. Annual Surveillance Report*. Sydney: National Centre in HIV Epidemiology and Clinical Research.

National Drug Strategy 1993. *National Drug Strategic Plan 1993–1997*. Canberra: AGPS.

—— 1996. *National Drug Strategy Household Survey: Survey Report 1995*. Canberra: Commonwealth Department of Health and Family Services.

Nolan, S. and Brady, N. 1996. No regrets on taking the job, says Penington. *Age*, 30 May.

O'Brien, S., Drake, S. and Hando, J. 1996. *Drug Trends: Findings from the Illicit Drug Reporting System*. Technical Report No. 38. University of New South Wales, Sydney: National Drug and Alcohol Research Centre.

O'Connor, J. 1973. *The Fiscal Crisis of the State*. New York: St Martin's Press.

O'Malley, P. 1994. Neo-liberal crime control—Political agendas and the future of crime prevention in Australia. In D. Chappell and P. Wilson (eds), *The Australian Criminal Justice System: The Mid 1990s*, Sydney: Butterworths.

—— 1996. Post-social criminologies. *Current Issues in Criminal Justice* 8(1): 26–38.

—— 1997. The politics of crime prevention. In P. O'Malley and A. Sutton (eds), *Crime Prevention in Australia*, Leichhardt: Federation Press.

O'Malley, P. and Sutton, A. 1997. Introduction. In P. O'Malley and A. Sutton (eds), *Crime Prevention in Australia*, Leichhardt: Federation Press.

Osborne, D. and Gaebler, T. 1993. *Reinventing Government*. New York: Penguin Books.

Parkin, A. 1996. The political process, parliament, and the uncertain triumph of liberal democracy. *Legislative Studies* 10(2): 43–51.

—— 1997. Liberal democracy. In D. Woodward, J. Summers and A. Parkin (eds), *Government, Politics, Power and Policy in Australia*, pp. 293–313, 6th ed. Longman: Melbourne.

—— 1998. Liberal democracy and the politics of criminal justice. *Australian Journal of Politics and History* 44(3), forthcoming.

Parliamentary Criminal Justice Committee 1996. *Report on a Review of the Criminal Justice Commission's Report on Cannabis and the Law in Queensland*. Report No. 37. Brisbane: Goprint.

Parliamentary Joint Committee on the National Crime Authority 1989. *Drugs, Crime and Society*. Canberra: AGPS.

Paternostro, S. 1995. Mexico as a narco-democracy. *World Policy Journal* 12(1): 43–4.

Penington, D. 1996. Why prohibition has failed and legal changes are necessary. *Age*, 16 April.

Phongpaichit, P. and Sungsidh P. 1994. *Corruption and Democracy in Thailand*. Chiang Mai: Silkworm Books.

Plutarch [*c.* 100 AD] 1914. Solon. In *Plutarch's Lives*. Vol. 1, pp. 447–55. Trans. B. Perrin. Cambridge, MA: Harvard University Press.

Police Service Weekly 1997. New Dosage Forms. *Police Service Weekly* 9(31), August.

Prasser, S. and Starr, G. 1997. *Policy and Change—The Howard Mandate*. Sydney: Southwood Press.

Premier's Drug Advisory Council 1996. *Drugs and Our Community*. Melbourne: Victorian Government.

Raine, L. and Cilluffo, F. 1994. *Global Organised Crime: The New Empire of Evil*. Washington, DC: Centre for Strategic and International Studies.

Rashid, A. 1997. Afghanistan cashes up through opium trade. *Canberra Times*, 10 May: 15.

Rein, M. 1983. *From Policy to Practice*. London: MacMillan Press.

Reuter, P. and Caulkins, J. 1995. Redefining the goals of national drug policy: Recommendations from a working group. *American Journal of Public Health* 85: 1059–63.

Roche, A. M., Evans, K. R. and Stanton, W. R. 1997. Harm reduction: Roads less travelled to the Holy Grail. *Addiction* 92: 1207–12.

Royal Commission of Inquiry into Drugs 1980. *Report*. (Chairperson: Williams). Commonwealth Government Printer.

Royal Commission of Inquiry into Drug Trafficking 1979. *Final Report: Volume 1* (Chairperson: Woodward). Government of New South Wales.

Royal Commission of Inquiry into Drug Trafficking 1983. *Final Report* (Chairperson: Stewart). Canberra: AGPS.

Royal Commission of Inquiry into the New South Wales Police Service 1997. *Final Report: Volume II: Reform* (Chairperson: Woods). Government of New South Wales.

Royal Commission of Inquiry into the Non-Medical Use of Drugs South Australia 1979. *Final Report* (Chairperson: Sackville). South Australian Government.

Royal Commission of Inquiry into Possible Illegal Activities and Associated Police Misconduct 1989. *Report* (Chairperson: Fitzgerald). Queensland Government.

Ryan, P. 1995. *Organised Crime*. Santa Barbara: ABC–CLIO.

Sackville Report. See Royal Commission into the Non-Medical Use of Drugs South Australia 1979.

Sampson, R. 1995. The community. In J. Q. Wilson and J. Petersilia (eds), *Crime*, pp. 193–216, San Francisco: Institute for Contemporary Studies.

Saunders, B. and Wright, J. 1994. Harm minimisation and drug education: A cautionary tale. Paper presented to the Alcohol, Drugs and Family Australian Professional Society on Alcohol and Other Drugs National Conference, Melbourne.

Schwartzkopf, J., Spooner, S. Flaherty, B. Braw, J. Grimsley, A., Scanlon, K. and Stewart, K. 1990. *Community Attitudes to Needle & Syringe Exchange and to Methadone Programs*. Sydney: NSW Department of Health. A 90/6.

Serio, J. 1993. Organised crime in the former Soviet Union: New directions, new locations. *Criminal Justice International* 9(5): 15–21.

Shannon, E. 1991. *Desperados: Latin Drug Lords, U.S. Lawmen and the War America Can't Win*. New York: Signet.

Shaw, T. M. (n.d.) Beyond complex emergencies and post-conflict peace-building: What links to sustainable development and human security? Unpublished paper. Dalhousie University.

Single, E. 1995a. Defining harm reduction. *Drug and Alcohol Review* 14: 287–90.

—— 1995b. AIDS, drugs and alcohol: Future directions. Paper presented to the Future Directions Conference on AIDS, Drugs and Alcohol, Delhi, India.

Single, E. and Lenton, S. 1998. The definition of harm reduction. *Drug and Alcohol Review* 17: 213–20.

Single, E. and Rohl, T. 1997. *The National Drug Strategy: Mapping the Future—An Evaluation of the National Drug Strategy 1993–1997*. A report commissioned by the Ministerial Council on Drug Strategy. Canberra: AGPS.

Slatem, S. 1998. The drug busters. *International Police Review* (March/April): 40.

Sterling, C. 1994. *Thieves World: The Threat of the New Global Network of Organised Crime*. New York: Simon and Schuster.

Stevenson, R. and Forsythe, L. 1999. *The Stolen Goods Market in New South South Wales*. NSW Bureau of Crime Statistics and Research.

Stewart Report. See Royal Commission of Inquiry into Drug Trafficking 1983.

Stokes, G. 1998. *Popper. Philosophy, Politics and Scientific Method*. Cambridge: Polity Press.

Sutton, A. and James, S. 1996. *Evaluation of Australian Drug Anti-trafficking Law Enforcement*. Criminology Department Report Series No. 128. National Police Research Unit, Adelaide.

Swain, M. 1999. *NSW Drug Summit: Issues and Outcomes.* NSW Parliamentary Library Background Paper 3/99.

Swiss Federal Office of Public Health 1999. *The Swiss Drug Policy. A Fourfold Approach for Special Consideration of the Medical Prescription of Narcotics.* Bern: Swiss Federal Office of Public Health.

Tingle, L. and Middleton, K. 1997. Withdrawal symptoms—How Cabinet caved in on heroin. *Age,* 23 August.

Turbiville, Jr., G. H. 1994. Operations other than war: Organised crime dimension. *Military Review,* January: 35–47.

United Nations 1992. The United Nations and Drug Abuse Control. New York, NY: United Nations.

United Nations International Drug Control Program 1997a. *Poppy Cultivation in Pakistan.* Briefing Note. Islamabad, February.

—— 1997b. *World Drug Report.* Oxford: Oxford University Press.

United Nations 1994. *Naples Political Declaration and Global Action Plan Against Organised Transnational Crime.* World Ministerial Conference on Organized Crime, Naples, Italy, 21–24 November 1994.

US Department of Justice 1995. Asian money laundering methods. *Burma Debate* 2(1): 34–5.

US General Accounting Office (GAO) 1996. Drug control: US heroin program encounters many obstacles in South-East Asia. *Burma Debate* 3(2): 24–34.

US Office of National Drug Control Policy 1998. *The National Drug Control Stragegy, 1998. A Ten Year Plan, 1998–2007.* Washington DC, USA.

US Senate 1992. *Asian Organised Crime.* Hearing before the Permanent Sub-Committee on Investigations of the Committee on Governmental Affairs, 3 October and 5–6 November 1991. Washington: US Government Printing Office.

US State Department 1997. *International Narcotics Control Strategy Report 1996.* Washington, DC: Bureau for International Narcotics and Enforcement Affairs.

—— 1998. *International Narcotics Control Strategy Report 1997.* Washington, DC: Bureau for International Narcotics and Enforcement Affairs.

Velleman, R. and Rigby, J. 1992. Harm-minimisation: Old wine in new bottles? *International Journal on Drug Policy* 1: 24–7.

Walker, J. 1995. Estimates of the Extent of Money Laundering in and through Australia. Paper prepared for AUSTRAC, Sydney.

Ward, J., Mattick R. P., and Hall, W. 1998. *Methadone Maintenance Treatment and Other Opioid Replacement Therapies.* Harwood Academic Publishers.

Wardlaw, G. 1982. *Political Terrorism: Theory, Tactics and Countermeasures.* Cambridge: Cambridge University Press.

Weatherburn, D. 1992. Crime and the partial legalisation of heroin. *Australian and New Zealand Journal of Criminology* 25(1): 11–26.

Weatherburn, D. and Lind, B. 1995. *Drug Law Enforcement Policy and its Impacts on the Heroin Market.* Sydney: NSW Bureau of Crime Statistics and Research.

White, R. and Haines, F. 1996. *Crime and Criminology: An Introduction.* Melbourne: Oxford University Press.

Williams Report. See Royal Commission of Inquiry into Drugs 1980.

Williams, P. 1997. *Progress of the National Drug Strategy: Key National Indicators.* Canberra: Department of Health and Family Services.

Williams, P. 1995. Transnational criminal organisations: Strategic alliances. In B. Roberts (ed.), *Order and Disorder After the End of the Cold War.* Cambridge, MA: MIT Press.

Williams, P. and Black, S. 1994. Transnational threats: Drug trafficking and weapons proliferation. *Contemporary Security Policy* 15(1): 127–51.

Williams, R. 1988. Politics, policy and crime: The Australian case. *Durham University Journal* 81(1): 41–6.

Wilson, J. and Herrnstein, R. 1985. *Crime and Human Nature.* New York: Touchstone.

Wodak, A. and Lurie, P. 1997. A tale of two countries: Attempts to control HIV among injecting drug users in Australia and the United States. *Journal of Drug Issues.* 27(1): 117–34

Wodak, A. and Owens, R. 1996. *Drug Prohibition: A Call for Change.* Sydney: University of New South Wales Press.

Wodak, A. and Saunders, B. 1995. Harm reduction means what I choose it to mean. *Drug and Alcohol Review* 14: 269–71.1

Woods Report. See Royal Commission of Inquiry into the New South Wales Police Service 1997.

Woodward Report. See Royal Commission of Inquiry into Drug Trafficking 1979.

Young, J. 1994. Incessant chatter: Recent paradigms in criminology. In M. Maguire, R. Morgan and R. Reiner (eds), *The Oxford Handbook of Criminology*, pp. 69–124, Oxford: Clarendon Press.

Index

users, 174, 181; and cannabis, 59, 169; and cocaine, 75–6; community-based approach, 170–82, 205, 206; cooperation between authorities, 53, 120; corruption, 5, 177, 189–90; cost of combatting drug trade, 26, 163, 202–3; focus on large-scale traffickers and supply reduction, 34, 98, 115, 138, 165–7, 192–3; and harm minimisation, 81–2, 98–9, 129, 168, 176, 181, 182; and harm reduction, 168, 169, 173, 175, 176, 181, 182, 206; and heroin, 62, 64–5, 193; high charge rate for use and possession of drugs, 165, 174; increasing powers and technology, 92, 93, 203; involvement with National Drug Strategy, 133; limits to, 56, 120; money laundering, 77–8; national review of specialist drug units, 163–8; objectives and outcomes, 165–8, 183; recommendations from the national review, 164, 168–9

League of Nations, 52

Lebanon, 38, 79

legislation: anti-opium, 8, 85, 89, 186; cannabis, 59–60, 90, 93–4, 154, 186; constraints on reform, 95–8, 105; currently in force in Australia, 85–8, 93; deeming provisions, 87; evolution of, 8, 11, 89–95; framework set by international treaties, 51; prospects for reform, 98–9, 191; setting appropriate penalties, 105, 195–6; *see also* decriminalisation

Lesser Antilles, 22

liberal democracy, 100–3, 104, 109, 112–13, 139, 152, 208

liberal-democratic institutions, 1, 5, 36, 101, 201, 203, 207

liberalism, 5, 8, 100, 101, 102, 113

Liberation Tigers of Tamil Eelam (LTTE), 39

Liberia, 38

Lin Mingxian, 20

Lo Hsiung-Han, 19

LSD (lysergic acid diethylamide), 53, 221, 222

M-19 (19th April Movement), 40

Mackay, Donald, 92

Mafiya, 24, 27, 32

Malaysia, 20, 46, 50

marijuana *see* cannabis

materialism, 16

MBDB (Eden), 65, 70, 71, 221, 222

MDEA (Eve), 65, 70, 221, 222

MDMA (Ecstasy), 49–50, 53, 65, 66, 67, 69, 70, 75, 105, 221, 222, 223

Medellin Cartel, 21, 24, 30, 31, 43

methadone programs, 117, 153, 184, 185, 194, 202

methylamphetamine, 65, 66, 67, 222

Mexico, 22, 25, 27, 38, 40, 42, 48

military security, 7, 37, 38–40, 56

Mill, John Stuart, 137

Mini-Dublin Group Meetings, 55, 215

Ministerial Council on Drug Strategy (MCDS), 107, 127, 130–1, 136, 142–3, 147, 185

Model Criminal Code Officers Committee, 87, 98

money laundering: as an international security and stability issue, 7, 16; in Australia, 58, 72, 78–9, 109, 203; controls over 53, 213, 214; defined and explained, 76–7; in Hong Kong, 48, 79; and integrity of financial institutions, 115, 118; law enforcement concerns, 77–8; links to global heroin and cocaine trade, 28–31; in South-East Asia, 46, 47

Mong Tai Army (MTA), 19–20

moralism, 3, 204

N-methyl-a-phenethylamine, 70

narco-democracy, 40–1

narco-terrorism, 31–4, 39–40

narcotic analgesics, 229

Nardoni Proti-Drogovy Central (NPDC), 24

National Campaign Against Drug Abuse (NCADA), 80, 129, 132

National Community-Based Approaches to Drug Law Enforcement (NCBADLE) Project, 170–3

National Council on Drugs, 147